FOR HOME AND COUNTRY

Studies in War, Society, and the Military

For Home and Country

World War I Propaganda on the Home Front

CELIA MALONE KINGSBURY

University of Nebraska Press | Lincoln & London

Portions of chapter 1 were originally published as "'In Close Touch with Her Government': Women and the Domestic Science Movement in World War One Propaganda," in *The Recipe Reader: The Recipe and Its Cultural Contexts*, ed. Janet Floyd and Laurel Forster, 88–101 (Aldershot: Ashgate, 2003), used by permission of the publisher, copyright © 2003 by Celia M. Kingsbury; and "'Food Will Win the War': Food and Social Control in World War I Propaganda," in *Edible Ideologies: Representing Food and Meaning*, ed. Kathleen LeBesco and Peter Naccarato, 45–64 (Albany: State University of New York Press, 2008), used by permission of the publisher, copyright © 2008 by SUNY Press.

Library of Congress Cataloging-in-
Publication Data

Kingsbury, Celia Malone.
For home and country : World War I
propaganda on the home front / Celia Malone
Kingsbury.
p. cm. — (Studies in war, society, and the
military)
Includes bibliographical references and index.
ISBN 978-0-8032-2474-2 (cloth : alk. paper)
1. World War, 1914–1918—Propaganda.
2. World War, 1914–1918—United States.
3. Propaganda, American. 4. Popular culture—
United States—History—20th century. 5. World
War, 1914–1918—Social aspects. 6. World War,
1914–1918—Psychological aspects. 7. Persuasion
(Psychology). I. Title.
D639.P7U63 2010
940.4'88—dc22
2009047702

Set in Iowan Old Style by Bob Reitz.

For Chuck

CONTENTS

List of Illustrations viii
Acknowledgments xi
Introduction 1
1. Food Will Win the War: Domestic Science and the Royal Society 27
2. "One Hundred Percent": War Service and Women's Fiction 66
3. VADs and Khaki Girls: The Ultimate Reward for War Service 105
4. "Learning to Hate the German Beast": Children as War Mongers 169
5. The Hun Is at the Gate: Protecting the Innocents 218
Conclusion: Learning to Love Big Brother—or Not 262
Notes 271
Bibliography 289
Index 301

ILLUSTRATIONS

All illustrations are from the author's collection.

1. "Sow the Seeds of Victory," James Montgomery Flagg. 7
2. "Keep the Hun Out," Billy Ireland 11
3. "For Home and Country," Alfred Everitt Orr 25
4. United States Food Administration uniform 34
5. "The Salvation Army Lassie," anonymous 44
6. "Sugar Means Ships," Ernest Fuhr .47
7. "Are YOU a Victory Canner?" Leonebel Jacobs 48
8. "Can Vegetables, Fruit, and the Kaiser too" 50
9. "She Helps Her Boy to Victory," anonymous 56
10. "Women of Britain Say—GO!" E. V. Kealey 81
11. "I Want YOU for the Navy," Howard Chandler Christy. . . .89
12. Edith Cavell's burial site. 107
13. "L'assassinio di Miss Cavell Inspira la 'Kultur,'" T. Corbella 108
14. Edith Cavell's victory over death, T. Corbella. 109
15. "We Need You," Albert Sterner. 111
16. Valerie Duval shoots a German soldier. 145
17. Black Cat Cigarette cards, nos. 1 and 13. 156–57
18. Black Cat Cigarette cards, nos. 32 and 43 158–59
19. Black Cat Cigarette cards, nos. 26 and 24 160–61
20. Black Cat Cigarette postcard 163

21. "Follow the Pied Piper," Macinel Wright Enright 170
22. The Kaiser as monster, James Montgomery Flagg 173
23. Davy and Dorfy with their animal friends 178
24. Lady Liberty's torch 180
25. "Oh please do! Daddy, Buy Me a Victory Bond," Joseph Ernest Samson 186
26. "My Daddy Bought Me a Government Bond," anonymous 187
27. "Our Daddy is fighting at the Front for *You*," Dewey 188
28. "Boys and Girls! You can help your Uncle Sam Win the War," James Montgomery Flagg 189
29. "Save your Child from Autocracy and Poverty," Herbert Paus 190
30. Storefront tea party 192
31. "Little Americans Do Your Bit," Cushman Parker 193
32. Soldier Bob, Florence Notter 197
33. Sheet music for "There's Nobody Home but Me" 198
34. "Fold-A-Way War Nurses" paper dolls 200–201
35. Dog saluting from *Les Soldats de la Grande Guerre*, Niké 205
36. French postcard of defecating child 207
37. Postcard of a child soldier 208
38. Postcard of German child soldier and his girlfriend 210
39. Impaled sausage from *Ten Little Sausages* 213
40. Sliced sausage from *Ten Little Sausages* 214
41. Back cover of *Ten Little Sausages* 215
42. "Hun or Home?" Henry Patrick Raleigh 221
43. "Hunger," Henry Patrick Raleigh 222
44. "Don't waste food while others starve!" L. C. Clinker and M. J. Dwyer 223
45. "When You Fire Remember This," W. A. Rogers 230

46. Edith Cavell 233
47. Sheet music for "Are You Half the Man Your Mother Thought You'd Be?" 248
48. Sheet music for "I'd Be Proud to Be the Mother of a Soldier" 249
49. Sheet music for "Britannia Needs You Like a Mother" . . 252
50. Sheet music for "That Family Called the U.S.A." 254
51. Cream of Wheat advertisement. 258
52. *Today's Housewife*, cover illustration. 259

ACKNOWLEDGMENTS

From a long list of friends and colleagues who have provided moral support as I completed this project, I would like to thank my department chair, Don Melichar, for his unflagging encouragement, and Dennis Muchisky for his support as well as his abiding interest in World War I. Also special thanks to Mary Hallab, Kevin Prufer, Sheryl Craig, Kathy Leicht, and Wayne Miller for asking the right questions and listening with grace to what must have been tedious answers. I am especially indebted to Gail Crump for writing letters in support of release time to work on this and other projects and to my former chair, Cheryl Eason, for endorsing my applications. I would also like to express my gratitude to the College of Arts, Humanities, and Social Sciences for granting that release time. To Lisa Schmidt at the University of Central Missouri's Academic Media Services go huge thanks for helping get my illustrations in order.

Additionally, thanks to Steve Trout for calling me several years ago to ask me to contribute an article to volume 6 of *Cather Studies*. Working with Steve and the University of Nebraska Press on that volume encouraged me to return to Nebraska with this book project. I am grateful to my editors, Heather Lundine and Bridget Barry, for responding to numerous questions, and to my anonymous readers for helping make this book the best it can be. Last but by no means least, thanks go to my husband, Chuck Martin, whose patience and love is limitless and whose editing indispensable. I couldn't have done it without you.

FOR HOME AND COUNTRY

Introduction

As a child of the sixties, I cut my philosophical eye teeth, as it were, on the lyrics of Bob Dylan. He expressed exactly my dissatisfaction with the culture of the Eisenhower fifties, still very much intact in small-town America of the sixties. While the Cuban Missile Crisis taught us to live for the moment, Vietnam offered more complicated lessons concerning the overlap of political strategy and strategy on the front lines. In 1965, the year T. S. Eliot died, Dylan released a sort of kitchen sink protest song that lambasted everything from war to materialism to the ubiquitous issue of middle-class morality. Aside from being the source of one of Jimmy Carter's favorite aphorisms—"He not being born / Is busy dying"—Dylan's "It's Alright, Ma (I'm Only Bleeding)" raises another issue, that of propaganda. Dylan cites propaganda along with hypocritical morality and greed:

> Old lady judges . . .
> . . . push fake morals, insult and stare
> While money doesn't talk it swears
> Obscenity, who really cares
> Propaganda, all is phony.[1]

In Dylan's view, propaganda includes everything promoting that vacuous fifties way of life, from advertising to TV sitcoms. Since Dylan whacked the establishment, other rock groups have used the subject of propaganda as a way of rejecting whatever happen to be current political trends. Green Day's "American Idiot," for instance, attacks contemporary militarism and, their word, paranoia. As the song goes,

> Now everybody DO THE PROPAGANDA!
> And sing along to the age of paranoia
> Don't want to be an American idiot
> One nation controlled by the media
> information age of hysteria
> Calling out to idiot America.[2]

Obviously not as iconic as Dylan, Green Day has become a spokesgroup for disillusioned youth who see in the contemporary politics of fear the same threat Dylan saw forty years ago in the politics of conformity. Whatever its subject, propaganda is the enemy, the destroyer of individual integrity.

In *The Peculiar Sanity of War*, I examined, among other things, the way rumor becomes or parallels propaganda on a very basic level. The First World War often turned rumors into atrocity stories, which in many cases found their way into print as "eyewitness accounts." The British "Bryce Report" is perhaps the best known collection of such otherwise undocumented atrocity stories. An official publication titled *Evidence and Documents Laid Before the Committee on Alleged German Outrages*, the Bryce report contains testimonials from Belgian refugees—farmers and other noncombatants as well as fleeing soldiers—of German atrocities as Germany advanced through Belgium in 1914. Most contemporary sources regard the Bryce Report as largely apocryphal. Addressing the Bryce report, Arthur Ponsonby argues, "At best, human testimony is unreliable, even in ordinary occurrences of no consequences, but where bias, sentiment, passion, and so-called patriotism disturb the emotions, a personal affirmation becomes of no value whatsoever."[3] Many of the atrocity stories became legendary, transcending even the force of rumor or the necessity of personal affirmation. Few civilians from the Allied nations doubted that Germany had left a path of mutilated civilians, including children, across Belgium or that given the chance, Germany would pursue its goal of carnage across the rest of Europe and Great Britain.

Modernism, Propaganda, and Blurred National Identities

Perhaps because of the war, literary modernism became an international moment in literary history. International issues informed most literature of the period and of the war itself. Vorticism had its roots in Italian Futurism and involved the British Wyndham Lewis as well as the American Ezra Pound in the magazine *Blast*, which published, among others, Ford Madox Ford and James Joyce. Ernest Hemingway, Gertrude Stein, F. Scott Fitzgerald, Djuna Barnes, and Edith Wharton lived in Paris between the wars, and Henry James and T. S. Eliot became British citizens. Joyce lived in Paris for a time after the war and published *Ulysses* there. Modernist writers seemed to have little need to settle in one place or to be governed by nationality.

Undoubtedly because of the war, ordinary citizens who seldom thought beyond the boundaries of their local communities learned the names and locations of places such as the Marne, the Argonne Forest, Paschendale, and Gallipoli. The American "Somewhere" series by Martha Trent, part of the focus of chapter 3, includes a novel and heroine for each of the Allied countries and sees that all the heroines cross paths "somewhere" in war-torn Europe. While cultural differences in the books are quite evident—Lucia Rudini is a goatherd—the novels serve two functions. First, they foster understanding and camaraderie between cultures, and second, they suggest the necessity for uniting to defeat a common enemy, one that will not be sympathetic to the virtue of young girls. But other wartime books also have transnational intentions. The children's book *Les Soldats de la Grande Guerre* is written in French and English; that is, the book was expected to generate patriotism in both France and England. The author and illustrator of *Ten Little Sausages*, which appears in chapter 4 with *Les Soldats*, lived in the United States and in England. Joan of Arc and Lafayette appear often in American sheet music and propaganda posters because they speak to the American values of liberty and national pride. The devastated Belgium appears on everything from U.S. Food Administration posters to recruiting appeals worldwide.

While not the primary focus of this study, literary modernism—largely ex-patriot, mostly male authored and antiwar—serves as perhaps the most prevalent meter of literary responses to the slaughter and bloodshed of conflict. And yet, women writers also addressed the horrors of war. Virginia Woolf's 1925 novel *Mrs. Dalloway* gives us the tragically shell-shocked Septimus Warren Smith, who years after the war loses his sanity, partly because the social structure he went to war to save has evaporated or never existed, and because the death and destruction he was helpless to prevent still haunt him. Vera Brittain's memoir *Testament of Youth* delves into war horrors and corresponding pressures from the home front to maintain the Victorian values that were miserably failing the war generation.

Perhaps most graphic and cynical of all the war novels written by women is Helen Zenna Smith's 1930 novel *Not So Quiet . . . Stepdaughters of War*. Smith, pseudonym for freelance writer Evadne Price, based the book on the actual diaries of a Voluntary Aid Detachment (VAD) ambulance driver, Winifred Young. The resulting novel is a blood-and-gore account of

"Smithy's" experiences driving an ambulance and later serving in a Women's Army Corps unit. The primary conflict in the novel is between Smithy and her mother, who uses the war service of her children to gain social status.[4]

These works and other equally powerful war works—among others the works of Rebecca West, H.D., and Radclyffe Hall—are the focus of a number of important critical studies of war literature. Two works of Dorothy Goldman instruct us in ways of reading the war and women's literature. *Women's Writing on the First World War* is a crucial anthology of women's contributions to the war canon. In *Women Writers and the Great War*, Goldman emphasizes the breadth of female perspectives on war when she declares that "women writers were like men in employing all the different modes of response available at the time—from Fussell's 'Great War Rhetoric' to modernist irony."[5] Jennifer Haytock's valuable feminist study of U.S. culture and literature during the war, *At Home, at War: Domesticity and World War I in American Literature* touches on many issues raised in my book. *At Home, at War* looks at both "sentimental propagandistic work" and a number of modernist texts, including those of Ernest Hemingway, Willa Cather, and Eudora Welty. Haytock argues that in these authors' work the domestic sphere and the trenches inform one another, that "domestic ideology . . . relies on, even as it helps to create, an ideology of war."[6] And yet ultimately, soldiers came to distrust those women who, by that ideology, had sent them off to war. Emphasizing the importance of domestic ritual in the lives of soldiers, Haytock correctly contends that "soldiers cannot escape the rituals through which the home operates."[7] Yes, and it is the need for home, for those primary familial relationships that propaganda capitalizes on to gain the trust of the men it seeks to recruit. While Haytock goes on to observe that after the war, "women became handy targets for soldiers' animosity," she also believes that the men took issue with the nation that had sent them to war and taught them to kill.[8] This cynicism, as we noted, informs much of modernist literature, the literary texts that so often become the focus of critical writing about the war. But the literary texts were only a part of the large body of writings about the war.

Outside the realm of modernism, much literature was written during the war, and this writing tells us in patriotic language what was happening or what was expected to happen on the home front. Informed by the language of propaganda, this literature and the culture that produced it is the focus of this study. World War I, on all sides, saw the first massive organized propaganda campaign of the twentieth century, the first deliberate and official effort to manipulate public opinion, an effort that was largely successful, according to wartime statistics. Second, among the Allied nations, there were a number of shared images and atrocity stories. As we have noted, national boundaries tended to blur in the unified effort to vilify, and thereby defeat, the marauding Hun. The most ubiquitous of these images is of the German, especially the Prussian, as a raping, child-butchering, cannibal ape who always sports a *Pickelhaube*, a spiked helmet, even though German soldiers stopped wearing the helmets in 1916 because of their high visibility. Rumors of atrocity stories spread in a weblike network from England and France and Belgium and Italy to the United States and to all the British colonies, which during the war were still numerous. Because propaganda imagery overlaps, and because Iowans and Alsatians, Londoners and Parisians, wealthy matrons and scullery maids were all united in their hatred of Germany, the focus in this study is not limited to specific nationalities or social classes. American, British, French,

FIG. 1. "Sow the Seeds of Victory," poster by James Montgomery Flagg, c. 1918.

and Italian propaganda all rely on the images I describe in the following paragraphs and are thus included with little distinction as to origin. As we will see, propaganda relies heavily on family relationships, and the family as a social unit varies little across cultural boundaries, especially in the Western countries. Additionally, where propaganda is designed to militarize children, I have included the occasional German image because the images are virtually identical to those used by the Allies. All warring nations rely on new and younger recruits, one of the true tragedies of war.

Propaganda posters from the First World War are stunning in their design. The United States used a number of major magazine illustrators of the day, including James Montgomery Flagg, Howard Chandler Christy, and Clarence Underwood. Flagg's small 1918 War Garden Commission poster "Sow the Seeds of Victory" (fig. 1) exhorts American women to "plant and raise your own vegetables." Beneath Flagg's rendition of Miss Columbia sowing seeds in a neatly tilled field is the caption "Every Garden a Munition Plant." While the permutations of this caption are virtually endless—the transformation of the backyard garden into a tool of destruction, for instance—the design carries well beyond the concept of the homegrown radish.

All combatant nations waged massive poster campaigns, a number of which we will examine in this book. Visible as it was, however, the poster campaign was only a small part of the effort to commandeer civilians. Recruiting posters, of course, drummed up volunteers for military service. But recruiting was one of many goals of the Allied propaganda campaign. Every war committee designed and published posters, pamphlets, cookbooks—materials designed to reach into every corner of American and British life. Yet clearly, propaganda did not stop with government publications. Sheet music complete with patriotic covers provided songs for inspiration, and popular magazines offered war fiction for young women and housewives who sought patriotic role models in the characters created by their favorite authors. Novels for adolescents and young girls placed their heroines in contact with spies and taught them how to fly the new airplanes. And children's books defined the war as a game and the enemy as a demon with horns and a tail. Games, paper dolls, and toys all made the war a part of daily play. And when women and children were not the target of propaganda, they were often used in propaganda to remind red-blooded men just what the war was all about. In her extensive history of the ways in which womanhood has been portrayed, *Imaging American Women: Ideas and Ideals in Cultural History*, Martha Banta explains: "When the occasion is war, and when the one catalyst required is will, then the American Girl (as Warrior Queen, Protecting Angel, or whatever) is ready to be pressed, vividly, into service, no matter the consequences."[9] Women, and by extension children, play an essential role in propaganda as subjects and as targets.

The purpose of this study is twofold. First, I briefly delve into the issue of propaganda itself. From the early works of Arthur Ponsonby and Harold Lasswell to contemporary college textbooks, it is my assertion that none has satisfactorily pinpointed the reason propaganda works. The term *peculiar sanity*, which came from Joseph Conrad's 1905 essay "Autocracy and War," attempted to explain the mass hysteria of war by looking at the function of rumor and paranoia. Victorian society operated to an extent through the use of rumor and gossip, and both forces continued to thrive during the war, feeding the hysteria and paranoia associated with legitimate fears of cataclysmic social change. In looking specifically at propaganda's role in determining human behavior, in creating the kind of milieu in which peculiar sanity can flourish, this study goes beyond the issue of peculiar sanity to examine basic social structures and the ways in which those basic structures serve the larger conglomerate, the state, and more crucially, the ways in which society's "innocents," women and children, become both a major focus of and a major tool of social manipulation. This volume focuses on several theories, not necessarily specifically connected to propaganda, which I believe help explain how a population, including women and children, can be motivated to behave in warlike ways. Second, we move on to review the specific propaganda, the official government versions and the perhaps more sinister privately issued variety, turning housewives into domestic soldiers and children into war mongers.[10]

Psychology: Not So Hidden Persuaders

In his 1957 study of propaganda, Lindley Fraser defines propaganda as "the activity, or the art, of inducing others to behave in a way in which they would not behave in its absence."[11] Fraser goes on to clarify his definition by excluding force or compulsion as forms of propaganda, although he does suggest that there exists a "border area which goes by the name of 'moral compulsion'—inducing people to do things utterly contrary to what they want to do by bullying, by threats, by social pressure, by *mere* tedious repetition."[12] That border or gray area here would seem to encompass most World War I propaganda, in which moral compulsion prevails. The moral choice between "Hun or Home"—the caption of a Henry Patrick Raleigh Liberty Bonds poster depicting an apish Hun figure pawing the corpse of a woman while her young daughter flees with a baby, her now-orphaned sibling (fig. 42)—is obvious and incontrovertible. "They" rape women and kill children. "We" have a moral imperative to stop them. A more subtle War Savings Stamps poster designed by cartoonist Billy Ireland of Columbus, Ohio, proclaims: "Keep the Hun Out!" (fig. 2). It does not depict women and children at all but sends a more

FIG. 2. "Keep the Hun Out," poster by Billy Ireland.

chilling message of the ultimate horror, the Hun on the doorstep, or in this case climbing through the window of a house. We see the gleeful Hun, bloody bayonet poised, from inside the window—we are most likely meant to assume a bedroom window. Flames billow behind him. That we do not see the women and children cowering in the room allows imagination to run wild and believe the worst.

Beyond the use of intellect necessary to understand literally the images presented by the propagandist, Fraser admits that the primary force contributing to the success of propaganda is emotional.[13] Clearly, the success of both posters depends on the emotions of young men who see themselves as the protectors of women and children, men who respond to this obvious sentimentality. The man who does not respond is a coward and a slacker, a virtual Hun himself. His choice to enlist becomes a visible and public response to the moral compulsion inherent in the caption "Keep the Hun Out!" Michel Foucault in *Discipline and Punish: The Birth of the Prison* speaks of the Panopticon, Jeremy Bentham's architectural construction, used in prisons to keep prisoners under constant surveillance, an unseen guard in a central tower from which all prisoners are constantly in sight. But according to Foucault, a Panopticon-like structure was historically used in villages to isolate plague victims.[14] As Foucault explains, "Bentham's Panopticon is the architectural figure of this composition."[15] But it is Bentham's figure that for Foucault becomes a "generalizable model of functioning; a way of defining power relations in terms of the everyday life of men. . . . The fact that it should have given rise, even in our own time, to so many variations, projected or realized, is evidence of the imaginary intensity that it has possessed for almost two hundred years."[16] The importance of the Panopticon as a form of surveillance is that it works whether or not a guard is actually present in the tower. If those being watched believe they are being watched, then the construction has served its purpose. Foucault goes on in his extension of the construction to call the Panopticon a "figure of political technology."[17] As such, the Panopticon serves as a model for the way propaganda functions. The imagined, or in some cases not so imagined, observation serves as the location of that visible and public response to the moral compulsion inherent in propaganda. The Panopticon is not necessarily the cause of the response, but it enforces the response. The Panopticon, or the idea of surveillance, channels the desired emotional response into a desired action. Both social and psychological forces are at work here as part of this perceived surveillance, this moral compulsion that by and large obliterates intellect, a process that I maintain can never be positive.

Recently it has become the habit of literary or social critics to refrain from making ethical judgments about historical practices, and thus the contemporary habit of viewing propaganda as a neutral phenomenon informs many studies on the subject. In his introduction to *Munitions of the Mind*, Philip M. Taylor contends that "there is no real point . . . in making moral judgments concerning whether propaganda is a 'good' or a 'bad' thing; it merely *is*."[18] While Taylor qualifies his words with the suggestion that it might be appropriate to judge "the intentions and goals of those employing propaganda," the distinction is problematic.[19] Whatever the specific goal, using emotions, including fear, to guide thought, or to prevent it, is antithetical to the idea of intellectual freedom and self-governance. The word *propaganda* originated with the desire of the Catholic church to "propagate" the faith. History has long documented the methods the church employed to achieve its ends, methods the contemporary church of course eschews. Still, the word carries the taint of bloodshed, a taint that it should retain. Our desire, then, to interrogate the power and potential dangers of propaganda necessarily keeps that taint at the forefront of academic study.

Predictably, both sociology and psychology have searched

for explanations for what appears to be aberrant behavior in the applications of and responses to propaganda. That both disciplines consider the obliteration of intellect a phenomenon to be studied underscores the idea that propaganda and its goals are destructive. That the totalitarian propaganda state is the focus of most twentieth-century dystopic novels, two of which I discuss in the next section, suggests the destructive nature of propaganda as well.

Freud and Jung: The Personal and Collective Unconscious

A number of propaganda analysts focus on psychological sources, both Freudian and Jungian, for the success of propaganda. In *The Age of Propaganda* Pratkanis and Aronson examine psychological theories, both behaviorism and psychoanalytical theory.[20] Addressing the question of behaviorism, the authors cite Pavlov and his research with dogs. Pavlov, of course, believed animals including humans could be conditioned to behave in specific ways. The authors allude to Aldous Huxley's *Brave New World* and Anthony Burgess's *A Clockwork Orange,* which demonstrate fictional examples of conditioning in totalitarian states.[21] And in terms of psychoanalytical studies, the authors refer to Vance Packard's groundbreaking work *The Hidden Persuaders,* to which we shall return shortly.

The Age of Propaganda only names *Brave New World* and *A Clockwork Orange,* but a brief look at the novels makes clear, if in a fictional sense, how conditioning works and how it can become a part of propaganda according to Fraser's definition of moral compulsion through "mere repetition."[22] In *Brave New World,* humans are conditioned in two ways. Embryos are first manipulated in utero, in this case a bottle on a conveyer belt. Society here is completely engineered, and embryos are designed according to the needs of society. As Henry Foster, a Hatchery employee, explains to a group of trainees, "We decant our babies as socialized human beings, as Alphas, or Epsilons, as future sewage workers or future . . . Directors of Hatcheries."[23] But conditioning continues beyond "birth." Hypnopaedia, "the greatest moralizing and socializing force of all time," is used to teach sleeping children everything from sex education to class consciousness.[24] Beta children learn that "we are much better than the Gammas and Deltas. Gammas are stupid," and so forth.[25] Bernard Marx, an Alpha Plus whose job involves conditioning but who is too intelligent not to think on his own, notes when he hears someone repeat a ubiquitous aphorism, "One hundred repetitions three nights a week for four years. . . . Sixty-two thousand four hundred repetitions make one truth."[26] Obviously, the hypnopaedia Bernard is referring to is a reliable form of conditioning only in novels, but repetition played an important role in war propaganda. Phrases such as "Doing your bit," "Safe for democracy," and "The war to end all wars," to name only a few, became part of every British and American vocabulary because they were repeated by politicians, journalists, generals, by everyone who had the public's attention. "Mere repetition," in a sense, is moral imperative.

But Pavlovian conditioning also appears in *Brave New World*. A group of Delta babies is conditioned with loud noises and electric shock to "grow up with what the psychologists used to call an 'instinctive' hatred of books and flowers" in order to keep them from reading or enjoying nature.[27] According to World Controller, Mustapha Mond, conditioning is necessary to provide stability. In his words, "No civilization without social stability. No social stability without individual stability."[28] Huxley published *Brave New World* in 1932 in that turbulent period between the wars when society was in many ways still reeling from the first war and at the same time deep in the economic depression of the late twenties. On both sides of the Atlantic, the massive propaganda campaign of the war remained in place to continue raising money and promoting food conservation after the war's end. Huxley's world vision, among other things, reflects the attempts at social control during and after the war.

Burgess's post–World War II *A Clockwork Orange* describes a perhaps more sinister form of conditioning called Ludivico's Technique, in which the violent teenager Alex is administered drugs and forced to watch violent films in an experimental attempt to curb his desire to rape and pillage. Before his conditioning is far advanced, Alex realizes that not only is he ill at the thought of violence, but he retches at the thought of sex, violent or not, and—as crucial to Alex—when he hears the music of his favorite composer, Beethoven, which has accompanied the conditioning. As the prison chaplain has warned him, he has ceased to be a man. Alex, in spite of his terrible past, has become a victim, the pawn of every political force, including rival ones, in the novel. As Pratkanis and Aronson put it, the novels "provide a futuristic glimpse of a bleak and scary world completely guided by behavioristic principles."[29]

As portentous as these novels are, they delve into only one method of psychological control. Clearly, there are others. Those Eisenhower fifties I alluded to earlier opened the doors to mass advertising on a scale never before imagined. Prior to the fifties, advertising had been largely limited to radio spots and print ads in magazines and newspapers. But in the fifties, television offered potentially larger audiences than other forms of media had afforded. According to sociologist Vance Packard in his 1957 masterwork *The Hidden Persuaders*, the post–World War II era saw "the use of mass psychoanalysis to guide campaigns of persuasion [to] . . . become the basis of a multimillion-dollar industry."[30] Companies seeking to advertise their products, according to Packard, sat "at the feet of psychiatrists and social scientists (particularly psychologists and sociologists) who [had] been hiring themselves out as 'practical' consultants or setting up their own research firms."[31] While Packard finds some advertising diverting and amusing, he argues that society has moved "from the genial world of James Thurber into the chilling world of George Orwell and his Big Brother."[32] But the world of Great War propaganda was not so genial or devoid of science. World War I propagandists had access to obvious forms of psychological manipulation to rouse patriotic sentiments; Freud was by then widely published.[33] According to Freud biographer Peter Gay, Freud found the war "too vile" and believed "people were behaving precisely the way that psychoanalysis would have predicted."[34] Freud's thoughts here are perhaps a tribute to his own theories; nevertheless, propaganda was pervasive, and according to Gay, Freud had declared that "the war had degenerated into a conflict more bloody than any of its predecessors and had produced . . . an outburst of hate and contempt for the enemy," which in Freud's case at the time would have been the Allies.[35] That hatred was felt by all combatant nations and was certainly fueled by propaganda, which, according to Lindley Fraser, had gone "from being an art, or craft, to becoming a (rudimentary) science,"—precisely what Packard feared about fifties advertising.[36]

Jungian interpretations of war mania, and thus of the force of propaganda, are not as preponderant as are Freudian discussions, yet they remain significant in examining human motivations. Sam Keen in *Faces of the Enemy: Reflections of the Hostile Imagination* explores the Jungian psyche for sources of that hostile imagination, the tendency of what he refers to as "homo hostilis" to create enemies.[37] The negative qualities we invariably assign to the enemy are reflections of what Carl Jung refers to as the shadow, in Keen's words, "the 'bad' self, which remains unconscious so long as it may be projected onto an enemy. By this sleight of hand, the unacceptable parts of the self—its greed, cruelty, sadism, hostility, . . . are made to disappear and are recognized only as qualities of the enemy."[38] Thus in World War I propaganda, Germans are depicted as rapists, cannibals, and mutilators of young children. Keen's admitted intention in writing his book is current; he hopes to "dispel the fog of propaganda and decipher the rhetoric that binds us to the illusions of the warfare system."[39] An admirable goal. All those subliminal urges boiling in the soup of the Jungian subconscious are here identified as part of the "normal" psyche and projected onto whomever is handy to create a ubiquitous enemy, one we can hate and kill with impunity and one we can teach our children to hate as well. While Keen's focus is almost exclusively Jungian, he does allude to the importance of social institutions as well. Keen believes that "creative thinking about war will always involve both the individual psyche and social institutions. Society shapes the psyche and vice versa."[40] Still, in Jung's depiction of the psyche's composition, archetypes are universal; they exist cross-culturally, and Keen describes similar archetypal images in cross-cultural propaganda. Keen's focus, then, remains psychological.[41]

Lawrence LeShan also examines what he calls the mythic quality of wartime perception. In *The Psychology of War: Comprehending Its Mystique and Its Madness*, LeShan declares that war involves "an essential change from our structuring the world in our customary way to our structuring it in the ways of a fairy tale or myth. The way-things-are, the rules for living, the morality that guides us: all of these qualities are very different during peacetime than during wartime."[42] LeShan couches this shift in terms of an us-versus-them view of the world. Of ten examples of the way wartime perceptions of humanity differ from those of peacetime, numbers nine and ten offer the best illustration of how the enemy is demonized by those perceptions. According to example number nine, during peace, "we can talk with those we disagree with. Negotiation is possible." During war, this belief mutates to the idea that "since the enemy is evil, he naturally lies. Communication is not possible. Only force can settle the issue. *We* tell the truth (news, education). *They* lie (propaganda)."[43] Perhaps more crucially in number ten, during peace we believe that "all people are fundamentally the same. Difference are quantitative." During war, however, "'We' and 'They' are qualitatively different, so different that the same actions are 'good' when we do them, and 'evil' when the enemy does them. There is doubt that we and they really belong to the same species."[44] LeShan insists that in making war, "it is individuals who act, not nations."[45] Yet individuals act believing that "we must identify ourselves with something larger than our skin-limited being; alone, we lose something of our humanness."[46] Like Keen, LeShan leads us then through the psyche to the idea of human community, the focus of sociology, at which we must take a closer look.

Sociology: Negative Positivism

Sociology also serves as a theoretical basis for propaganda analyses. Public opinion emerges when the institutions that desire to control it shape potentially diverse social groups into an unthinking mass. Most often, this shaping is political, and it is achieved through some form of propaganda. Political sociologist Harold Lasswell defines propaganda as "the control of opinion by significant symbols or, to speak more concretely and less accurately, by stories, rumours, reports, pictures and other forms of *social* communication. Propaganda is concerned with the management of opinions and attitudes by the direct manipulation of social suggestion rather than by altering other conditions in the environment or in the organism."[47] Like Fraser, Lasswell appears to exclude force as a form of propaganda. Contrasting civilian life with military life, Lasswell concludes, "Civilian unity is not achieved by the regimentation of muscles. It is achieved by a repetition of ideas rather than movements. Propaganda is the method by which this process is aided and abetted."[48] Arthur Ponsonby also alludes to the idea of a regimented public. Indeed, Ponsonby is so adamant in his descriptions of social control that he almost seems to rule out the idea of psychology at all, seeing instead an uneducated mass that will believe whatever it is told. His expressed aim in writing his book—one similar to Sam Keen's—is that "the common people may be more on their guard when the war cloud next appears on the horizon."[49] Unfortunately, propaganda is much more effective than a small book published ten years after the war. Ponsonby's declaration that "the public can be worked up emotionally by sham ideals" certainly calls his optimism into question, as does his continued assertion that "a sort of collective hysteria spreads and rises until finally it spreads and gets the better of sober people and reputable newspapers."[50] Given the number of questionable articles the *Times* published as fact and the number of British intellectuals who immediately joined the war effort or signed on to work with Lord Northcliffe at Crewe House, either hysteria spread faster than Ponsonby might have anticipated, or those "sober people" are just as susceptible to mass hysteria as that proverbial "mass." As he continues to indict governments for using lies, Ponsonby declares that "a moment's reflection would tell any reasonable person that such obvious bias cannot possibly represent the truth. But the moment's reflection is not allowed; lies are circulated with great rapidity. The unthinking mass accept them and by their excitement sway the rest."[51]

I turn now to that mass and its function within the social structure. In the world of sociology, much has been made of mass society. C. Wright Mills in his major opus *The Power Elite* addresses the issue of the mass society as part of his definition of the power elite. According to Mills, the concept of the "Great American Public" that was crucial to eighteenth-century concepts of democracy, and is still, as he puts it, "used as the working [justification] of power in American society," is a "set of images out of a fairy tale: they are not adequate even as an approximate model of how the American system of power works."[52] In place of the "Great American Public" exists perhaps a modified version of the mass society. Mills explains that four criteria must be considered to establish the difference between a public and a mass society. First, "the ratio of the givers of opinion to the receivers" must be considered. In a public, opinion flows freely in all directions. When opinion is dependent on mass communication, the classical concept of the public begins to disappear. Second is the ability to respond to an opinion without fear of reprisals, including "conventional sanction," gossip, ostracism, and potential loss of employment.[53] Mills's third criterion is the connection between public opinion and political action, "the ease with which opinion is effective in the shaping of decisions of powerful consequence."[54] During wartime, of course, including both world wars, the public has little to do with decision making. The American public, for instance, had little to do with the decision to drop atomic bombs on Japan. Finally, Mills addresses the extent to which "authority" penetrates into daily life. As examples, he refers to the Nazi system of informants and Soviet cell structure. We might add the fictional example here of children informing on their parents and everyone else in Orwell's *1984*.

In Mills's view in 1956, "we have moved a considerable distance along the road to mass society."[55] Because American society is not yet totalitarian, Mills declines to address it as a mass. And yet the almost universal war fervor during the Great War, the suggestion that slackers should be ferreted out and dealt with accordingly, the attempt to eradicate the use of the German language, and the suggestion from Roy Rutherford Bailey's Captain Tick-Mouse that children should "help Uncle Sam catch the slackers" are all suggestive of totalitarianism.[56] What was true for Mills in 1956 may not have universal application in the twenty-first century, as Alan Wolfe points out in his afterword to *The Power Elite*. Nevertheless, his theories can shed light on basic social structures, both now and during the Great War. Because the war was conducted on such a grand scale, mass armies were required. Masses of men and equipment had to be moved and moved quickly. As we have noted, mass propaganda for the first time motivated public opinion to the degree that these goals were accomplished.

Given the emergence of what appears to have been a mass society, at least at the time, and given the use, intentional or not, of some pretty obvious psychological tools, the efficacy of First World War propaganda becomes almost comprehensible. But more should be said of the workings of social structure before we move on to a review of Great War propaganda. Basic in terms of classical sociological theory is the sometimes overlooked work of Ferdinand Tönnies. Tönnies indeed wrote much on the subject of public opinion both before and after World War I. But it is his earlier work *Community and Society* (or *Community and Civil Society*, depending on the translation) that ultimately sheds most light on the construction of propaganda. Like the later works of Mills, Tönnies's work on public opinion deals with the concept of the mass society and the formation of opinions.

Tönnies also names ways public opinion can be suppressed, or at least how the expression of opinions can be suppressed or "checked"; in other words, Tönnies distinguishes between opinions and the expression of opinions.[57] While thoughts are "free," Tönnies concludes that "the expression of thoughts and views—and especially their public, that is, their consciously planned dissemination (propaganda, agitation)—is a free act that one can successfully order or prevent."[58] When a community speaks with a single voice, propaganda is often responsible, and the expression of dissident thoughts is checked with a religious zeal. In fact, Tönnies connects religion and public opinion as he elaborates on the idea of suppression and demonization. As he explains, "Real Public Opinion and religion both vilify a deviant opinion as a sin. Even though they are not interested in having a deviant opinion expressed or disseminated ("propagandized"), its assessment (i.e., its rejection) is based on *having* the opinion."[59] As we have observed, failure to condemn the Hun, to fight him in whatever capacity possible, is tantamount to being a Hun or a demon.

While his work on public opinion sheds light on the thrust of propaganda, Tönnies's earlier work *Community and Society*, in which he defines the sociological concepts *Gemeinschaft* and *Gesellschaft*, sheds even further light on the way propaganda influences public opinion. Gemeinschaft, translated as "community," and Gesellschaft or "society" represent two basic human relationships: primary, or friends and family, and secondary, such as a store clerk, someone with whom the city dweller deals, even on a recurring basis, but with whom there is no other connection. According to the theory of Gemeinschaft, or community, primary relationships are "an original or natural condition which is preserved in spite of actual separation."[60] Three primary relationships are the matrix of community or, as Tönnies puts it, its embryo: the relationship between mother and child, that between spouses "in its natural or general biological meaning," and that between siblings.[61] We shall return to these three groupings. The Gesellschaft, or society, is an "artificial construction" that Tönnies views as negative in the sense that everyone is "isolated and there exists a condition of tension against all others."[62]

The state is an example of society, or Gesellschaft. It is a group of loosely connected human beings who, to contradict LeShan momentarily, feel only a sense of competition with one another. Given Tönnies's designations, we might wonder about the question of propaganda and how the state uses it to create unity, to make the larger civil society seem to be one big community, a kind of family. In *Women and War*, Jean Bethke Elshtain argues that "to create a grand civic entity, local identities must be shattered or muted; individuals must become entangled with the notion of a homeland not as the local community into which one is born but as a vast entity, symbolized by flags, oaths of allegiance, constitutions (in some cases), and wars *against* others."[63] But in fact in propaganda, local identity is never muted; it is expanded into the idea of a unified homeland, a collection of nuclear families that have the same needs and the same values no matter what their actual location. In popular sheet music, for instance, individual states in the United States represent members of the family, and in Great Britain, the colonies are depicted as the "children" of Britannia. The state, the Gesellschaft, achieves its purpose of unity by using the three primary relationships that form the Gemeinschaft in much of its propaganda. That is, the Gesellschaft appropriates the Gemeinschaft for its images of propaganda. As we examine posters, sheet music, and children's books, we will see depicted ad infinitum relationships between mother and child. The earlier alluded to "Hun or Home" (fig. 42) is an example of that unit

FIG. 3. "For Home and Country," poster by Alfred Everitt Orr.

ripped apart by the evil Hun. We also see relationships between husband and wife—Orr's "For Home and Country" comes to mind, picturing a soldier/husband embracing wife and child (fig. 3). And finally, we see relationships between siblings, in which everyone is made to feel a sibling, wife, or mother to every soldier. We also see young brothers and sisters working together for the war effort—*Captain Tick-Mouse* characters Davy and Dorfy, for instance (fig. 23).

Although sociological theory has its origins in the late nineteenth century, the basic social structures it defines exist, perhaps unfortunately, in many of the same ways they have for centuries. Perhaps they, like Jung's archetypes, arise out of the human psyche. Perhaps. At any rate, these theories give us an idea of how elemental are the images of propaganda and why humans are eager to die for them, or to kill for them. With these thoughts in mind, then, let us move on to the propaganda itself. The first three chapters present propaganda meant to bring women into the war effort, as wives and mothers or potential wives and mothers. At the government and corporate level, we see the campaigns of the U.S. Food Administration and the corresponding British League of National Safety, as well as the Red Cross and the YWCA, to name a few. At the private level, we delve into magazine fiction and romance novels meant to enlist both married and single women into the war effort. Next we explore in chapter 4 the vast store of material directed toward children. From textbooks to war games, no area of childhood escaped the scrutiny or the reach of war propaganda. Finally, we turn to propaganda that seizes on those images of the innocent, on the noncombatant as fodder for Hun atrocities. Like Arthur Ponsonby, like Sam Keen, my ultimate hope is that if we look at enough propaganda, we will know it when we see it, and we will know why it raises the hair on the backs of our necks.

ONE

Food Will Win the War

Domestic Science and the Royal Society

Two of the primary relationships Tönnies describes in his theory of Gemeinschaft depend on the involvement of women, in one case as wives and in the other as mothers. Since the two are irrevocably interconnected in Western society, much war propaganda focuses on the responsibilities of women to civilize their men and to feed and educate their children. From the days of the Temperance and Suffrage movements, women upheld the idea of their moral superiority, and the advent of the First World War allowed that idealization to continue. In some cases, of course, that moral superiority played out in pacifism. But by and large, women assumed a pivotal role in maintaining the morale of the home front. New methods of food preparation and new products designed to make life in the kitchen easier formed the basis of the propaganda campaign to enlist the housewife in the moral role she was born to play.

Wives and Mothers: Salvation in the Mixing Bowl

Herbert Hoover assumed the duties of director of the United States Food Administration at its inception in August of 1917 and immediately set about mobilizing the food industry, restaurants, and the home kitchen to adopt his new plans for food conservation. Hoover adamantly rejected pleas from European Allies to institute food rationing. As he recalls in his introduction to William Clinton Mullendore's *History of the United States*

Food Administration, "voluntary action has the great value of depriving those who can afford it and not those who have no margin for sacrifice."[1] Hoover's rationale appears to have its foundation in the knowledge that the poor, those with no margins for sacrifice, could not afford many of the food items that rationing would have controlled in the first place. Those who could not eat cake were not a part of Hoover's grand scheme. But middle-class women were very much a part of it. Hoover tells us that "the women of the country were called upon for this service and, under the leadership of the very able women who headed the Conservation Division in Washington, directors were appointed to collaborate with the state and county administrations and a network of committees was established engaging several hundred thousand women. A campaign secured from 14,000,000 families . . . signed pledges to carry out the conservation programs suggested by the Food Administration from time to time."[2] Beyond controlling the press, as we shall see shortly, Hoover established a system of hands-on coercion that was impossible for the patriotic woman to resist, and a system of voluntary compliance that enlisted food distributors and manufacturers—that is, the corporate end of food production.

Products such as Crisco, Calumet Baking Powder, and Campbell's Soup and the propaganda campaign to enlist women are directly linked to the U.S. Food Administration and its efforts to manipulate the sale and distribution of food as well as its consumption. Albert N. Merritt, a member of the Food Administration staff, in his 1920 book *War Time Control of Distribution of Foods*, details in great length the pressures applied to manufacturers and distributors of food as well as food retailers. In a chapter called "Voluntary Propaganda," Merritt alludes to a potato surplus that occurred in the summer of 1918. According to Merritt, "potatoes could not be exported, and as there was such an acute shortage of wheat a most energetic campaign was conducted through the wholesale and retail dealers to push the sale of potatoes, and to urge their use by the consumer in the place of wheat."[3] Many of the wartime bread recipes call for the use of potatoes, and according to Merritt, the "campaign resulted in the avoidance of the complete loss of millions of bushels of this important food commodity, with a corresponding saving in wheat for export."[4] In other words, housewives bought potatoes. Other works also confirm the efficacy of propaganda. In his *History of the United States Food Administration* Mullendore substantiates on a national scale the effects of the Food Administration's campaign. While the first pledge card drive failed because it lacked the appropriate methods of distribution, a detail Hoover omits from his introduction, the second drive, according to Mullendore, "actively enlisted between thirteen and fourteen million homes in the United States."[5] Hoover proudly relates this detail, and David M. Kennedy confirms it in his cultural history of World War I, *Over Here: The First World War and American Society*.

On the state and local level, the Food Administration campaign involved women's clubs and local leaders to achieve its end. Ivan L. Pollock, writing of the Food Administration's activities in Iowa, describes a massive pledge campaign involving most of the women's clubs in the state. According to Pollock, "a total of one hundred and eleven meetings were held in the thirty-six towns and cities visited, with a total attendance of more than one hundred thousand people."[6] While these texts may be a sort of after-the-fact propaganda, they do chronicle the efforts at enforcing food conservation without rationing and depict the popularity of "doing one's bit."

Domestic Science, the Modern Kitchen, and America at War

Well before the war, the kitchen became a way to challenge wives and mothers to become better homemakers and, in so doing, reinforced the gender roles inherent in the Gemeinschaft. In her incisive study *Perfection Salad: Women and Cooking at the Turn of the Century*, Laura Shapiro examines the movement generally known as "domestic science," which found its way into many home kitchens. Domestic scientists sought to educate women in the new science of nutrition, to engage industry to produce labor-saving, nutritious food products, and to establish, in Shapiro's words, "the link between science and housework."[7] Shapiro argues, and later propaganda texts bear her out, that women were believed to be responsible for the moral well-being of the American character. Old-fashioned housewives who refused to take advantage of modern conveniences, she maintains, "bore the responsibility for the failings of the American home, failings that seemed to lead directly to poverty, disease, alcoholism, unemployment, and all the other social miseries apparent at the turn of the century."[8] But the woman who understood the importance of calorie and nutrition charts, the woman who used scientifically tested recipes, held the keys to the nation's future. Americans sought in the germ-free modern kitchen the cure for all of the nation's ills.

The domestic science movement continued well into the century and appears full-blown in World War I propaganda. Even before America entered the war in 1917, and perhaps anticipating that eventuality, the domestic science movement took on a military zeal. In *The Margin of Happiness: The Reward of Thrift*, published in 1917 but written before America's entry into the war, Thetta Quay Franks asks for women's participation in a nationwide endeavor in much the way Herbert Hoover does after the establishment of the Food Administration later that year.

Her pleas indeed foreshadow Hooverization, the popular name given to Hoover's plan to conserve food without the use of rationing.[9] Insisting that women have vast powers in matters of national importance, Franks asks, "How many women realize the dignity and value of their position as guardians of the national health, spenders of the national wealth? Much of the power and influence of a nation lie [sic] within the keeping of its women. How many American women have learned to think nationally?" Among what Franks lists as "some of the nation's most urgent problems" that she believes women can solve are "the high cost of living, the increasing death rate from organic disease, and the rising divorce rate."[10] Poor housekeeping, in fact, according to Franks, is responsible for the increase in the divorce rate in the United States.[11] To substantiate her assertion, she cites an article from the *Newark Evening News* of March 28, 1916, which states: "Women's ignorance and neglect of homemaking arts were pointed out as a leading cause of family desertion, at a conference yesterday afternoon of social workers." The "proof" for this conclusion is a statement made by a Mr. Gascoyne, who declares that "much of the blame for the delinquent husband rests on the undesirable home conditions caused by the presence of an untrained wife."[12] If a husband strays, the fault inevitably lies with the wife. Inherent in this assumption, of course, is the idea that men will instinctively misbehave without the civilizing influence of an intelligent and highly skilled woman.

To avoid the inevitable disgrace of incompetence, Franks goes on in her book to instruct women in the ways of intelligent housekeeping by suggesting, among other things, that all packaged food be stored in glass jars with etched or painted labels.[13] She suggests that a grocery list be prepared on the typewriter and maintained in alphabetical order.[14] As to the arrangement of the kitchen itself, all utensils must be hung from hooks for easy access, such that all similar utensils are "placed together in orderly fashion and each has its allotted hook and must be replaced after it has been used."[15] Since many women were also responsible for managing the family budget, Franks details specific suggestions for shouldering that responsibility and at the same time repeats her belief that homemaking is a "social service." A budget allotment for "betterment," including books and the theater, she believes, "has ethical as well as economic values," because "love of home and all that home stands for is the only safeguard for the nation against the growing tendency to evade the responsibilities of home life."[16] In this interesting example of circular reasoning, Franks links national interests and national security with morality and the home, Gemeinschaft with Gesellschaft. The Victorian ideal of progress reverberates in the American connection to science and invention, to the notion that the kitchen range could save the world.

In the chapter "Cooking as a Science," Franks suggests just that. Here she links, in some cases correctly, improper diet with diseases such as heart disease. Using charts to compare the death rates in the United States with death rates in England and Wales, Franks concludes that Americans eat too much meat, too much sugar ("twice as much as Europeans do"), and too little whole grain flour.[17] While we might applaud what sounds like a sensible and modern approach to eating, we cannot overlook either the militancy with which she presents this "scientific" material or her strong connection between food and morality. Eating too much meat, according to Franks, "overworks the liver and kidneys in their effort to eliminate the poisonous products produced by the excess."[18] In Franks's hands, statistics become ammunition. Once America entered the war, the ammunition was turned directly toward victory. As the cover of a Calumet Baking Powder recipe book proclaims, "Food will win the war. Don't waste it!"[19] And food, well organized and well prepared, will win the war, not only against the Germans but against sloth and gluttony, against a multitude of sins for which Franks has no tolerance. Salvation, as she sees it, lies in the alteration of public opinion, which of course Franks attempts to do. But her ultimate goal is to reach the American woman, to convince her that the application of scientific methods to cooking is a patriotic duty, war or no war, and that ultimately the responsibility for the well-being of her family and her country is hers. In what amounts to a manifesto at the chapter's conclusion, Franks asks, "Must we not conclude that cooking must be practiced as a science in order to guard the future health of the nation? . . . How long will American women leave the deciding of the national eating habits to chefs and cooks in whom this wealth of valuable knowledge is lacking?"[20] In tying the kitchen, the center of the home, to the success of the nation, Franks establishes before official propaganda does the juxtaposition of the values of the Gemeinschaft onto the Gesellschaft. Home and country are already irrevocably linked.

In terms of practical application, Franks details the organization of Classes in Cooking and Household Efficiency through the Civic Committee of the Women's Club of Orange, New Jersey. Cooking Lesson 2 includes instruction in the preparation of scalloped cabbage, cauliflower au gratin, and boiled carrots, illustrating Domestic Science's love of the simple and the presumed ignorance of the students, forty-four housewives and twenty-two housemaids. Striking here are a number of details, not the least of which is the popularity of

FIG. 4. Photograph from a stereopticon showing the United States Food Administration uniform.

the classes. The twenty gas burners available in the Domestic Science Department of East Orange High School, rented for the sessions, could not meet the enrollment demands, so two women looked on each week rather than working directly with the recipes. U.S. government publications supplied the recipes for every session. And finally, the women were dressed in identical uniforms that included "a very becoming cap like those worn by professional nurses" (fig. 4).[21] This uniform or one very much like it would soon become the uniform of that literal "American Army of Housewives," the "soldiers of the kitchen"; that is, any woman who mailed in her pledge card to the U.S. Food Administration, a card signaling her acceptance of government intervention in the kitchen.

Home Cards and Cornmeal: The U.S. Food Administration and Official Propaganda

Once America entered the war in 1917, the campaign for scientific cooking became part of Hoover's campaign linking food conservation with military victory. Posters, books, and magazine articles all ask women in the name of national security to conserve food, to prepare food at home once again, to use "foods obtainable near home," and to see that "large quantities of perishable foods" are preserved for later use.[22] The labor-saving products, canned goods, and prepackaged foods they had for the past decade been encouraged to use in their food preparation were earmarked for shipment to war. Using the language of domestic science, U.S. Food Administration propaganda brought women into direct contact with the war by urging them to enlist in that "American Army of housewives."[23] As culinary soldiers, women were held responsible not only for the moral salvation of the country through housekeeping but for its military salvation as well.

And the duties of the patriotic housewife were well defined. Hoover, in an appeal published in the August 1917 issue of *Ladies' Home Journal,* "What I Would Like Women to Do," speaks directly to American women about food shortages in Europe and ways to rectify them at home. "Every woman," he writes, "should feel herself definitely engaged in national service in her own kitchen and in her own home." Alluding to the new domestic science, Hoover goes on to insist: "The intelligent woman of America must make a proper study of food ratios, so that the most nutritious foods will appear in their proper proportions on the home table."[24] Hoover's entreaty is followed by an article on baking bread from wheat substitutes. Wheat was one of the commodities most needed in war-ravaged Europe, making conservation of wheat flour at home a top priority. In case the housewife might take lightly the appeal to her sense of patriotic duty, the *Journal* feature included a pledge card to be snipped out and sent to Hoover and the Food Administration. The American woman was thus drawn into the war effort and was brought, as the subtitle for both articles proclaims, "in Close Touch with Her Government."[25]

Women who did not subscribe to the *Journal* could find pledge cards everywhere. David. M. Kennedy, in *Over Here*, a study of American culture during the war, mirrors earlier statistics that more than half a million volunteers went door to door distributing pledge cards.[26] In addition to those fourteen million families who signed and returned pledge cards, seven thousand hotels and restaurants also joined the cause.[27] For women the canvassers missed, the Food Administration placed pledge cards in other likely places. *War Cook Book for American Women*, a Food Administration publication, includes a pledge card as well as an explanation of what the pledge entails. Beyond staying in close touch, the American woman is asked to "remember the needs of the nation as told to them by the Food Administration." Obedience is the key here. Agreeing to perform "war service in the home" removes much of the element of choice from questions of homemaking. Signing the pledge "is not a promise to [do] some particular thing, but an agreement to follow directions."[28] Indeed, the Food Administration's Home Card gives very specific instructions for compliance.[29] In addition, the *Cook Book* introduction emphasizes paying attention to "conditions that vary from day to day," explaining, "In the spring, for example, when the stock of potatoes ran low, the directions said: Eat rice; but when the potato crop was harvested, the directions said: Eat potatoes, the rice is wanted for the Army."[30] While civilian needs would generally take a back seat to those of fighting forces, and food shortages were a constant reality, especially in Europe, the tone of this appeal issued on behalf of the "cause of honor and democracy" is that of Orwellian newspeak. The implication is that the housewife does not have the necessary tools to plan menus based on availability, and therefore, she must be reminded of her patriotic duty.

Food and the War: Textbooks and the University

On the college front, *Food and the War: A Textbook for College Classes* also provides lessons in basic nutrition. Written for students of both genders, *Food and the War* begins with an appeal to each from Hoover. While the letter to "college men" does carry the request to "obey the food regulations," it also implores young men to use "every legal means [to] prevent their violation by others" and to "be aggressive agents of the Food Administration wherever you go." University women, on the other hand, are admonished largely to pursue domestic science. The letter to "college women" states: "All our questions now center in food; its production, its distribution, its use, its conservation. The more you know about these things, the more valuable you will be, and the greater will be your service to humanity. We urge you to pursue those studies which deal with food, and to train yourselves for real leadership."[31]

Food and the War was prepared with the advice of professors from many of the nation's top universities, including an associate professor of food chemistry from the University of Chicago and an associate professor of social ethics from Harvard. Ethics aside, the text itself reads much like a textbook in domestic science and is undoubtedly designed to produce more "leaders" like Thetta Quay Franks, more authors of war recipe books. In the back, "A Laboratory Manual" includes chemical experiments involving food items, instructions for food preparation including recipes using substitutes for wheat flour and sugar, and a detailed assignment for a student demonstration of one of the cooking processes involved. Suggested topics include the preparation of cheese soufflé for meatless meals, wheatless biscuits, and white sauce made from a wheat substitute.[32] Thus the students are themselves prepared to pass on these techniques to other culinary soldiers.[33]

And many did. The Woman's Council of National Defense at New Hampshire College of Agriculture and the Mechanic Arts, in cooperation with the Food Administration, published a series of leaflets "in behalf of the food emergency work." The first leaflet, Extension Circular No. 21, deals with the use of fats. In a preliminary note, the federal food administrator for New Hampshire, Huntley N. Spaulding, admonishes women to take up the call to culinary arms when he declares, "There is no greater opportunity and responsibility before the women of New Hampshire households than that of helping to conserve food supplies for our country and for our allies. . . . The lessons . . . are worthy of your earnest attention and observance."[34] Recipe 8 in this first leaflet is a formula for making soap from fats and lye, a practice we might suspect had vanished from the American home, except perhaps from the most rural, by the end of the nineteenth century.[35] We can only guess how many New Hampshire households actually resorted to the use of lye soap, but we can assume the leaflets contributed to the already large body of propaganda aimed at women and devoted to food conservation through domestic science.

Thetta Quay Franks herself continued to promote domestic science on all fronts. In the back of *The Margin of Happiness: The Reward of Thrift*, G. P. Putnam's Sons placed an advertisement for her next book, *Household Organization for War Service*. A short description of the new book repeats the subjects covered in *Margin* and notes that the new book includes information on "economic substitutes for meats," a subject appropriate to wartime cookery. But foremost in the ad is the assertion that "America expects every woman to do her duty." This proclamation simply rephrases Franks's assertion that the American woman is responsible for the well-being of the nation, and it is reiterated in ladies' magazines, in much of the war propaganda published by the U.S. Food Administration, and in food advertisements that also supported the war effort.

The press, at least in matters of food conservation, became a virtual arm of the U.S. Food Administration. Mullendore, in his *History of the United States Food Administration*, devotes a section in the chapter on conservation to "Co-operation of the Press," a condition he calls "fundamental." Because the Food Administration did not trust the accuracy of the press, which included "the great dailies of the cities" as well as "the larger magazines," Hoover appointed an "Educational Director" whose job it was to send out press releases.[36] According to Mullendore, "special articles for journals, magazines, and trade papers were reviewed and corrected by those in charge of the work under consideration. Inaccuracies were thus guarded against, and the public learned that it might rely with confidence upon the accuracy of information given out."[37] In other words, the Food Administration was writing articles and sending them out to magazines and newspapers with the expectation that the materials would be published as they were. Hoover's article in the *Ladies' Home Journal* is a case in point. Mullendore's assertion that the press "gave evidence of their appreciation of this opportunity for service by making a special effort to give publicity to news of the Food Administration," is another masterpiece of Orwellian newspeak.[38] Even in light of "shrinking" food supplies, the idea of a "free" press publishing government-authored articles is bound to raise red flags and illustrates how coordinated war propaganda was.

Ladies' magazines, thereby prompted, sounded the call to culinary arms. *Ladies' Home Journal* brought the demands of Hooverizing into every middle-class American home, and the more specialized domestic science journals also responded to America's need to conserve. *American Cookery: Formerly the Boston Cooking-School Magazine of Culinary Science and Domestic Economics* promoted the appeals of the Food Administration by including wartime recipes and menus and patriotic vignettes and poems alongside its articles on home decorating, as in the August–September 1918 feature "Harmony in the Breakfast Room."[39] The bound volume of the journal for 1918, through its articles and advertising, reflects changes in food shortages and Hoover's efforts to influence consumption in the home. In a news release of May 27, 1918, Hoover had asked that "all those whose circumstances permit shall abstain from wheat and wheat products in any form until the next harvest."[40] In the August–September issue of *American Cookery*, editor Janet McKenzie Hill, author of *War Time Recipes*, ponders the "word from the United States Food Administration" asking for further limitations on the consumption of meat and chicken.[41] The request to abstain from the use of wheat flour results in the inclusion of bread, cake, and cookie recipes using everything from rice flour to rye flour. In the "Queries and Answers" section, extolling the virtues of rice flour, Hill questions the patriotism of housewives who fail to conserve wheat. Instead of using half rice and half wheat flour in recipes for white cake, Hill maintains, "If one's desire to serve her country is of more importance than the color of the cake served, use barley or rye flour to replace the wheat flour."[42] Hill had been doing just that for most of 1918. In the section "Seasonable and Tested Recipes" from the

February issue, she includes Corn Flour Parker House Rolls and Barley Biscuits as well as sandwiches made of cream cheese and decorated with crossed strips of pimento to remind diners of the Red Cross.[43]

And of course, the patriotic woman will comply. If not, she runs the risk of censure, of ridicule. In the February issue, an article called "The Basis of Victory" by Ladd Plumley once again places the burden of victory on the American housewife when it asserts the idea that "well-cooked food . . . is what will bring quick and complete victory to America." Because of the food problem, Plumley demands that women and girls must become more absorbed in cooking than they have been in the past. And there is no room for failure or incompetence. Plumley staunchly maintains, "If she is not an efficient cook, cannot make good bread, cannot make good pie, cannot make good cake, she should blush for herself. If she is not a good cook, she should take up cookery . . . as a serious study." Plumley goes on to say that even trained nurses should be able to cook because a "well-fed patient has many times the chance of recovery than the wounded soldier who is served with ill-prepared food or has an insufficient diet."[44] While the food situation in Allied Europe was in places dire, it was also dire in Germany. More important, however, is the suggestion that food alone could be the source of victory. Such an oversimplification ignores questions of weapons, manpower, strategy, and even weather—all the factors that together determine which side wins a battle and ultimately a war. In addition, the suggestion that trained nurses would take time away from their duties to cook meals is short-sighted at best. We might also suppose that Plumley would not make the same suggestion for male doctors.

Yet an editorial from the March issue agrees with Plumley.

Reporting news that "the girl students in six hundred American colleges" are going to be taking classes in cooking, no doubt using *Food and the War* as a text, the editors go on to laud the plan and to assert that "thousands of bushels of wheat and other foodstuffs will be saved by this campaign, it is estimated." Beyond war-related benefits of these courses, the editors echo Thetta Quay Franks in suggesting that the introduction of domestic science as a serious course of study for women will result in "vastly improved and healthier conditions of home life throughout the land."[45] The moral superiority of women is indeed pervasive, and the home remains the backbone of the state.

If the editorials, articles, recipes, and menus are not sufficient to convince the readers of *American Cookery* to conserve food, the magazine also includes poems and vignettes demonstrating the need for compliance. The March issue, furthering the argument for domestic science education, includes a vignette, "On 'Having a Case'" by "The Wiser Person." In this little story, an inexperienced housekeeper, faced with the problem of her "girl's" day off and hungry men to feed, relies on eggs and bread. Confiding to her neighbor, The Wiser Person, the young wife admits her panic. Versed in domestic science, The Wiser Person enumerates—in enough detail for readers to duplicate—the emergency dishes the untrained woman could have prepared had she had a case of canned soup on hand in her pantry. All the "recipes" involve stretching canned soup by diluting it, mixing it with stale bread for a "scallop", or using it to add variety to egg dishes and soufflés. Convinced, the young wife rushes off to order a case of soup from her grocer.[46] Beneath the vignette, a "poem" to Herbert Hoover, "A Hoovercessional!" by Caroline Louise Sumner, proclaims:

But since this is the edict stern,
If we would conquer Kaiser B,
To disobey we'll quickly spurn!
We'll all respond to Hoover's plea!
O Mr. Hoover, we're won o'er,
We'll starve for "FREEDOM EVERMORE!"[47]

Other magazines offered similar articles. The November 1918 issue of the *People's Home Journal,* published before the armistice on November 11, includes a Food Administration–approved menu for Thanksgiving dinner, along with recipes for the preparation of the menu. The "sensible economical, wholesome feast" is intended to maintain "the spirit of true economy necessary to be observed to help win the war."[48] Opposite the Thanksgiving feature an advertisement for "Yeast Foam" boasts an attractive young woman dressed in the uniform of the Food Administration saluting over a perfect loaf of bread.[49] In all of these attempts to Hooverize the American housewife, practitioners of domestic science join forces with the U.S. government and with industry in what amounts to a full media blitz. No "responsible" woman could ignore the call without risking the epithet "slacker." Sheet music, a popular medium for propaganda, also reflects food service. The "Salvation Army Lassie," the subject for a ubiquitous poster as well, is the focus of the 1919 fundraising song "Don't Forget the Salvation Army (My Doughnut Girl)." The smiling, helmeted woman on the cover of the sheet music holds a huge tub of doughnuts. The lyrics, "officially endorsed and adopted by The Salvation Army" tell of a woman who was "as brave as a lion but meek as a lamb" as she delivered coffee and doughnuts to "the sons of Uncle Sam." The doughnuts, provided as a result of food conservation at home, were admittedly an important part of

FIG. 5. "The Salvation Army Lassie," poster, anonymous.

Allied morale. For this reason, according to its publisher, the song was "the only secular song number to which [the Salvation Army's] unblemished seal has been affixed" (fig. 5).[50]

Targeted for service at home and service abroad, women found themselves the subject of additional scrutiny in research devoted to female strength. Since women were being asked to perform in traditionally male areas aside from the kitchen, including the War Garden in both the United States and Great Britain, the image of women as the "weaker sex" needed to be overshadowed by that of a more robust figure capable of the war work she was expected to do. The Sunday magazine section of the *St. Louis Post-Dispatch* on October 21, 1917, includes an article that focuses on the research of Dr. Dudley A. Sargent, a "noted authority" from Harvard, who declares that women are physically superior to men and only seem otherwise because they choose to hide their strength. Sargent's reasoning is specious; nevertheless, he argues that women could "make as good soldiers as men."[51] Women, he declares, are "biologically . . . more of a savage than man, more of a barbarian," and therefore have "a greater proportion of physical endurance."[52] The unnamed author of this article calls this statement "one the fair sex may find rather unflattering."[53] While this research does not aim directly at food consumption, it follows a cover drawing by Lee Conrey depicting frontline soldiers opening "A Box from Home." In the drawing, two immaculately clean soldiers share a pie baked and shipped by what we can assume to be a Food Administration recruit. And in case anyone takes Sargent's argument too seriously, the back page of the magazine is devoted to the "Season's Latest Hats," in which no woman could possibly engage in physical activity.[54] The kitchen here is still the most appropriate area of service, at least for the middle-class woman, and food conservation is the most important realm of feminine endeavor.

Women, including those from the middle class, were nevertheless occasionally asked to perform physical labor as well. Since many farm laborers had enlisted, women were expected to take their places, as women had in factories, actions Sargent would no doubt have endorsed wholeheartedly. An article in *Leslie's Weekly* for March 30, 1918, suggests that farm work is appropriate for three groups of women. Surprisingly, the first group listed is educated women: college students and teachers who were free for the summer and wanted to do patriotic service. The second group, "working women, strong, but unskilled," makes a logical choice for proposed farm work, as do seasonal factory workers, who make up the third group. Such a "camp" at Bedford Hills, New York, overseen by Miss Ida H. Ogilvie, professor of geology at Columbia, according to the author, "proved beyond a doubt that women can do agricultural work" and that the presence of college women was crucial to maintain the morale of the working-class women.[55]

Newspaper supplements nevertheless largely supported saving wheat. In the *North American* of Philadelphia on Sunday, April 14, 1918, Mrs. Anna B. Scott, its "cooking expert and food economist," proposes what she calls her "50-50" plan, asking housewives to use "in every recipe that calls for wheat flour only one half the amount stipulated, substituting for the remainder something that will admirably take its place." According to Mrs. Scott, the 50-50 plan used less wheat than "even seven wheatless meals a week" without depriving diners of bread.[56] This sixteen-page supplement includes copies of six Food Administration posters, printed where advertisements for products might otherwise appear.

The Food Administration's poster campaign vehemently urges conservation and participation. Paul Stahr's "Be Patriotic" shows Lillian Gish, or a Gish look-alike, as Miss Columbia, arms outstretched, asking the American woman to "sign your country's pledge to save the food." As we have seen, others draw demarcation lines between allies and the enemy. A stunning poster, "Sugar Means Ships" (fig. 6), portrays the careless

FIG. 6. "Sugar Means Ships," poster by Ernest Fuhr.

woman—the woman who does not do her bit—not only as the enemy but as the mythic devourer of men. In the poster, the Food Administration employs several images to enlist the aid of women as consumers and at the same time to indict them for waste. The woman illustrated is not a champion of domestic science; she is not in close touch with her government. In one corner of the poster, opposite a black cloud labeled war, a smartly dressed woman who is larger than life sips from a soda glass that merges into the ocean and becomes a vortex into which ships, some bearing the label "soldiers," threaten to slip. "Sugar Means Ships," the poster warns. "For your beverages," it continues, ships that should carry soldiers and supplies would be required to carry sugar. Women should therefore reduce their consumption of sweetened drinks. In the corner labeled

FIG. 7. "Are YOU a Victory Canner?" poster by Leonebel Jacobs.

war, a soldier summons the ships to "Hurry!"—before they are sucked up by the careless and thirsty woman who may not heed the call to duty.

Munitions workers and a number of YWCA volunteers were literally involved in the war both in the United States and "over there." On the home front, measuring spoons served the cause of conservation and thus fed starving soldiers and children. A War Garden Commission poster depicting Miss Columbia proudly displaying home-canned goods asks, "Are YOU a Victory Canner?" (fig. 7). But one War Garden Commission booklet directly involves the housewife in the violence of war by asking her to "Can the Kaiser," to "Back Up the Cannon by Use of the Canner."[57] The booklet, innocuous enough itself, contains instructions for the latest and safest methods of canning and drying the produce from the Victory Garden. But its cover employs an image from an earlier poster of Kaiser Wilhelm stuffed into a pickle jar (fig. 8). Ludicrous enough on the surface, this pickled effigy calls up images of cannibalism, of which the Germans were in fact suspected, and once again illustrates the ubiquity of a number of propaganda images and stories. Foreshadowing the grim reality of the Second World War, a famous atrocity story that became part of World War I propaganda was of a so-called corpse factory where bodies of German soldiers supposedly emerged as glycerin for weapons and food for hogs and poultry. According to Paul Fussell, a similar rumor, not necessarily German, placed the factories on the British side. Fussell believes the story grew out of a mistranslation—probably deliberate—of the German word *Kadaver*, a word most often used to refer to the corpses of horses rendered for fat and by-products in German rendering plants.[58] In spite of German protests that the word was never used to refer to human remains, the *Times*, citing dictionaries to

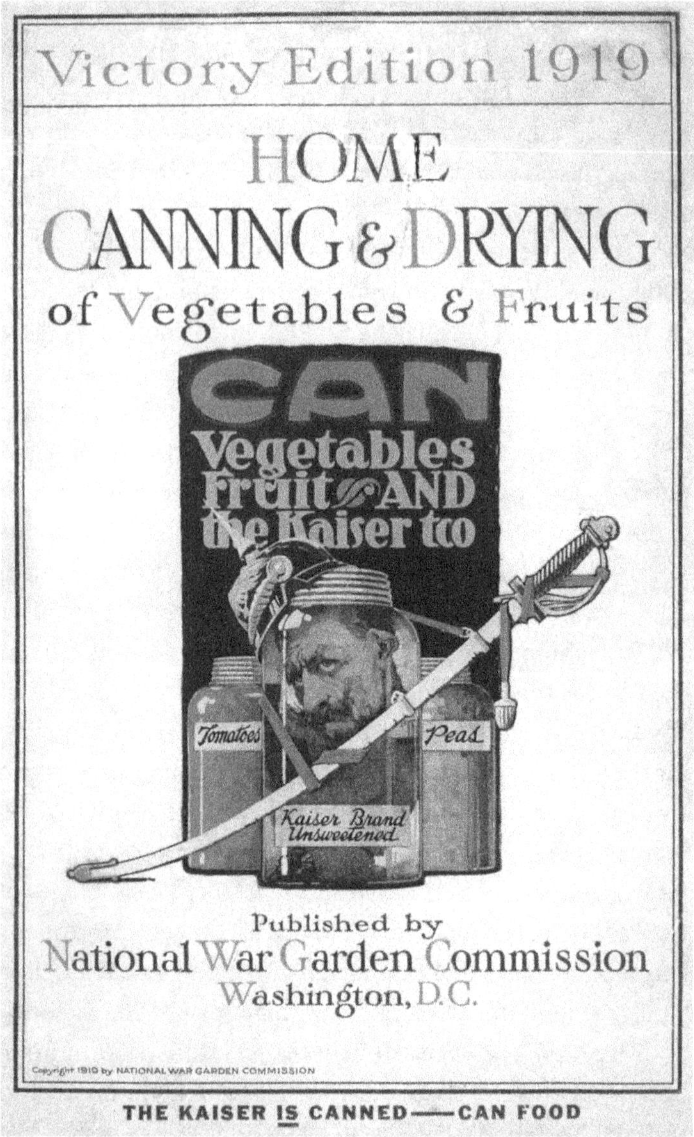

FIG. 8. "Can Vegetables, Fruit, and the Kaiser too," cover illustration from the National War Garden Commission cookbook *Home Drying and Canning*.

show that it was, continued to publish articles on the subject, and the British government allowed the rumors to be spread to the Allies.[59] In a *Times* article on April 20, 1917, two weeks after America's entry into the war, a British sergeant claimed that a German prisoner had told him about the factories. The British soldier stated that "this fellow told me that Fritz calls his margarine corpse fat because they suspect that's what it comes from."[60] In his analysis of propaganda stories in *Falsehood in War-Time*, Arthur Ponsonby suggests this story was fabricated by Brigadier-General Charteris, who continued to deny responsibility for it as late as 1925.[61] Regardless of its origin, the corpse factory rumor fired the patriotism of citizens on both sides of the Atlantic. The can-the-Kaiser image further employs this rumor by appearing to make a joke of implied cannibalism, this time of course with the German leader as the by-product.

Crisco and Corn Syrup: The Food Industry

Hooverizing American women also became the goal of many American businesses. Through their advertising campaigns, manufacturers of food products assisted the Food Administration in drafting women into home front service. Calumet Baking Powder along with other manufacturers of baking powder published recipe booklets containing recipes using alternatives to wheat flour. In addition, the booklets published letters and manifestos written by leading domestic scientists of the day. Calumet's booklet opens with a message signed by Maude Marie Costello, who was "of the Domestic Science Branch of the University of Chicago." Costello invites housewives to "Enlist in the Army for the conservation of food and not . . . wait to be 'Drafted'".[62] Royal Baking Powder dedicates its recipe book to "the housewives of the United States who are assisting the Government in its work through the Food Administration."[63]

The Food Administration's own pamphlet goes into specific detail about the location of food shortages, specifically in Belgium, where women and children were reputed to be starving.[64] The Food Administration poster "Hunger" by artist Henry Patrick Raleigh (fig. 43), illustrated in Anna B. Scott's newspaper supplement, graphically dramatizes Belgium's plight by depicting an emaciated mother nursing a baby. The poster then asks Americans to eat less wheat, meat, fats, and sugar. These coordinated publications once again placed much of the burden of conservation on the average housewife. The recipe booklet itself, repeating the directions on the Food Administration Home Card, urges housewives to plan two wheatless days, Monday and Wednesday of every week; one wheatless meal every day; one meatless day, Tuesday; one meatless meal every day; and other culinary sacrifices. And again in copy paralleling a Food Administration poster, citizens are asked to "remember that every flag that flies opposite the enemies' is by proxy the American flag."[65] The corresponding poster depicts the flags of the Allies and asks Americans to "Support Every Flag that Opposes Prussianism—Eat Less of the Food Fighters Need." The recipe booklet admonishes the housewife: "If we are selfish or even careless, we are disloyal, we are the enemy at home."[66] While food conservation was an important part of the war effort, the suggestion that noncompliance or carelessness made a woman "the enemy" employs the idea of surveillance, channeling the desired emotional response into a desired action by invoking a moral compulsion that by and large obliterates intellect, and in fact implies that women, average citizens, cannot realize on the basis of rational observation that conservation is appropriate.

In response to Hoover's pleas to cut wheat consumption, recipes for war breads, "victory" breads, and "50-50" breads abounded. Janet McKenzie Hill, editor of *American Cookery*, explains in the introduction to her book *War Time Recipes* that the "U.S. Food Administration allows the name of 'Victory Bread' to be applied to any bread containing twenty percent or more of wheat substitute."[67] Copyrighted by the Procter and Gamble Company, manufacturer of the then new lard and butter substitute Crisco, *War Time Recipes* uses Crisco in every recipe. Since Hoover had also demanded, "Use no butter in cooking," Procter and Gamble could advertise its own product and remain patriotic at the same time, basically the goal of the Food Administration's move to enlist producers of food products. But food manufacturers were not the only businesses that advertised and provided war recipes at the same time. Dr. D. Jayne and Son of Philadelphia, makers of Dr. D. Jayne's Family Medicines, published booklets instructing housewives in "The Preserving of Fruits," "How to Do Pickling," and, related to the wheat shortage, preparing "War Breads." Adjacent to an advertisement for Jayne's Expectorant, cooks could find recipes for Rice Bread and Arcadian Valley Bread made of cornmeal and rolled oats.[68] In the short preface at the beginning of the booklet, Dr. D. Jayne's Family Medicines admits that the goal of the publication is to "bring again to your notice the merits of our preparations." But since there is a war on, the preface explains, "it has been our unremitting effort to supply much needed information of such a kind, and in such a manner, as would be worthy of a business which has seen four great wars in its lifetime."[69] On the cover of the recipe book, a rosy-cheeked housewife in a white apron hands a loaf of home-baked bread to Uncle Sam, who holds her in a fatherly embrace and, because she is a dutiful daughter, regards her with a kindly expression.

Already established as a way of admonishing women, the domestic science movement provided a means through which the U.S. Food Administration and other patriotic organizations could reach the average housewife with their pleas for conservation, their demand for patriotism, and their insistence on participation in the war effort. Through posters, cookbooks, and ladies' magazines, women were recruited as surely as if they were doing battle on the front lines. For so long the moral torch bearers of the nation, women were asked to win the war with food—in Hoover's words, to "bring to a successful end the greatest national task that has ever been accepted by the American people."[70] Given the habit of holding the housewife responsible for the physical, moral, and fiscal health of the nation, it should come as no surprise that she might be held responsible for the outcome of the war as well.

The wife, the mother, and in some cases the sister of the soldier, women who until 1920 still lacked the vote, would stand tall as the defenders of the hearth. Indeed, Martha Banta, in the preface to *Imaging American Women*, alludes to the Columbian Exhibition in Chicago in 1893, where visitors could observe a hundred-foot statue (a sixty-five-foot woman on a thirty-five-foot base) of the Republic. According to Banta, the statue was the centerpiece of the exhibition, emblematic of both the country and gender at the time. Banta quotes an observer, James B. Campbell, who declares that "the features of the statue had a look of proud contentment and happiness, as if there was nothing left to be desired in her existence."[71] The archetypal woman, the "statue of the Republic represented the type of the nation. The form was that of the female, the type of American womanhood writ large. The sex and the race came together as a visual emblem of the greatness (physical size and moral force) of a nation which had 'nothing left to be desired.'"[72] Also included in Campbell's praise of the Republic is the description of a then current scientific study that had set about proving that

Eve was two hundred feet tall, what Banta calls the "physical immensity of the Original Woman."[73] By 1917, the optimism of the Columbian Exhibition had been lost in the fervor of war propaganda, but the idea of woman as moral force remained. The elevation of the wife and mother to mythic proportions continued, perhaps without that look of contentment, in the propaganda image that cast her as her nation's savior.

The Royal Society and Mrs. Peel

In Great Britain, food control became part of a power struggle on the part of university scientists. Members of the Royal Society saw the war as a way of gaining a permanent position of importance in the British government and its decision-making process. The belief, according to historian Andrew J. Hull, was that "all policy questions were essentially scientific questions," a reflection of late nineteenth-century positivism and, according to Hull, an extension of public science, the belief that science should influence policy.[74] Royal Society members thus found their way onto committees involving the development of weapons and other war-related research. In spite of the ulterior motive of control, the Royal Society became in a roundabout way the guardians of working-class well-being when it came to food consumption. Their actions were based in part on the work of members D. Noël Paton and W. H. Thompson, who prior to the war had done dietary studies of the working class involving food consumption and metabolism.[75] The purpose of these studies was to establish the number of calories, generally derived from bread, necessary to maintain a high level of productivity. Although Paton argued against the importance of vitamins in diet, these were scientifically important, if class-informed, studies. In the words of William Bate Hardy, biological secretary of the Royal Society during the war, "food is fuel, and

FIG. 9. "She Helps Her Boy to Victory," anonymous.

. . . the quality of fuel supplied fixes the output of work."[76] This let-them-eat-bread cynicism in relation to the working class did lead to a rejection of mandatory rationing of flour while other commodities—tea, margarine, bacon—were ultimately rationed.[77]

This thinking also ignored or failed to anticipate the obvious reality, reflected in earlier efforts at voluntary rationing—that the British poor, like the American poor, could not afford inflated war prices for meat, rationed or not. According to Arthur Marwick in his cultural history *The Deluge: British Society and the First World War*, during the war some heavy laborers ate as much as fourteen pounds of bread a week, the equivalent of a two-pound loaf a day.[78] Mandatory rationing in Great Britain, never a reality in the United States during World War I, followed at least two efforts at voluntary rationing, including a propaganda campaign to limit that essential bread consumption by the working class. Established in late 1916, the British Ministry of Food, via the doomed efforts of highly unpopular Controller Lord Devonport, initiated the voluntary rationing campaign. A poster aimed at working-class women depicts an aproned housewife with the caption "She keeps the family to victory rations and prevents waste" (fig. 9). She is, of course, measuring flour, the commodity so important to the maintenance of her family.[79]

As in the United States, few British publications based on the conservation methods of domestic science address working-class needs. Instead, most magazine articles and cookbooks were designed to recruit middle-class women as much as they were to instruct. Dorothy C. Peel, in her 1917 *Eat-Less-Meat Book*, does cite two studies of the diet of British laborers—*Poverty: A Study of Town Life*, by Seebohm Rountree, and *Life and Labour of the People in London*, by Charles Booth. Both, according to Mrs.

Peel, draw the same conclusion: "(1) The diet of the middle classes is generally more than adequate; (2) that of the well-to-do artisan is on the whole adequate; but (3) that of the labouring class is seriously inadequate."[80] These studies echo the findings of Paton and Thompson, but Mrs. Peel, after devoting several pages to these rather obvious statistics, goes on to address the needs of her middle- and upper middle-class readers by devising menus that "contain the ample quantity of nourishment to which well-to-do people are accustomed, which do not depart unnecessarily from the usual style of living demanded and appreciated in England, and which yet lessen the strain on the nation's supply of meat, wheaten flour and sugar."[81] The war need not interfere with everyday life if women paid attention to culinary details.

Middle-class sacrifices in both countries involved the use of newly devised recipes; Marwick calls them "culinary innovations."[82] On both sides of the Atlantic, science becomes the key to maintaining a middle-class lifestyle for the duration of the war, and in doing so, science also places war work within the confines of the home and the kitchen. Peel, who believes that any "intelligent" person can learn to cook "after a few weeks of scientific teaching," still prepares food largely from scratch, albeit with fewer eggs and less cream, although both are still present.[83] Many U.S. creations also begin with basic recipes, then recycle leftovers in combination with convenience items such as canned soup. Harbingers of the American favorite, tuna noodle casserole, these recipes not only reflected food science; they used relatively new products—Campbell's Soup, as we saw illustrated in "On 'Having a Case,'" and the new lard or butter substitute, Crisco. A *Saturday Evening Post* advertisement for Crisco offers Janet McKenzie Hill's *War Time Recipes* to readers for "10 cents in stamps," and praises Hill for "dedicating this new book to the American Woman" and creating recipes that "use successfully all the flours substituted for wheat."[84] Other war cookbooks, like that for Dr. Jayne's Family Medicines, sanction nonfood products related to health. "War-Time Cook and Health Book" published by Lydia E. Pinkham Medicine Company declares on its back page, "Women's Service Requires Health and Strength." The way to achieve this freedom from headaches and other female ailments is to use Lydia E. Pinkham's Vegetable Compound. Each page of the cookbook includes recipes and testimonials from users who swear to the compound's value. And of course, printed at the very beginning of the book is the directive from Herbert Hoover to conserve food.[85] Science, industry, and government unite here to regiment the behavior of American and British women, to promote war service but in a traditional and womanly manner.

Food and Literary Fiction

Food also plays a role in wartime fiction, reflecting both widespread concerns over its continuing availability and its place in war propaganda. And of course, food continues to serve as a delineator of social class, depicting the desire of middle-class housewives to conform as culinary soldiers, to remain socially acceptable, and perhaps upwardly mobile. Much literature published during the war lacks the cynicism of postwar works, which strip from war experience the jingoism of propaganda, as for instance British poet Wilfred Owen did even during the war.[86] In postwar novels, propaganda becomes a source of conflict between those who remain safely on the home front and those who agree to "do their bit" without any indication of what they are about to face. Food as an instrument of propaganda, then, becomes an important part of the war experience as it begins to appear in literary works published both during and after the war.

In *Mr. Britling Sees It Through*, published during the war and highly successful on both sides of the Atlantic, H. G. Wells depicts upper-class indifference to possible food shortages and the desire to keep the war from disrupting everyday life. Immediately taken by war fervor, Britling is incensed when, on August 4, 1914, the day war is declared, one of his neighbors drives up in her car, which is loaded with food and other staples. Waving at the Britlings excitedly, she explains, "I thought I'd tell you. I've been getting food." The neighbor, Mrs. Faber, is contributing, of course, to the possibility of panic by hoarding. Irate because her grocer refuses to sell her more than a dozen cans of sardines, Mrs. Faber does plan to can the peas in their kitchen garden, but her hoarding would eventually become illegal. In her car are "two sides of bacon, a case of sugar, bags of rice, eggs, a lot of flour."[87] Britling says to his wife, "And that . . . is how England is going to war! Scrambling for food—at the very beginning."[88]

Still, among the many things Britling must cope with during the early days of the war, food is never an issue. While he may be uncertain about his foreign investments, Britling has the means to take in and feed an upper middle-class Belgian refugee, Mr. Van der Pant, whose wife is temporarily misplaced in England. She and their children have been sent to England earlier and are safe but, because of bureaucratic bungling, cannot at the moment be found. Dining with the Britlings on the first evening, Van der Pant notices that they are serving a Moselle. Apologetically, Britling asks, "Do you care . . . to drink a German wine?" Van der Pant replies that the wine is good and "after the peace it will be Belgian."[89] We can assume the wine has come from Britling's cellar, stocked before the war, but the dinner once again suggests that "usual style of living" to which Dorothy Peel alludes.[90] Only those middle-class women who perhaps need to gain status from their patriotism must make a show of conservation. These are the women at whom, as we have seen, much propaganda was aimed, and one of the places where propaganda was most effective. Pledge cards mailed to Herbert Hoover, window cards placed conspicuously in the front window for the neighbors to see, and the U.S. Food Administration uniform all assure inquiring eyes that the woman of the house is doing her patriotic duty. British matrons visibly "did their bit" by holding recruiting meetings, and as discussed in chapter 2, young women took to the streets to present white feathers, symbols of cowardice, to any able-bodied male not in uniform.

HELEN ZENNA SMITH'S *NOT SO QUIET . . . STEPDAUGHTERS OF WAR*

Food becomes especially important as a tool of control when it becomes a reward for desired wartime behavior, as is depicted in Helen Zenna Smith's novel *Not So Quiet . . . Stepdaughters of War*. First published in 1930, *Not So Quiet* is the grim chronicle of a Voluntary Aid Detachment ambulance driver's experiences.[91] Smith, pseudonym for freelance writer Evadne Price, obtained the war journal of a VAD by the name of Winifred Young, who had turned over the diary with the stipulation that Price remain faithful to its tone. Even though it was published twelve years after the war's end, the novel's emotional turmoil emerges directly from the war via the diary. Price's fictional account graphically depicts the horror and suffering of war and the insurmountable rift between home front and front lines, a rift maintained by propaganda, social pressure, and in the case of the VADs, food deprivation.

First, we should acknowledge that a frontline position will

by nature be spartan. But the conclusions of the Royal Society's food studies also apply here. William Bate Hardy's assumption that "food is fuel, and . . . the quality of fuel supplied fixes the output of work" must, and in most cases does, inform the decisions of those supplying food to troops. For much of the war, for instance, the British were able to provide the men in the trenches with a daily ration of rum for their morning tea. Not so the ambulance drivers in *Not So Quiet*. In the opening pages of the novel, as one of the drivers prepares beef broth for the women, Smithy remarks that they are always hungry, that in fact they survive on "[beef broth], biscuits, and slab chocolate" sent from home (10). The canteen food is "vile at best" (10), and Smithy's descriptions of the food are indeed disgusting. Not only is the food badly prepared, but "one is liable to find hair-combings in the greasy gravy; bits of plate leavings from the day before and an odd hairpin" (51). On top of the bad cooking, ingredients fall into the category of mystery meat, what Smithy calls "sinister looking joints of some strange animal" that the drivers "often go outside in groups to examine" (51). Because of the immense responsibility of the drivers—ferrying wounded and dying men in the dark on icy roads, often under enemy fire—logic might dictate better treatment. Indeed, Smithy comments that the "hospital orderlies say they would never stand our rations." She goes on to explain that the orderlies "have Army rations, of course" (51). The key here is the reliance on the home front for what should be treats but become sustenance. Beef broth and chocolate have never been expected to feed an army, but the unwillingness to acknowledge that these middle-class women are doing work that is both essential and exhausting—they are only civilians doing their bit—keeps them hungry.

At the root of the VAD's ill treatment is not only that desire to enlist civilians in the war effort but the focus, also reflected in the United States, on demanding war work of middle-class women—people Smithy refers to as "refined women of decent education" (50). Middle-class women, aware of that historical burden of moral superiority, are in fact easy targets. Eager to please, eager to exert their moral superiority on wounded soldiers, and always reluctant to complain, the drivers, Smithy argues, are "the only class that suffers in silence, that scorns to carry tales. . . . We dare not face being called 'cowards' and 'slackers,' which we certainly shall be if we complain" (50). Home, in this case, becomes a threat, not a solace, the place where they will be disgraced if they return prematurely. The Panopticon, the home front, is most definitely "a way of defining power relations," and the VADs are at the bottom of the hierarchy.

Smithy's words address another aspect of middle-class compliance—the hope that contributions to the war effort will enhance social status, will grant upward mobility to those who seek it, as Smithy's mother does. Mrs. Smith is a rabid warmonger who will do anything to out-recruit her neighbor Mrs. Evans-Mawnington. Mrs. Smith's letters to Smithy shamelessly reflect the competition between the two: at one point Mrs. Smith "has seventeen more recruits than Mrs. Evans-Mawnington up to date" (76). That these numbers reflect potential casualties, men maimed or killed, means little to either woman. Because their money was earned in manufacturing—jam in the Smiths' case—both women seek enhanced social status through the war service of their children. Mrs. Smith has no idea, nor does she wish to, of the horrible conditions under which her daughter lives; she does not fathom the devastation Smithy lives with daily. Smithy has quickly perceived the force of the jingoism that is prevalent back home. A brave VAD, she is one of England's "splendid daughters," who must not write home that she does not "believe in God or them or the infallibility of England or anything but bloody war and wounds and foul smells" (30). Smithy believes telling the truth would result in being called a "silly hysterical little girl," or ultimately being disowned, as Smithy is. The truth can never win out over jingoism when upward mobility is the prize.

Price's novel reflects the power of propaganda on a middle class desperate to be socially accepted, to remain an essential aspect of the Gesellschaft. Propaganda and its promise of enhanced social status as a reward for good behavior keep the VADs within view of the Panopticon—under constant surveillance—and at the same time imply their complicity. The role of food then becomes one of coercion, a way for those on the home front to maintain power. Food in the form of the care package becomes a function of the Panopticon, as a way of maintaining surveillance. As a reward for "doing their bit," the packages serve as a kind of bribe, while at the same time reminding the recipients of their complicity. Bovril and biscuits become part of the system of surveillance. As the drivers drink the last of a bottle of Bovril, someone points out, "If there isn't a parcel soon with a new supply we go out empty tomorrow" (21). The new supply arrives with a letter from Smithy's aunt, who is leaving her money to Smithy because she is "so *pleased* with [Smithy's] patriotism and noble example to all girls of [her] age" (79). If Smithy remains compliant, she will receive more than potted meat for her service; she will become an heiress.

Like the food scientists who argued for ample bread for working-class families to keep them productive, civilians on the home front used food as a way of eliciting desired behavior. The occasional jar of potted meat and tin of ginger tea biscuits compelled VADs to continue working "under conditions no professional scullery-maid would tolerate for a day" (50). Housewives back home, whether supervising servants or doing the cooking themselves, were unwilling to relinquish their moral grip on household and family, and thus joined the fight by using domestic science to prepare tasty but patriotic meals. Campbell's Soup and meatless meals became a way of life for a society that had dined in splendor roughly twenty years before. Dietary sacrifices became a specific way to "do your bit" and avoid the censure of those prying eyes that supported the mechanism of the Panopticon. Whether under the auspices of the British Ministry of Food, the U.S. Food Administration, or zealous parents, food becomes a powerful political force. Because it is a necessary commodity, food served the cause of social control as well as any other source of propaganda. Food also served Herbert Hoover well, rewarding him in 1929 with the U.S. presidency.

In all of these circumstances, the state or Gesellschaft manipulates the primary relationships of women to their husbands and children, as well as their secondary relationship to the state, weaving the two together until they become inseparable. As we shall observe, authors of popular fiction employ the same tactic privately to maintain war fervor in the home at the fever pitch necessary to the continuation of the war.

TWO

"One Hundred Percent"

War Service and Women's Fiction

Post–World War I fiction and personal narratives are known, sometimes erroneously, for their cynicism and bitterness. Fiction written during the war, with few exceptions, is of an entirely different ilk. Magazine fiction, especially concerning women's war service, lacks cynicism altogether and either promotes participation in ways that correspond with official propaganda or uses the plight of women, especially Belgian women, to advance the idea of war service. To achieve its ends, magazine fiction relies heavily on clichéd images of women: good ones, who might temporarily stray but eventually recognize the error of their ways; wealthy, careless, even evil ones who do not redeem themselves thus; and saintly ones who are pure for the duration of their lives, which are often brief. The good women are the ones who rise to the call of both family and state, who sacrifice themselves and their men to defeat the bloody Hun. Certainly these stereotypes are not new; they are, in fact, archetypal—the fairy godmother and the wicked witch of fairy tales—and perhaps, as Keen argues, they may be imbedded in social institutions. Keen's claim that "society shapes the psyche and vice versa," undoubtedly raises a chicken-and-egg dilemma, yet the stereotypes persist within ideal social structures.[1] Domestic science, as we have seen, makes use of similar clichés in belittling the housewife who cannot cook and blaming her for whatever bad behavior her husband may exhibit. While the stereotypes may reveal the occasional variation for the sake of suspense, in war fiction, the call to duty and sacrifice remains constant.

Long before official American involvement in the war, American magazines included both fiction and nonfiction promoting, at the very least, sensitivity to the predicament of many Europeans.[2] Events such as the invasion of Belgium and the sinking of the *Lusitania* on May 7, 1915, provided source material for official and unofficial propaganda. One of the most brutal of the "official" stories was that of the handless Belgian baby, the child deliberately mutilated by advancing German soldiers. Arthur Ponsonby in *Falsehood in War-Time* devotes a chapter to the story, which he declares "everyone wanted to believe, . . . and many [people] went so far as to say they had seen the baby."[3] Newspapers on both sides of the Atlantic reported the story as fact and also published photographs of the baby. According to Ponsonby, *Le Rive Rouge* published two photos, one in September of 1915 and one on July 26, 1916, which depict German soldiers eating the hands.[4] Newspapers also vilified the Kaiser in stories and he was burned in effigy frequently in the United States. *Critica* in Buenos Aires published a drawing supplied by the Allies in which the Kaiser forces women to turn over their children so that he can chop off their hands. Underneath the picture a caption reads, "Suffer little children to come unto me."[5] We will shortly see these images repeated in Wallace Irwin's short story "One of Ten Million." Robert Graves in *Good-Bye to All That* also addresses the question of handless babies. Claiming to have seen children without both hands and feet, Graves believes the wounds were "merely the result of shell-fire, British or French shell-fire as likely as not," rather than German bayonets, a point to which we shall return in chapter 5.[6] As Ponsonby points out, however, neither seems plausible. In his words, "No one paused to ask how long a baby would live were its hands cut off unless expert surgical aid were at hand [sic] to tie up the arteries (the answer being, a very few minutes)."[7] But the propagandists' regard for the truth is negligible, and stories involving women and children are too hard to resist. As we observed earlier, according to Ferdinand Tönnies, primary relationships are the foundation of the Gemeinschaft, and propaganda uses those relationships to invoke a sense of community and of threat to the community. Mothers separated from their children or children from their parents and atrocities committed against either group illustrate the most detestable of those threats. Among the posters employing the sinking of the *Lusitania* is Fred Spear's "Enlist," which depicts a drowned mother submerged with her baby in her arms.

The Good, the Bad, and the Wealthy: Female Stereotypes in War Fiction

Few could ignore the paradigm of a drowning mother and baby and the threat it implies, and few did. In 1916, two years into the war and after the sinking of the *Lusitania*, even urbane publications such as *Metropolitan* and *McClure's* began to reflect war mania. The September 1916 issue of *McClure's* begins with a story by Porter Emerson Browne, "Mary and Marie." "Mary and Marie" begins with the line: "This is not much of a story," and in fact it is not. Browne, who was a frequent contributor to *McClure's*, quickly became one of the war's most vehement supporters. Indeed, we will encounter his work later as we examine children's literature. Author of plays, stories, and satirical pieces, including the highly sentimental play *A Fool There Was*, Browne was well known for crafting melodrama, both on and off the stage. Historically, *A Fool There Was* is his most recognized work. The play was based on Kipling's poem "The Vampire," which begins with the lines:

A fool there was and he made his prayer
(Even as you or I)
To a rag and bone and a hank of hair.[8]

The poem describes a man who leaves his family for a femme fatale and is then summarily dumped. In 1915 *A Fool There Was* became a film starring Theda Bara, the film that made her career and gave us the slang term *vamp*. In an article in the September 1909 issue of *Everybody's Magazine*, Browne writes of creating melodrama, "Don't be afraid of seasoning too highly, nor of cooking too fiercely. You can't do it."[9] Browne is speaking of drama here, but his recipe applies to the story "Mary and Marie," which is not only melodramatic and stereotypical but rife with sentimentality. The story contrasts the lives of two young women: Mary, a wealthy American, and Marie, a young Belgian rustic. According to the narrator, Mary's country "sat idly by, selfish, self-satisfied, . . . squandering vacuously in self-pander all [her] riches of honor and courage and dignity," while Marie's "went to war to save her gentle soul from dishonor."[10] Marie's father is an innkeeper and her life is bucolic. Between her chores at her father's inn, she communes often with the nearby river, her "friend." But one day the Germans cross the bridge over the river, kick the family's trusted plow horse, and kill Marie's father, Papa Michard, and her brother as she looks on helplessly. Marie flees to the river but decides she must warn other villagers that the Germans are coming. She is caught, raped, and left to die. Marie has just enough strength to crawl back to the river, where she departs this war-torn world in peace. Mary, of course, back in New York, parties and pays for her entertainment with money her father has made on munitions—as he puts it, "one of the stocks that those darned fools over in Europe are boosting by killing one another." If it keeps on, he tells her, they will soon have a house in Newport.[11] Of course, Marie and not Mary provides the obvious connection to the religious imagery here. Marie is both saintly and virginal, in spite of having been ravaged by the ruthless Huns. The drunken Mary, at the end of the story, is a figure no proper woman would emulate, unless of course she is wealthy enough to escape reproach. The figure of the evil "vamp" also reverberates here. Mary may not be a literal vampire, but she and her money-hungry father are in fact feeding off the blood of a devastated Europe.

An early supporter of American involvement in World War I, Browne had already published a number of short pieces on the war in *McClure's*. But the rest of the magazine does not reflect the kind of war fervor Browne promotes. With the exception of a poem, "Epitaph for a German Soldier," which appears on the second page of "Mary and Marie," war images are notably absent. Other fiction for the month includes a story by Sophie Kerr, "That Parkinson Affair," and "Bridges Burned," a story by Mary Browne Donoho, "a new Southern writer who gives an old situation a fresh twist."[12] The advertisement for Ivory soap opposite "Mary and Marie" depicts a clean modern bathroom and a well-dressed woman and beribboned little girl. In fact, the advertisements seem to involve women like Browne's Mary. A Packer's Tar Soap ad describes "Margaret's carelessness—and her hair." The ad's illustration is of an upper middle-class bedroom and three women, one obviously Margaret, doing her hair as the other two look on approvingly. Perhaps not as wealthy as Mary, the women in the ads nonetheless demonstrate the superficial concerns for beauty and self-protection reflected in the story, and a concern for fashion that continued through 1918, despite the war. Browne's aim here clearly is to shame female readers into becoming the selfless patriotic heroines of later war fiction and propaganda. While Ivory soap might survive war scrutiny,

Rogers Brothers Silverware depicted on the back cover would not. And the noble black horse, the mount of a stunning beautifully dressed woman on the cover, most likely will be drafted into military service. As the ads suggest, Americans were not yet ready to devote all their attention to a European war, but the vehicle for later propaganda is certainly in place. Images of marriageable women and mothers and children, as well as of the prosperous home, abound here. The sentimentality of Browne's story, the image of the virtuous and self-sacrificing girl, is consistent with the tone of the magazine.

Married and Dangerous

The idea of the selfish and unethical woman of wealth, a woman like Browne's Mary, is repeated in the Dana Gatlin story "New York Stuff," which appeared in the March 1918 issue of *McClure's Magazine*. Like the New York of the Browne story, Gatlin's New York is all superficial glitter. In the opening paragraph, Gatlin quickly informs her readers that New York is "too engrossed with her materialistic provender, the things which can be judged in terms of dollars and cents, which can be bought and sold; the things which, in the destroyed or partially destroyed cities of Europe, the very hand of distraction has proved to be but ephemeral baubles after all."[13] And indeed, one of those ephemeral baubles, a ruby necklace, becomes the focus of the story. One new element in the Gatlin story is the image of the dangerous married woman who corrupts, or tries to corrupt, the innocent girl or her beau, or both, an image that also appears in Worrall and Terry's play/novel *The White Feather*, although with a twist. Also a stereotype, the dangerous married woman is the antithesis of the self-sacrificing wife or mother who is the heart of the Gemeinschaft and the model for war service. The threat the dangerous woman poses is tantamount to the threat of the enemy to the stable family unit. There is no place for this disruptive figure in the Gemeinschaft, although she may have, or have had, a husband. The dangerous woman refuses to operate within the strict family structure, and thus she appears in these stories as a further source of evil. Because there is a war on, good will triumph over evil in magazine fiction. To celebrate the endurance of the conventional family, at least in this Gatlin story, the dangerous woman gets her comeuppance.

"NEW YORK STUFF"

In "New York Stuff," the good but temporarily dazzled Nora Starr has gone to New York from a place called Cherryvale to pursue a career in art, selling drawings and magazine covers to magazine editors. From the very beginning in the clichéd name Cherryvale, we see small-town values pitted against the city's lack thereof. To her complete surprise, the innocent Nora is taken up by a married "society" woman when the two meet at a "War Charity Bazaar." Predictable from the first word in its character development, the story takes us into the world of Fanny Gentry, who "owned two motor cars and a pearl necklace, and . . . exhibited her Pekingese at dog-shows" (13), but is in fact not real "gentry." Readers must guess from Fanny's lifestyle that she lives to an extent beyond her means, and Fanny encourages Nora to do the same. Fanny persuades Nora to give up her room in a "respectable" boarding house for an apartment in a residential hotel overlooking Central Park and to buy expensive dresses on credit. Nora has some qualms about getting in over her head, especially since "events were happening at the minute which called for a whole world's mourning" (13). Reflecting Cherryvale's "small town" principles, Nora, as propaganda would have it, transfers her feelings for her own community to the larger community that is in distress. Until she is distracted by Fanny, Nora willingly performs the war service that Fanny performs to attract attention.

Nora also wonders about Fanny's behavior, which is "boisterous" according to small-town Cherryvale standards. But because her head is turned by Fanny's attention, Nora ignores her reservations. Even Fanny's flirtation with Dickey, a single man of old family, becomes to Nora "the New York way," since Fanny's husband only makes jokes about it (13). Dickey, who tolerates Fanny and clearly cares about Nora, tries to warn her on more than one occasion and refers to the Gentrys' crowd as "bounders" (55). References to the war occur every time Nora does something she knows is shallow or when she suffers pangs of guilt for squandering her talent and money trying to please Fanny instead of doing something about the war. The ephemeral bauble Gatlin refers to, the ruby necklace, appears one evening when Nora arrives at the Gentry home for a dinner party wearing a new red satin dress and a violet corsage sent from Dickey. Although Nora does not tell Fanny where the corsage came from, Fanny clearly guesses and jealously removes it, then "loans" Nora the ruby pendant. When Nora demurs, Fanny declares, "You're surely not one of those silly prudes who thinks we should all go round looking like frumps, just because there's a war!" (56). While Nora lacks the "spiritual energy" to argue with Fanny, she is put off by Fanny's "sneering tone" and reminds herself that while "there were many foolish and futile methods of showing 'patriotism' afloat just then, . . . they were efforts in the right direction" (56). Unlike the hollow patriotism of Fanny's war service, Nora's sense of duty and empathy are genuine. Nora is out of place in the world of the story, and her predicament is that of every good girl gone temporarily awry. Eager to appear urbane and to please Fanny, Nora gives in and wears the necklace, which of course, she "misplaces."

The loss of the necklace becomes a wake-up call for Nora. Since she is still a woman of integrity underneath all that glitter, Nora insists on paying back the twenty-two hundred dollars Fanny paid for the necklace, a feat that will require her to give up her high-priced friends. Here, Fanny's character becomes apparent, if it were not already, when she tells Nora that she bought the necklace with a one-thousand-dollar check from her father and "was dunned to death before I got the balance paid" (57). Fanny lacks the small-town value of paying off debts in a timely manner, or better yet, not having debts at all. Nora has wondered why Fanny always seems short of cash and is constantly trying to get money from her father, who is supposedly wealthy, but Nora has again chalked it up to the New York way, a way that has come to represent the worst of the larger community, the Gesellschaft.

At this point Nora's conscience gets the better of her, and she makes a speech about the war and her own lack of participation in it: "I'm in no position to do *anything* that I should," she tells Fanny emotionally. "All the suffering in France and Belgium—every time I hear stories of those poor children, my heart bleeds! But, what's the good of your heart's bleeding if you do nothing really to help? Do you know that, all this time I've been squandering money so foolishly, I've never given one cent to any war charity?" (57, italics Gatlin's). Fanny is at first speechless, then sarcastically calls Nora's words "very creditable sentiments," further illustration of Fanny's frivolous character. Nora, on the other hand, reveals that she is serious about her intentions by breaking off with Fanny and all of her crowd, including Dickey, an action that, not surprisingly, garners Fanny's approval. The plot twist here further reveals Nora's goodness and Fanny's evil. Nora moves back to a boarding house, works hard on her drawings, and begins earning more money, enough to pay her bills and send Fanny a small payment on the necklace.

While this story lacks the unabashed sentimentality of the Browne story, it comes close in its conclusion. As her luck would have it, one day Nora receives the largest check she has ever had for her work and gets a letter from Dickey, forwarded from Cherryvale, where he believes Nora has gone. In her jubilation, Nora writes a two-hundred-dollar check to Fanny and resolves to take it to her. Not at home, Fanny is dining at the Plaza Hotel, and Nora goes there, where she finds Fanny and Dickey together. Nora is not surprised to find Dickey there, but she is shocked to see Fanny wearing the "lost" ruby pendant. Dickey, who is a good sort after all, knows Nora is upset about something and abandons Fanny in the Plaza. Outside, he tells Nora, "Something hideous [is going on]!—I sense it" (57). Readers do not learn whether Nora gives some of her newly earned money to war charities, but for her sentiments and for her conformity to the ways of the Gemeinschaft, Cherryvale, she marries Dickey, the wealthy husband of good family, while Fanny must return to her bounder husband and friends, who have no values. Readers might even suspect that given the right circumstances, Fanny would abandon her own home for Dickey and his wealth. While the word divorce may have been too strong for *McClure's* fiction at the time, Fanny's jealousy of Nora and her absolute desire that Nora "dump" Dickey suggest Fanny has set her sights on winning him and his money without regard for any moral issues that might arise. Fanny's complete lack of integrity, her willingness to endanger the family unit by her pursuit of Dickey, is closely tied to her insensitivity to war issues. Fanny is not the married woman of war posters and sheet music. Like Mary of "Mary and Marie," Fanny will do anything to get money, even lie and steal from a "friend," or worse, divorce her husband. Both Fanny and Mary are concerned only with their own amusements and care nothing for Belgian children, handless or not.

Released almost a year after the beginning of American involvement in the war, this issue of *McClure's* is almost entirely devoted to war issues, and is, in fact, called *McClure's Win-the-War Magazine*. On the editorial page, contributors including Dana Gatlin and Porter Emerson Browne comment on editor Frederick L. Collins's "plans for making McClure's a Win-the-War magazine," as Collins explains. Browne, in typical hyperbolic fashion, declares, "The subordination of all considerations, private, personal, financial, to the end that victory shall be ours, speaks magnificently for the spirit and patriotism of both owners and editors. You are again pioneers on the trail . . . all America should, and soon must, be pursuing."[14] Describing the changes in outlook at *McClure's*, Collins declares in an oxymoronic paragraph that the new *McClure's* will be "not a gloom magazine,—not a propaganda magazine,—not a government bulletin,—not a mouthpiece of parties or societies or movements,—just the same old *McClure's* in attractive appearance and entertainment value, but with every page framed to do its part in helping our boys abroad to win the war by stimulating, encouraging and strengthening the patriotic spirit of the folks who must stay at home."[15]

But like pornography, we must know propaganda when we see it, and this is it. Even the Ivory soap ad opposite the editorial page reflects the war, depicting not an upper middle-class woman but a soldier pulling a bar of Ivory from his kit. The copy tells readers, "That boy of yours will think of home every time he washes if you put a cake of Ivory soap in his comfort kit." First, the copy invokes the idea of the Gemeinschaft, the family unit that will be maintained by patriotism and soap in the face of the evil Hun. Second, the copy ignores the fact that in the trenches, a bar of soap is virtually useless. An additional soldier drying his hands on a clean white towel makes the war look like Boy Scout camp, perhaps because the truth of the trenches itself challenges the sanctity of the family unit.

Other ads and articles echo *McClure's* Win-the-War policy. Among the nonfiction articles, "Uncle Sam's Flour Barrel" describes the flour mills in Minneapolis, and "It's the Huns!" provides a firsthand account of air raids in London. "It's the Huns!" champions the "splendid, contemptuous fearlessness" of Londoners in the face of German air raids.[16] Sharing space with it is an advertisement for *The Rape of Belgium*, a book by Hugh Gibson depicting German atrocities and the "murder" of Edith Cavell, a British nurse who was executed for helping French and British prisoners escape from a hospital in German-occupied Belgium. Offered through *McClure's* book department, the book is available for a trial inspection and can be paid for in two installments. Like "Mary and Marie," the ad demonizes Germany in an illustration of a fainting woman being crushed by a fist bearing the German eagle insignia, and according to the copy, the book "faithfully pictures for you the wreck and crimes the Prussian perpetrates in his lust for conquest."

THE WHITE FEATHER

A second depiction of the dangerous married woman, or in this case widow, occurs in Lechmere Worrall and J. E. Harold Terry's creation *The White Feather*, which appeared in a number of guises. Performed as a play that opened on December 10, 1914, under the name *The Man Who Stayed at Home*, the work was also "novelized" and published in 1915. The play ran for almost two years at the Royalty in London and was also performed in major cities in the United States under both titles, although the play reappeared in the United States under the title *The White Feather* and had apparently by then been "Americanized."[17] It is to the novel *The White Feather*, which maintains the same plot as the original play, that I refer here.

The play is billed both as a comedy and as a "spy thriller." The initial *New York Times* review of Saturday, February 6, 1915, claims the play was written in a hurry, which it must have been to hit the stage within barely five months of the war's beginning. According to the *Times* reviewer, parts of the play are "funny without meaning to be." One of the questionable scenes that occurs early in the plot development and gives the novel its title has to do with a young girl and a basket of white feathers, the symbol of cowardice presented to able-bodied men who were not in uniform.

In the scene, Daphne Kidlington, who never reappears, shows up at the resort hotel on the English Channel where our heroine, Molly Pollock in the novel and Molly Preston in the play, is staying with her father, a justice of the peace in the novel, and her fiancé Christopher Brent, who by September of 1914 has not yet enlisted. Daphne wants Molly to go out with her to dispense white feathers, but Molly's father expresses disapproval. Mr. Pollock asks Daphne, "What good do you suppose you are going to do by setting the men's backs up, eh?"[18] Undeterred, Daphne presents a white feather to Brent, who uses the plume to clean his pipe and makes a joke about the innkeeper's refusal to let him pluck her pigeons, foreshadowing the revelation that among the pigeons are carrier pigeons that deliver messages to the Germans. Molly is incensed at Daphne for shaming her fiancé, and Daphne is incensed at everyone else, and when asked to leave, she storms off down the lane trailing feathers. Mr. Pollock, still disapproving but softening his position, tells the group, "Some of her feathers may be deserved, but she goes the wrong way to work" (25). Miss Myrtle, spinster and old "friend" of Mr. Pollock, says to Brent, "Painful as it has been to me to witness your ordeal, I hope that the significance of it will make you think." Mr. Pollock, moving farther away from disapproval as Miss Myrtle quickly retreats, replies, "I don't often agree with that cat of an old maid, but I must say I think she is right this time," and he too retreats before Brent can respond. The farther into the plot we go, the more antagonistic Mr. Pollock becomes toward Brent, until he finally decides to forbid Molly to marry him. What Molly, Miss Myrtle, and Mr. Pollock/Preston do not know at the moment Daphne presents the white feather is that Christopher Brent is an officer in the British Secret Service and is at the inn to uncover a German plot to blow up ships in the harbor. Audiences, because of the billing of the play, must have sensed that Brent is the hero in disguise—he wears a monocle to appear foolish—but the response to the patriotic gesture of giving the white feather, and playing the scene for comedy, could have been risky and suggests the *New York Times* reviewer was correct in his assertion that the play was hastily written. Two issues appear at cross-purposes here. Mr. Pollock's eventual refusal to allow Molly to marry a "slacker" illustrates the pressure on all young able-bodied men to enlist and the rabid patriotism that we have already seen on the home front. Still, the idea of an uppity young woman publicly shaming even a slacker was distasteful to the Victorian generation that was sending its young off to war.

Historically, the response to the white feather is a debatable issue. Historian Nicoletta F. Gullace, in a lengthy article published in the *Journal of British Studies*, suggests that ultimately the white feather campaign may not have been as well received as it perhaps was at the outset of the war—that is, when the play was written. "The Order of the White Feather" originated on August 30, 1914, when Admiral Charles Penrose Fitzgerald came up with the idea of shaming young men into enlisting by having middle-class women, initially in Folkstone, hand out white feathers to "slackers." According to Gullace, "the practice occurred, much as described in both contemporary and postwar accounts, but . . . its meaning, seriousness, and symbolic load were greatly enhanced as the war drew to a close and people began to count the dead."[19] In other words, women's complicity in the casualties was duly noted as postwar cynicism evolved.[20] Since the war, feminist scholars as early as Virginia Woolf have seen the memory of the white feather campaign as, in Gullace's words, "more a product of male hysteria than of actual female practice" (180). Male hysteria or no, the campaign was prevalent enough to spread to the colonies. In the documentary "Killing Fields: The First World War," an episode of *People's Century*, Australian Edward Smout recalls enlisting to fight as a citizen of the British Empire. "If you'd stayed a year or two longer [at home]," Smout laughs, "you'd have got a white feather from the girls—no it was the thing to do."[21]

But as we are learning, the white feather campaign was only one of many ways in which women were coopted into war service as part of propaganda campaigns. Gullace herself alludes to one of the most famous British recruiting posters from the Great War, "Women of Britain Say—GO!" a poster that uses images of upper- and working-class women and a child, all watching as the troops march off to war (fig. 10). British and American war songs use the voice of womanhood to recruit, mostly by invoking men's sense of duty to their mothers. Songs portraying mothers sending men off to fight include the British "Your King and Country Want You," a song intended for the colonies, "Britannia Needs You Like a Mother (Would You Turn

FIG. 10. "Women of Britain Say—GO!" poster by E. V. Kealey.

Your Mother Down?)" and the American "America Here's My Boy," "If I Had a Son for Each Star in Old Glory (Uncle Sam, I'd Give Them All to You)," and "A Mother's Liberty Loan"; we will examine these songs more fully in chapter 5. While they do seem to be written largely by men, they parallel the tendency of propaganda to employ women to achieve its purpose in the way that the white feather campaign literally did. Even though white feather bestowers might be, in Gullace's words, "bold and impudent [enough] to brave disapproval" (182), as is Daphne Kidlington, the concept that these women were uppity contradicts propaganda imagery and other historical references to women's participation in war fervor. What we see here is a social conflict between encouraging female impudence and appearing unpatriotic. In *The White Feather*, the idea of the slacker Christopher Brent becomes as disgusting to Molly's father as a female who forgets her place.

Edward Smout's laughter as he alludes to the white feather does suggest a sort of uneasiness with the idea of public shame, but the source of his unease is not clear. The notion that "it was the thing to do" suggests a much broader public disapprobation of shirkers and a seriousness that went well beyond a young woman's disapproval. Shortly after admitting that he agrees with Miss Myrtle about Brent's white feather, Mr. Pollock declares that "I disapprove entirely of such methods. . . . If a man cannot or will not hear his country's call, he must either be able to give a reasonable excuse to his friends or be prepared to sacrifice their esteem. . . . Impertinent young women have no right to force such explanations by employing emblems of cowardice" (83). That women were both specifically and symbolically tied up with that disapproval is precisely the focus of this chapter. Whatever the response to the Order of the White Feather and their followers, shirkers were universally shunned and loathed because they were leaving their women to the mercy of the evil Hun, and everyone knew from the stories that came out of Belgium early in the war what the evil Hun did to women. We have seen an example in "Mary and Marie," and this is clearly the message in *The Rape of Belgium*. Given the historical context, then, it might seem that whatever comedy grew out of the white feather scene may have provoked an uneasy laugh like Smout's, one in which the misogyny of the moment is ultimately overshadowed by patriotism. When Christopher Brent cleans his pipe with the emblem of cowardice, he is deliberately playing the fool to cover his actual purpose at the inn. He also does so when he allows his bath tub to overflow into the sitting room below, an act that conveniently moves the guests out of the room to thwart the German spies. Both acts pave the way for his "accidental" shooting of his landlady's carrier pigeon as it flies off with a message for the Germans. Brent knows he is earning the censure of his friends, but he must act the part to maintain his cover. We might also add that this is popular drama, a play billed as a spy thriller. Taking audience expectation into account, the playwright cannot allow the leading man to remain a fool for the duration of the play. The audience is with Brent from the very beginning and can therefore laugh at his antics.

A second strike against Christopher Brent is his apparent flirtation with the widow, Miriam Lee, who has arrived the evening prior to the white feather incident. Mr. Pollock suspects that Christopher has known Mrs. Lee previously, and indeed he has. Brent tells Molly that he knew Mrs. Lee's husband in South Africa, which is true, but the dangerous Mrs. Lee is also a British spy. Taking up for Christopher later in the day at tea, Miriam asks Mr. Pollock why he did not receive a white feather from Daphne. Mr. Pollock alludes to his age and "great responsibilities of a private nature," which he cannot divulge

(86). While Molly is involved in adjusting the ill-fitting uniform of newly enlisted Percy Pennicuik, who has just taken Molly for a tour of a nearby military camp, Christopher walks off after Miriam, to Mr. Pollock's amazement. Turning on Christopher, Mr. Pollock protests, "That fellow Brent has no sense of decency or shame whatever. . . . His brazen effrontery about the white feather at tea is nearly equaled by Mrs. Lee. Cross-questioning me like that indeed! And now look at 'em! Might have known each other for years! An outrageous flirtation, I call it" (88). Mr. Pollock cannot cope with unmarried women other than his daughter, and Miriam is the worst sort of unmarried woman—much worse than the merely annoying Miss Myrtle—because she is still young enough to be attractive, and since she has previously been married, she has experience with men as well. Miriam also contradicts Mr. Pollock; that is, she is an independent thinker. All these circumstances make Miriam a threat to the family unit, the local community of vacationers, and Miriam's past makes her a prime suspect as a German spy, a threat to the larger community, the state, as well.

By the time Mr. Pollock has uttered the word *flirtation*, audiences or readers have seen the Marconi Christopher and Miriam have found hidden in the fireplace and used to receive a message from German spies trying to communicate with the innkeeper, Mrs. Sanderson, who is also a German spy and a threat to both the local community and the state. The upshot of the message on the Marconi is that the Germans are planning to blow up troop transports crossing the channel that evening. Audiences must now trust Miriam, except for the remote possibility that she is a counter-spy, which is very remote because Mrs. Sanderson, her son Charles—actually employed by the British Admiralty, the waiter Fritz, and the sinister Fräulein Schroeder, all spies, do not include her in their conversations until she poses as a German spy to take suspicion away from Christopher. As Christopher must play the fool, Miriam must play the dangerous widow to protect Christopher and their attempt to foil the German plot.

Christopher's final act of buffoonery is "accidentally" shooting Fritz's last carrier pigeon as it flies off with a map of a British minefield taped to its leg. The Marconi destroyed and the pigeon dead, the spies must resort to burning the inn and its inhabitants as a signal to the German submarine anchored off the coast. One of Miriam's finer moments occurs when she must play the femme fatale and a German spy to save Chris from Molly's interrogation after Molly finds in Miriam's room the map taken from the dead carrier pigeon. Charles Sanderson, Mrs. Sanderson's son and the mole who stole the map from the Admiralty in the first place, has attempted to divert attention away from himself and has told Mr. Pollock that someone, Mrs. Lee, or possibly Chris, has stolen the "document" and could be a German spy. Partially telling the truth to Molly, Miriam reveals how she and Chris met in South Africa and Chris rescued her from her "brute" of a husband. Miriam's only lie is that she has gone to work spying for Germany after Chris bails her out of her bad marriage. She is willing to be thought the temptress and corrupter of Chris to prevent Mr. Pollock, who has the authority as a justice of the peace, from arresting Chris before the real spy ring is broken up. Sarcastically brilliant, Miriam claims to have stolen the map that Chris has admitted to stealing rather than explain that the map came off the pigeon. She says of him, "How perfectly delicious of you! . . . and how exactly like you! Who says that chivalry is dead?" (185) Miriam also makes Sanderson believe she is a German spy, and in this way gains the trust of Mrs. Sanderson and Fräulein Schroeder, whom she traps by driving them to town to the police station.

Gradually Chris reveals his position to everyone, and all is well. But the contrast between Molly and Miriam, the world-weary spy, persists until the end. Christopher Brent loves Molly for her frailty and ignorance, and he even tells Miriam that he wonders what Molly will be like when she loses her innocence, "when things happen that will make her grow" (45). Miriam suggests, "Nothing ever may happen. . . . Englishwomen have a most remarkable faculty of becoming wives and mothers and still floating on through life in bland ignorance" (45); that is, they will always be useful to the family and the state. By plot's end, Molly has changed, but she never acquires the sophistication of Miriam. In a brief moment of bonding after Molly has learned the truth, Miriam tells her she will need to be a support for Chris to lean on. At the very end, Molly pulls herself up to do just that, but Chris believes he is allowing her a "tender delusion" (282), something Miriam no longer needs from a man.

Totally melodramatic, *The White Feather* uses every possible stereotype. The sinister Fräulein, the evil German personified, insists that the English should all burn in the fire and even slips Miss Myrtle, a stereotypical spinster, a sedative. "A mere nothing," Fräulein declares. "It will but insure sound and healthy sleep" (203). Her intention is to drug Miss Myrtle to guarantee her demise in the fire. When she understands at the police station that she has failed in her mission, Fräulein swallows the obligatory cyanide capsule and is driven back to the inn, where the whole household observes her gruesome death, a death that takes far longer than it should, given the poison she ingests. Fräulein dies supposedly in service to the state, but because she is an evil Hun, she lacks the compassion normally afforded to her gender. Her suicide, often considered a cowardly act, renders her useless to her own nation. She fails as a woman and as a spy.

Molly and Miriam are both examples of good women who sacrifice for the state, but Molly is the perfect example of the child/woman men marry, even if Miriam is more interesting. Christopher Brent is not seeking an equal like Miriam in marriage; he wants a woman he can love "for not knowing anything about life," so that he can "teach her about it" (45). He believes Molly is like the water sprite Undine, who gains a soul when she marries the knight Huldbrand. He tells Miriam, "She won't go through life without getting a soul; and we all know that means pain and grief and tears" (45). And Molly is also Galatea-like—first a creation of her father and then Chris. When Chris comes close to insulting Mr. Pollock to Molly, she responds "resentfully" because "she was only nineteen and she had been brought up by Mr. Pollock to consider everything that he himself said was right and admirable" (51). Molly is neither as strong nor as independent as Nora Starr of "New York Stuff" because she has been raised by a father who does not wish her to be. As Miriam has pointed out, Molly is brought up to "[float] on through life in bland ignorance" (45). The end of the play and the Undine references suggest that if she does not float in bland ignorance, it will be at Chris's discretion. Most definitely, it is not the dangerous woman but the woman like Molly—who needs to be saved, whether from the evil Hun or from herself—who is the strongest force as a propaganda tool. She is the adhesive that holds together the Gemeinschaft and more significantly, when she serves as Chris's backbone, the state at war.

Married and Dutiful

The Edna Ferber story "One Hundred Percent" presents a much different picture of the married woman than "New York Stuff" and "The White Feather." Emma McChesney Buck is a sort of superwoman, a remarried widow or divorcee—we are never told which—with a grown son and grandchildren. Nevertheless, Emma is still young, pretty, and vibrant as well as smart. Before marrying the owner of the T. A. Buck Featherloom Petticoat Company, Emma was a traveling sales representative for the firm. Unable to play the role of the stay-at-home Fifth Avenue matron after her marriage, Emma still goes in to the business several hours a day, making the business very much a family endeavor. When the United States enters the war, Emma immediately rises to the official challenge. Ferber devotes the beginning of the story to a humorous exchange between Emma and T.A. over their two subscriptions to the *New York Times*. As a war economy, Emma decides to eliminate one subscription, and the comedy of errors over sharing the paper at breakfast establishes Emma as a woman who needs to read the paper and the couple as a good-natured and congenial pair who share a relatively equal relationship. Resigned to the need for two papers, Emma declares, "I'm willing to eat trick bread and whale meat and drink sugarless coffee, but I draw the line at hating my husband for the price of a newspaper subscription. White paper may be scarce, but so are husbands. It's cheaper to get two newspapers than to set up two establishments."[22] But the humor in the story is relatively short-lived. Emma dons a uniform and goes out to do war work, but not before first applying her skill and intelligence to the collar of the flannel shirt the company is making for women's war uniforms. Garnering the disapproval of the head designer, Emma takes a pair of scissors to scraps of fabric as she observes, "Somehow a woman in a flannel shirt always looks as if she had quinsy [severe tonsillitis]. It's the collar. They cut them like a man's small-size. But a woman's neck is as different from a man's as her collarbone is" (12). Emma's new design is immediately popular. The head of the uniform department in the store where

FIG. 11. "I Want YOU for the Navy," poster by Howard Chandler Christy.

the uniforms are sold tells Emma, "All these women warriors are willing to bleed and die for their country, but they want to do it in a collar that fits, and I don't blame 'em" (12). If women are going to die, they want to look good doing it. The concept of femininity is key here and is closely linked to much war propaganda. Among the most stunning of the war posters are those of Howard Chandler Christy, whose "Christy girls" are both feminine and slightly seductive but never threatening (fig. 11). The department store clerk is suggesting to Emma that if women can go out looking like a "Christy girl," then so be it. Fashion will never completely take a back seat to war because clothes are part of the social construction of femininity. Women's uniforms, even those of the Red Cross nurse, all conform to the dictates of fashion and of modesty.

Emma's war work takes her away from both the company and T.A. Her son Jock is an advertising executive in Chicago, and his wife has just given birth to their second child. Jock is anxious to enlist but does not because of the new baby. Fisk, Featherloom's sales representative for the Midwest, wants to enlist, but his wife Gertie, former head stenographer at the company, has just lost a child and is not quite well. T.A., also eager, admits he is jealous of Emma's uniform, that in fact he is "jealous of every buck private in the army! I'm jealous of the mule drivers! Of the veterinarians. Of the stokers in the transports. Men!" (58). Too old for active service, T.A. admits that he has been offered a job in Bordeaux doing merchandising, something he is highly qualified to do, but he says to Emma, "I couldn't ask you to go back to the factory" (59). In one fell swoop, Emma realizes that her war work is keeping three able-bodied men—Jock, Fisk, and T.A.—from the war. Her solution is to bring Jock's wife and children to New York to live with her so that Jock can enlist. Emma will take over the Midwest territory, a job that had been hers before she wed T.A., so that Fisk can enlist. And as an act of family unity, the company will pay Gertie's salary as a stenographer until she is well enough to come back to work. Finally, as Emma explains, "Mr. T. A. Buck goes to Bordeaux. Old Emmer takes off her uniform and begins to serve her country—on the road" (59). When T.A. tells Emma, "Gad, . . . you're glorious!" (59), Emma says, "Glorious nothing! I'm going to earn the living for three families for a few months, until things get going. And there's nothing glorious about that, old dear" (59). In spite of what Emma says, here the Gemeinschaft exists in all its glory. Family matriarch and businesswoman Emma mobilizes those around her to serve the state while serving it tirelessly herself. She tells T.A. as they part at the train station, "I want everyone to get into [the war] one hundred percent, so it'll be over sooner; and because we've won" (60). Still, the war defines everything and is the only reality. "These last three years have been a dream—" she says, "a delusion" (60). Emma is doing the upper middle-class equivalent of going to work in a munitions factory, only for no pay; she is actually giving up her uniform for families, both her workers' and her own. Fisk, T.A., and her son Jock will be at risk, but that is the ultimate sacrifice the family must make for the state.

"The Great Adventure," a Theodore Roosevelt editorial in the same issue of *Metropolitan*, praises women like Emma for sending their husbands and only sons to the war. In keeping with the hyperbolic style of most war editorials, Roosevelt declares:

> These gallant men at the front are high of soul, as they face their fate on the shell-shattered earth, or in the skies above or in the waters beneath; and no less high of soul are the women with torn hearts and shining eyes; the

> girls whose boy lovers have been struck down in their golden morning, and the mothers and wives to whom word has been brought that henceforth they must walk in the shadow.
>
> These are the torch-bearers; these are they who have dared the great adventure.[23]

Roosevelt wrote these words roughly four months after his son Quentin was shot down and killed during a major German assault on the Western Front. According to Martin Gilbert, Quentin was near-sighted and as rumor (possibly apocryphal) had it, "tacked on to the German squadron rather than his own at the end of an aerial engagement."[24] Roosevelt's comments on Quentin's death echo the editorial from *Metropolitan*. Even in his grief he declares, "Only those are fit to live who do not fear to die, and none are fit to die who have shrunk from the joy of life and the duty of life." The words remain today on Roosevelt's monument in Washington.[25]

Clearly Ferber's story illustrates, not only in the character of Emma but also in Jock's wife Grace and Fisk's Gertie, the willingness to subjugate the needs of the family to the needs of the state—the belief in Roosevelt's message; indeed the story might be a fictionalization of the editorial, except we see only the enlistments, not the potential maimings or deaths. Like the mothers in the song titles mentioned, Emma, Gertie, and Grace are eager to give up their men, to risk their men's lives as propaganda demands.

The Spinster as War Monger: "A Star in the Window"

The attitudes of Emma, Gertie, and Grace pale in comparison to that of Miss Lydia Hale, protagonist of the Dana Gatlin story "A Star in the Window." Reminiscent of Kipling's Mary

Postgate, Miss Hale is a genteel spinster of old New England family, the last of the Hales. Although we are not told if this is the family of Nathan Hale, Miss Hale's fighting spirit is worthy of the name. Miss Hale lives in the old family home in a state of moderate decay. She is a sort of godmother to the son of her former sweetheart Seth Braddock, who ran off to China after a lovers' quarrel and never returned. The son, also Seth, is in his early twenties, just out of college. The story opens when town millionaire Peter Unruh, a German American and "a covetous old man . . . who had hoarded all his life for a rich, envious, selfish, secure old age," sends his lackey and a huge machine to Miss Lydia's to purchase two huge box trees, or boxwoods.[26] The trees stand on either side of her front lane, trees that "had been seedlings long before the Revolution" (24). Miss Hale sends Unruh's men packing when Seth arrives with the news that the Germans have sunk the *Lusitania.* While pulling up centuries-old bushes cannot parallel the destruction of a passenger ship, the suggestion is that Germans have no respect for life or tradition other than their own. The normally gentle Miss Hale, "all white and shaken," calls the perpetrators "monsters—devils—the filthy monsters!" (24). Extraordinarily virulent, Miss Hale first of all assumes that the United States will enter the war without delay, and then laments the fact that she has "no one to send! Oh, if only I were a man!—if there were *any* Hale to go!" (24). Seth assures her that he will go for the Hales and the Braddocks, a promise that comforts Miss Hale to the extent that she is "sustained by the feeling that she ha[s] sent a man to the war" (24). Since Miss Hale's assumption about U.S. participation in the war is hasty, Seth must go to Canada to enlist, "to fight for all that lifts man above devil-brutes" (26).

Miss Hale's war fervor escalates as Seth is wounded. But the news of his hospitalization is dwarfed by gossip that Peter

Unruh has acquired the mortgage on the old Braddock place and intends to foreclose. Miss Hale employs her Yankee ingenuity and sells Unruh her boxwoods for twenty-five hundred dollars, enough to pay the overdue mortgage payment and "furnish the poor boy a few needed luxuries" (36). While he is there, Unruh sets his sights on Miss Hale's Chippendale grandfather clock, another artifact she will end up bartering, but Miss Hale is happy that "Peter Unruh's own money . . . had saved from his clutching fingers the home of her soldier" (36).

The final pages of the story contain at once some of the most jingoistic and tragic dialogue of all the stories under consideration here. The timid Miss Lydia Hale makes Ferber's Emma Buck seem entirely reasonable. Almost a year after his first wound, Seth is again wounded—this time a bayonet wound in the shoulder and a shattered knee that Seth cannot remember injuring. The knee is so bad that Seth is sent home from the Canadian forces just as the United States finally enters the war. Justifying her sale of the boxwoods to Seth, Miss Hale tells him, "You were my fighting-man. Seth—the Hale's fighting-man in this war when the world needs brave men as it never needed them before. I'd almost have died, Seth, if I couldn't have been in it. And I was in it—because I had *you* in it" (37). But Seth's sacrifice to date is not enough for Miss Lydia, who comes from a "'fighting family'" (37). She finds a surgeon who can repair Seth's knee for the price of the Chippendale clock, which she sells to Unruh. Wounded, healed, and patched up again, Seth once more goes to war, this time in an American uniform. When he demurs at the thought of selling the clock, Miss Lydia hushes him. "Oh, Seth, Seth! Don't you know—? Would you stop me from sending my soldier across for America—would you?" Miss Lydia's words elicit a "silent look more martially resoundant [sic] than fife and drum" (37).

When Seth departs, Miss Lydia hangs a service star in her window, hence the story's title. Perhaps the haste of the story's conclusion adds to the poignancy of Seth's situation, but the way Miss Lydia hustles him off barely rehabilitated so that she can be "in it" is astonishing even in the face of rampant war fervor. The likelihood that Seth will not return is great, but Miss Lydia would rather he perish than sit out the remainder of the war at home, a circumstance that would prevent her from being "in it." The star in the window is Miss Lydia's only concern.

Some bitterness about the role of all women in the enlistment process does surface in the works of three major antiwar poets, Robert Graves, Siegfried Sassoon, and Wilfred Owen. Graves, in his nonfiction account of the war, *Good-Bye to All That*, speaks of war fervor at home when he returned wounded after having been initially reported killed in action. Graves quotes a letter from "a little mother" printed in a local newspaper as an example of the insanity he perceived on the home front. Some critics and historians doubt the authenticity of the letter; nevertheless, its tone rings true. In the letter, addressed to a pacifist soldier who had written an antiwar letter to the same paper, the little mother declares that "there is only one temperature for the women of the British race, and that is white heat . . . . we women pass on the ammunition of 'only sons' so that when the 'common soldier' looks back before going 'over the top' he may see the women of the British race at his heels."[27] While Graves refrains from commenting on the letter beyond calling it "newspaper language," his use of it as an illustration of war madness is clear.[28]

Wilfred Owen in the poem "Disabled," written from the point of view of a quadruple amputee, speaks of the soldier's reasons for enlisting at the age of seventeen. Aside from being drunk after winning a soccer game, the soldier acknowledges that he has also signed up "to please his Meg. / Aye, that was it, to please the giddy jilts."[29] But perhaps the most bitter of all the antiwar poems is Siegfried Sassoon's "Glory of Women." The first stanza lambastes women for their participation in war fervor.

> You love us when we're heroes, home on leave,
> Or wounded in a mentionable place.
> You worship decoration; you believe
> That chivalry redeems the war's disgrace.
> You make us shells. You listen with delight,
> By tales of dirt and danger fondly thrilled.
> You crown our distant ardors while we fight,
> And mourn our laurelled memories when we're killed.[30]

Yet what Sassoon describes here is exactly the attitude engendered by war propaganda, and the attitude reflected in Miss Lydia Hale's behavior. Certainly Miss Hale does not need the social status that might accrue from the very visible star in the window. Indeed, her war fervor derives from her own family tradition, a tradition the boxwoods link to the American Revolutionary War, which they pre-date. America once fought for its freedom from a colonial power and Miss Hale does not differentiate one enemy from another. Peter Unruh may be stereotypical of German "Kultur," but Miss Hale's attitude suggests that she would be up in arms if the enemy were once again the British. Miss Hale's family loyalty is indistinguishable from her loyalty to the state. She serves as an example to all those women who wish to gain the kind of status Miss Hale possesses, even if she is a bit down at heel. As a good woman, she is willing to part with her possessions, including her "son," because whatever she may or may not own, she will always be a Hale. Unlike the wicked Fanny Gentry, who is all about status and possessions,

Miss Hale is real gentry and must behave as her name dictates. The star in the window says she is a woman to be emulated, that family and the state really are inseparable during war, that any woman worth her salt will sacrifice her men without question.

Nightmares, Babies, and Cannibal Germans

One propaganda story that appeared in the pages of *McClure's* in December of 1917, before the magazine adopted its Win-the-War policy, actually outdoes the later "A Star in the Window" in its use of propaganda. "One of Ten Million," by Wallace Irwin, author of "humorous" poetry and novels and creator of the racist column "Letters of a Japanese Schoolboy," begins with a description of the first year of married life for Mary and Bob Hamilton.[31] Bob is a bookkeeper in a "tool-works," and although his future is promising, the couple occupies a small apartment in a building without an elevator. Mary is something of an airhead whose chief goal is "that their home should remain intact, that they should move into a larger flat each year, gathering Colonial furniture as they went; that Bob should wax fatter and fatter in the commercial world; that their first child should be a boy and their second a girl."[32] As the story opens, Mary is pregnant with that first child and "ill a great deal those several weeks preceding the climactic event of her life" (15). Mary's plans, including the birth of the child who does turn out to be a boy, do not acknowledge the war that has just been declared, and she makes it clear to Bob that he must claim an exemption when he registers for the newly implemented draft.

Several days before the child is born, Bob carelessly drops a propaganda flier in the bedroom where Mary is confined, and she cannot get the image on the flier out of her mind. The cartoon depicts Kaiser Wilhelm as a mechanical monster, a "sort of machine-made dragon, created of steel and iron and armor-plate, with forty-two centimeter guns belching flame from his nose" (15). That Mary knows what a forty-two-centimeter gun is seems highly unlikely; still, the image haunts her along with the caption, "He's Looking toward America" (15). Mary throws the flier on the floor, but it lands face up where she continues to gaze upon the caricature. Mary is definitely not the war monger that Miss Lydia Hale is, nor is she a resourceful matron like Emma Buck. Mary wonders, "What two straws did they care whether the French held a place called Verdun or handed it over to the Crown Prince and saved a lot of bother for everybody?" (15). Like Molly Preston of *The White Feather*, Mary needs to awaken from her childish complacency, and in this case the birth of a child and a drug-induced vision of hell suffice.

Readers must guess early on that Bob does not claim an exemption as he has promised. His explanation includes the jingoistic phrases repeated in the press and propaganda publications and a nod to public pressure. Before the baby is born, he tells Mary, "Somebody's got to [go], or we'll just all stay home and invite the Kaiser over here" (15). When Mary realizes he has not claimed the exemption, he justifies himself by saying, "If you only knew what a man's up against nowadays. I simply couldn't try and worm out of it. I'd seen too many slackers and cry-babies snooping around for an excuse to dodge service. I couldn't bear to be put among the girls" (16). Mary calls him on this need to be manly, but to no avail. Bob knows that Mary's mother is wealthy enough for Mary and the child to be taken care of if he does not return, and he is so adamant and Mary so stricken that Mary's doctor arrives to give her a sedative. Drifting in and out of sleep, Mary hallucinates that the figure of the Kaiser from the propaganda flier takes shape in the room and speaks to her. In an image of the vulnerable woman repeated often in propaganda, Mary sees herself "clad . . . in her night-apparel and holding her baby to her breast" approaching the Kaiser, who asks questions about her children (58). Without Mary providing the name, the Kaiser writes in his "War Account Book," about which he claims, "Irresponsible foreign writers have called this our Butcher's Book, but the name is irregular." When Mary inquires why the Kaiser is writing her child's name in the book, he replies, "I am going to eat him, of course" (58).

Throughout the war, Germans were depicted as cannibals, including the propaganda story of the corpse factory, in which German corpses were ostensibly rendered into fat for everything from munitions to margarine. In this case the Kaiser himself is the personification of the devouring German war machine. When Mary kneels to pray, the Kaiser stops her and prays himself that "Gott of the Vaterland . . . bless this feast" he is about to enjoy and "make the flesh of the child tender" for his palate (58). Shameless in its depiction of Queen Victoria's grandson, the story concludes with Mary telling the Kaiser, "I'll fight you—I'll make my husband fight you," at which point she awakens to find her mother and the baby by her side (59). Mary's final act is to summon Bob once again, this time to tell him when he says he has not asked for an exemption, "Thank God!" (59). Incidentally, the story is illustrated by Clarence Underwood, creator of a number of propaganda posters during the war. The illustration shows Mary cowering in her bed while the impressionistic figure of the Kaiser, sword drawn, looms over her, his gloved finger pointing toward her head. Oddly enough, her wise old monocled doctor, dispenser of sedatives, looks on thoughtfully, his chin in his hand.

It is noteworthy that both the stories depicting women as

intellectually shallow are male-authored, but all the characters are stereotypical, and the stories end either with marriage or with the women sending their men off to fight, or ultimately both. In each case the family becomes the Kaiser-fighting unit; like the Hale family for the duration of its history, the middle-class family is mobilized in the service of the state, which propaganda has tied to the local or domestic sphere. The Gemeinschaft serves the Gesellschaft because the Gemeinschaft has been instructed to believe its cohesion depends upon that service. The baby-eating Kaiser must be held at bay, or as the Billy Ireland poster "Keep the Hun Out" suggests, Huns will be at the bedroom window of every middle-class home in America.

In spite of the war fiction included in this issue, for instance "The White Morning: A Torrential Novel of Modern Germany," not all the advertising had switched over to war subjects. The Ivory soap ad touts the product for cleaning oriental rugs, and an article on "the woman playwright" precedes "One of Ten Million." While America had been at war for more than six months and the Food Administration and other propaganda departments were in place, the war was not yet ubiquitous. Moving public opinion is an arduous process, and as we have seen, the propaganda designed to achieve that end was broad in its scope. From Hoover's Food Administration campaign to the War Bond and War Saving Stamp movements and, of course, the enlistment drive, all areas of private life became fair game. After a brief look at the effect of the war on ladies' fashion, which remained central to the social construction of femininity and continued to command space in ladies' magazines, we will see how propaganda reached out to younger and younger converts, offering the excitement that only war can provide.

Metropolitan and *McClure's* magazines offered readers more or less literary fiction; Willa Cather, after all, worked for *McClure's* until 1912. Both published the occasional story by Kipling, or on rare occasions, Conrad. Ladies' magazines also published fiction. The December 1914 issue of *Cosmopolitan* boasts a Dana Gatlin story, "The Mating," alongside a feature on Egypt by Rudyard Kipling. None of the pieces reflects the war, although it was into its fifth month and was supposed to be over by Christmas. Even the post-*Lusitania* June 1916 issue of *McCall's* devotes most of its pages to dress patterns. But by September of 1917, the *Delineator*, a magazine published by the Butterick pattern company, declares on its cover, "The New Factors in National Life have produced New Fashions." Trends include cutting up last year's dresses according to new patterns and using less fabric for new garments. Both are part of the new war economy, but both also address the need for women to remain attractive and feminine, appropriate to their propaganda image, even under the stress of war. Economy of dress in these magazines parallels economy in the kitchen. The first article in the September 1917 *Delineator* is a message to American housewives from French women about economical cooking, including recipes for rabbit stew, pig's feet, and tripe. Further into the magazine, a Campbell's soup ad shows one of the Campbell soup kids saluting and sporting a hoe for tilling the home garden. An accompanying poem declares:

> We are all doing our bit
> To help Uncle Sam make a hit.
> With food from our farms we strengthen his arms
> By making the nation more fit.[33]

A feature, "Our Thrift Series," is devoted to food conservation.

More in tune with the idea of compulsory service, the *Delineator*'s "Women's Preparedness Bureau" offers advice to small towns for organizing women for war service, among other things by taking a door-to-door census during which census takers would "record the name and address of every woman, what work she can do best, how much time she is prepared to give the Government, [and] whether or not she is a wage-earner." This information is to be filed on index cards under skills. Given the modern paranoia about computer-generated information banks, this idea, like many others herein described, still seems Orwellian. But the plan does not stop there. "Girls" between the ages of sixteen and thirty are to be organized "under true military rules and regulations and [to be put] to work in squads under the direction of one of their own members—the petty officer of the day."[34] The article is illustrated by a photograph of two women feeding calves out of buckets. Among the jobs these "girls" will perform are helping poor women with their housework and "help[ing] any other committee in the town that happens to be pressed with work."[35]

Like the pressure on Bob Hamilton of "One of Ten Million," the pressure on all women, but especially younger ones, moves well beyond joining the White Feather brigade. In the following chapter we see the call for Red Cross nurses and canteen workers and fictionalized accounts of their adventures. But magazines demand of the housewife sacrifices in the kitchen and in her clothing budget, while at the same time demanding she remain fashionable. "Women, War and the New Fashions" shows among its featured patterns two pseudo-military styles, one a khaki trench coat and the other, to demonstrate "war's brighter side . . . a new suit of service—blue homespun trimmed with gold braid and buttons."[36] As if war actually had a brighter side, the industrious housewife will make these dresses, cut simply to reduce the use of fabrics, and she will still perform war service as well.

By March of 1918, in addition to doing her bit "by simplicity," women are instructed in methods of remaking old dresses into new "remade dresses that gratify the craving for new clothes and satisfy your war-time conscience."[37] Eleanor Chalmers, author of the article, offers to provide advice to women about remaking dresses if they will write in with their measurements and such details as whether the dress is "for yourself or your mother," supposedly a nod to age-appropriate dressing. Much of this March issue is devoted to war subjects. The cover, unlike the cover for September 1917, is a propaganda drawing of a mother pointing out details on a map of Europe to her uniformed son. Her knitting waits on the edge of the map while the son's toy soldiers stand beside it on the table. The opening article debates the question of women in combat by looking at the battalion of Russian women, the Battalion of Death, that did in fact fight in World War I. After raising obvious questions—such as "How did German marksmen feel when they knew their bullets were sinking into woman-flesh, destroying motherhood?"—the article concludes that it is wrong for women to go into battle, but that the Russian women "had to do it."[38] According to Professor Ross, chair of history at the University of Wisconsin, once the author's history professor and now a traveling companion in Russia, "if it has come to the point in this war where women are going to shoulder rifles and become soldiers and live in the mud and kill and die, our civilization has reached a lower stage than any known in human history."[39] In this economy, women must continue to remake old dresses and learn to cook dishes with rabbit, and they must remain men's inspiration, but they must let the men do the fighting. And if women die in their roles as nurses, ambulance drivers, or canteen workers, they must do so in a well-cut blouse.

Following the article on women in combat, "American Women in Battalions of Life" contrasts the Russian women with the more civilized Americans who perform auxiliary service, such as manning switchboards. Clearly the emphasis here is on remaining "womanly" and dressing well while performing socially sanctioned war service. Even the no-nonsense Red Cross in its own magazine of August 1918 features a seven-page photo spread called "Service Uniforms of Red Cross Workers."[40] From the dress white to the summer outdoor uniform, all are stylish and closely resemble the war wear in the *Delineator*. After all, no soldier wants to be nursed by a sloppily dressed woman. The pretty woman will no doubt encourage him to get well sooner so that he, like Seth Braddock, can once again be off to the front.

With the exception of the Russian soldiers, women are instructed in propaganda and popular fiction to do their bits so that the men can do theirs. According to their social roles, women must remain feminine in their performance of duty and in their manner of dress. None of the materials under consideration here ever loses sight of the "reality" that women are first of all wives, mothers, and sisters, a central component of each of the three primary relationships Ferdinand Tönnies describes in his theory of Gemeinschaft. Professor Ross's hyperbolic statement about the condition of a society that sends women into battle, knowingly or not, points to that essential role of women in traditional social structure. While war may tax that structure, the state also takes advantage of it to compel its citizens, contradictorily, to divert their energies away from the family. Potential wives and mothers, young women who have not yet assumed adult roles, share equally in the responsibility of performing war service. We now move on to look at these women and the promise of a home and family implied as a reward for answering the call.

THREE

VADs and Khaki Girls

The Ultimate Reward for War Service

The military-style uniforms of the Red Cross and the U.S. Food Administration offered a way for adult married women to identify themselves as participants in the Great War, as supporters of those men in their lives who also had war work to accomplish. Already wives and mothers, adult women like Emma Buck of "One Hundred Percent" perform war service because propaganda demands it, or because the jobs their husbands once performed need filling. But the war offered special responsibilities and rewards for unmarried women, who while maintaining enough femininity to remain attractive to men were reinvented in popular fiction in military terms. The heroines of popular fiction perform strenuous tasks, even kill, as do their brothers, in the name of the state. These militarized young girls have exceptional talents, but their talents never exceed the boundaries of local society. They may be smart, beautiful, strong, and even athletic, but nevertheless, at war's end, each is still very much a young lady in terms of cultural expectations. She does not let her war adventures turn her either into a tomboy or, worse, a Blue Stocking, and for her restraint and modesty she is rewarded with the ultimate prize, a husband or a male protector. Alongside the soldier, the talented young woman becomes a necessity to the state, because she serves it in both of its aspects—the local community, represented by family, and the larger political community, represented by the warring state.

Possibly the most prominent female martyr of the war was British nurse Edith Cavell, and indeed, a large portion of chapter 5 is devoted to the novels and films focusing on that martyrdom. Cavell, aged forty-nine, was executed rather hastily in October of 1915 after she was tried for helping French and British soldiers escape from a hospital in German-occupied Brussels. While some literature uses words such as "shelter" to soft-pedal her actions, Cavell herself never denied that she aided in the escapes, an action that clearly violated the presumed neutrality of the medical profession. Still the public outcry over her execution was massive and virulent, to the extent that her co-conspirators were spared the same fate. The issue, of course, was that the barbarian Huns had shot not only a woman but a nurse. Cavell became a rallying cry in Great Britain and in the United States. Leonard Dawson, a character from Willa Cather's war novel *One of Ours*, cites three reasons for enlisting after the United States enters the war: "Belgium, the *Lusitania*, and Edith Cavell."[1] Postcards of her initial burial site in Belgium circulated, one of which includes a small grainy photo of Cavell in the upper left-hand corner (fig. 12). Italian postcards also featured Cavell's execution in Art Deco drawings of her and the image of Death (figs. 13 and 14). After the war Cavell's body was returned to England, and according to Martin Gilbert, "crowds, including large numbers of school children, watched her coffin go by, carried on a gun-carriage." Cavell was also honored with a statue, voluntarily guarded by civilians, near Trafalgar Square.[2]

Cavell's value as a recruiting tool continued even into World War II. A still from the 1939 film *Nurse Edith Cavell*, a remake of the controversial 1928 silent film *Dawn*, appears in an ad recruiting women for war service in the April 17, 1944, issue of *Life Magazine*. The still of Cavell shows the nurse escorted to her

FIG. 12. Postcard of Edith Cavell's burial site in Belgium.

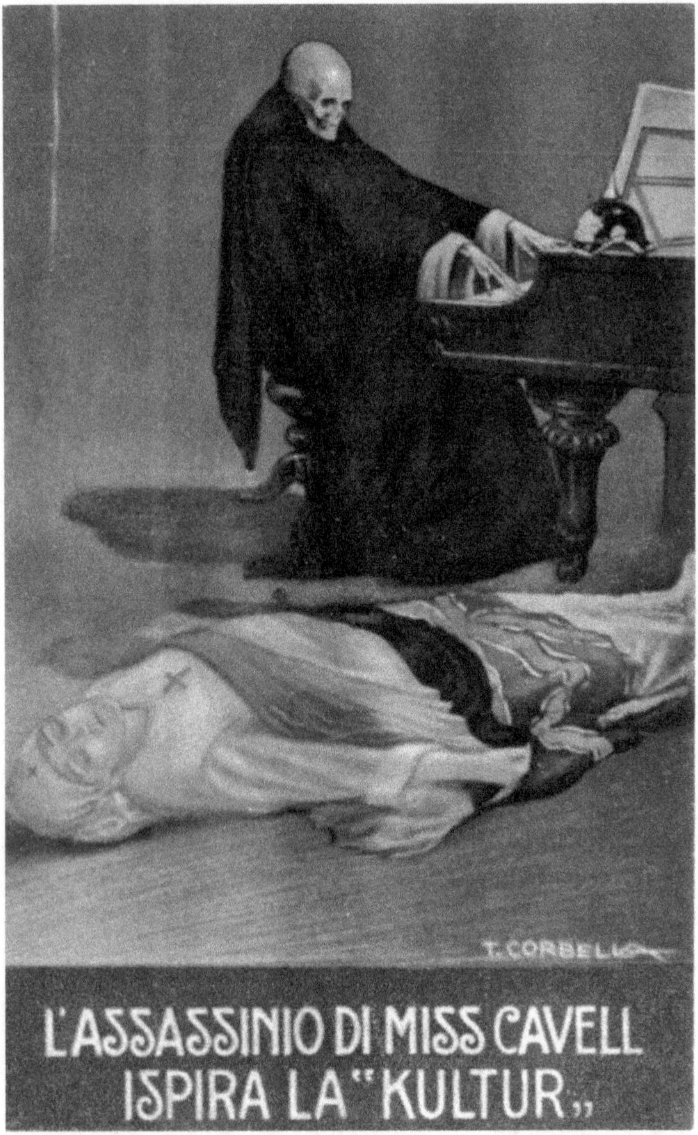

FIG. 13. "L'assassinio di Miss Cavell Inspira la 'Kultur,'"
Art Deco postcard by T. Corbella.

FIG. 14. An Italian Art Deco postcard by T. Corbella depicting Edith Cavell's victory over death.

death by a pickelhaube-clad German soldier and a chaplain, in reality not British as the ad claims but the American Reverend Horace Gahan. The caption includes a portion of Cavell's last remarks: "Tell [the women of my country] that in time of war, Patriotism is not enough."[3] The implication of the passage is that like Cavell, women must be prepared to die for the cause of the Allies. Unfortunately the ad, but not the film, omits the significant and arguably pacifist part of Cavell's statement. Cavell tells Gahan, "They have all been very kind to me here. But this I would say, standing as I do in view of God and eternity: I realise that Patriotism is not enough. I must have no hatred or bitterness towards anyone."[4] Clearly this attitude does not make a strong statement in favor of military service, nor does it depict Germans as the beasts recorded in propaganda stories, thus the omission of the words from the *Life Magazine* ad. While the film closes with Cavell's words superimposed over the 1919 memorial service, the juxtaposition of the words and the congregation singing the hymn "Abide with Me" actually makes her act of forgiveness an even stronger propaganda statement. The ubiquity of Cavell's manufactured image as a beautiful young nurse—Anna Neagle, the actress who plays Cavell in the film, is conspicuously younger than forty-nine—speaks to the power of propaganda and to its innate ability, when convenient, to ignore large portions of the truth, and to its power in its use of women to achieve its goals, in this case of enlisting young girls who wish to emulate Cavell's heroism. As the film demonstrates, the mythologized image of Cavell endured well beyond her death and becomes an even stronger force for enlistment from the grave—strong enough, in fact, to give Cavell the mythic status of a twentieth-century Joan of Arc. An American Red Cross recruiting poster by Albert Sterner depicts a ghostly white-robed figure embracing a young

FIG. 15. "We Need You," poster by Albert Sterner.

woman in street clothes. The figure points to a nurse tending to a wounded man while the young woman in street clothes looks admiringly at the specter (fig. 15). Although the caption "We Need You" does not identify the apparition as Cavell, the image certainly calls on her memory. No better persona than that of Cavell, especially Cavell risen from the dead, could remind potential nurses of their duty to the state.

War songs also sang the praises of nursing. Two songs in particular, "The Rose of No Man's Land" and "I'm Going to Follow the Boys," champion the nurse as the flower of womankind. The second stanza of "The Rose of No Man's Land" declares:

> Out of the heavenly splendor, Down to the trail of woe,
> God in his mercy has sent her, Cheering the world below;
> We call her "Rose of Heaven," We've learned to love her so.

The refrain concludes, "Mid the war's great curse stands the Red Cross Nurse, She's the rose of 'No Man's Land.'"[5] Cast in the image of Cavell, the more-than-saintly woman, posed on the sheet music in a ray of heavenly light, serves as a model for young girls to emulate. But the image of the nurse is not all saintly. She is, as the song says, sent to spread cheer, and that cheer necessarily involves the occasional dance or perhaps a kiss. "I'm Going to Follow the Boys" tells the story of a young woman who has had many beaux, but now they have all gone to war. The refrain combines the desire to have fun with the willingness to serve; soldiers need female company, and the hope on her part is that she will be rewarded with the hand of a charming officer when the war is over. The song's refrain promises:

> I'm going to follow the boys—over there—Any-where
> I don't care. I'm just dying for one little dance,
> But all my dancing partners are 'Some-where in France,'
> I never nursed anyone,—I'll admit,
> But I'm strong to do my bit, And if one little kiss or more
> Can help them win the war, Why I'm going to follow the boys.[6]

As emerges from the stories and novels examined in this chapter, the marriage plot, the union of the hero and the heroine at the end, prevails. While Edith Cavell died unmarried at the age of forty-nine, that part of the myth, like her forgiveness at the end of her life, is generally excluded. The image of the nurse, the nurturer, married or marriageable, is among the most powerful because it taps into all three primary social groups of the Gemeinschaft—wife and husband, mother and children, and sister and brother. If husband and brother are primarily absent during war, leaving the home front to women and children, the empty space at the table, as it were, echoes loudly. Sweaters and socks were knitted and bandages rolled to remind the men of the home they had temporarily left behind.

"Twenty-Two"

Because of the basic nature of the call to nursing, much literature written for adolescent girls and young adult women features nurses as heroines. The June 1917 issue of *Metropolitan*, which features an article by Teddy Roosevelt called "Put the Flag on the Firing Line," also headlines a "20,000 word love story" by Mary Roberts Rinehart.[7] "Twenty-Two" depicts the young Jane Brown, who is in training to become a nurse because, in the words of the head nurse, "every girl wants to wear a uniform and be ready to go to the front if we have trouble."[8] The "if we have trouble" suggests the story was penned before April of 1917, yet the war is the reason Jane is following in the footsteps of Edith Cavell. Jane is only nineteen and is doing her best to follow the rules and learn her career when three complications intervene. First a dashing young male patient known by his room number, "Twenty-two," becomes interested in Jane. A second problem arises when a young working-class man from Jane's home town is brought to the hospital unconscious with a head injury. Finally, and also conveniently, a potentially contagious case is admitted and the hospital is quarantined.

Like the plot of Porter Emerson Browne's story "Mary and Marie," the plot of "Twenty-Two" is predictable and clichéd, and the characters are stereotypes. Twenty-two, whose real name is Middleton, has been brought in with a broken leg and minor burns suffered when the wall of a burning warehouse fell on him. Middleton is very wealthy and is not employed because he does not need to be. In a morphine-induced haze, he tells Jane Brown that he is a journalist and got too close to the burning building trying to get a story, when in fact he was just driving past and stopped to gawk. He also invents a girlfriend, Mabel, which he immediately regrets. In spite of being something of a ne'er-do-well, a poor little rich boy, Twenty-two is not irredeemably bad, only mischievous. When he lies to Jane about being a journalist, he admits to himself that "he had been getting awfully bored with himself since he left college. Everything he tried to do, somebody else could do so much better. . . . [H]e would have been a journalist if he could, or at least have published a newspaper. He knew what was wrong with about a hundred newspapers" (9).

In spite of its predictability, "Twenty-Two" is at moments humorous. Once his leg is in a cast, Middleton persuades the staff to let him sit in a wheelchair, and he sets about trying to find Jane Brown, who is no longer assigned to his station. Private patients are prohibited from entering the section of wards where Jane is working, and Middleton steals old Mr. Simonds's cane to remove the sign that declares the prohibition. Alphabetically, "(a) Twenty-two . . . engag[ed] that gentleman in conversation, possessed himself of the cane. (b) Wheeled back to the elevator. (c) Drew cane from beneath blanket [covering his legs]. (d) Unhooked sign with cane and concealed both under blanket"

(10–11). When Twenty-two finds Jane and tries to tell her Mabel was a figment of his morphine-blurred imagination, the cane and the sign fall to the floor, at which point Jane reveals her humanity by walking out into the hall and laughing.

Complication number two arises when a handyman of sorts, Johnny Fraser from Jane's home town, is brought in with a serious head injury. The wound, according to the Senior Surgical Interne, who is up to date on medical procedures and also incidentally interested in Jane, needs trepaning, but old Doctor Willie, also from Jane's home town, refuses to authorize the surgery. While Jane idolizes the old physician, she understands that the Senior Surgical Interne is correct in his diagnosis, and here Jane's real conflict begins.

The staff cannot operate without Dr. Willie's orders, nor can they say anything to Dr. Willie without being dismissed. On more than one occasion Jane speaks to Dr. Willie herself, but she comes to understand that "to him she was still a little girl. She probably would always be just a little girl to him" (56). Complication number three, a potentially contagious case, results in having the hospital quarantined, a "literary" device that creates of the hospital an insular community. Trying to attract Jane's attention and to compete against the Senior Surgical Interne, Twenty-two comes up with two ideas: first an evening concert at which Jane plays the piano, and then a newsletter, the *Quarantine Sentinel*. Through the *Sentinel*, Jane shames the Staff by writing a letter advocating surgery for Johnny Fraser, in spite of Dr. Willie's reluctance. Jane, of course, is kicked out of nursing school the day she would have become an official trainee, but Johnny is trepanned and saved, and Twenty-two declares his love, which Jane reciprocates.

Thematically, the story focuses on the selfless young woman who intends to answer her country's call, yet she relinquishes her career, if not for love, for ethics. The story also pits small-town values against those of the metropolitan community. Here, interestingly enough, small-town values only partially triumph. The aging and inflexible Dr. Willie represents all that is bad about the local community—ignorance and a sanctimonious pride in that ignorance. But Jane's ethics also originate in the local milieu. Jane knows she will be dismissed for speaking out against Dr. Willie; nevertheless she does so, because she realizes that as a nurse trainee, she is expendable. Prevented from serving as a nurse in the war, Jane is still rewarded with a wealthy husband. Like Nora Starr of "New York Stuff," Jane insists on ethical behavior where it does not always exist, tragically in this case in a hospital. The message seems to be that even without serving, Jane will receive the reward of marriage because she possesses the correct political zeal and the guts to act on her principles. The family unit is maintained, although we might imagine Twenty-two later serving in the war at Jane's urging and Jane directing her servants in the practice of domestic science to save food, or donning a uniform herself, as does Emma Buck.

In Great Britain, the Voluntary Aid Detachment offered a way for upper middle-class women to serve without going through formal nurse's training. As we saw in chapter 1, VADs not driving ambulances were basically nurse's aides, who often did not have the respect of the Red Cross nurses and nuns who staffed war hospitals, and accordingly were assigned the most menial tasks, such as scullery work. Obvious exceptions are Vera Brittain, who actually did nursing and whose journals do not repeat the litany of propaganda found in popular fiction, and the fictional Helen Zenna Smith, whose initial story was based on the diary of a VAD ambulance driver. Still, in some cases the volunteer work of necessity became more substantive than dishwashing and offered the potential reward of a husband, or at least the propaganda of popular fiction led young women to believe a man might be waiting at the end of the war.

Dorothy, VAD and the Doctor

Written in the epistolary style, *Dorothy, VAD and the Doctor*, by Scottish author Captain R. W. Campbell, creator of "Private Spud Tamson" and other Kiplingesque works, was published in a paperback format. The novel begins with a letter from Dorothy Deene to her friend Topsy, in which Dorothy explains that she has decided to be a VAD, largely because the uniform is the most dashing of war service dresses. Dorothy is also "really keen on getting into the officers' ward," because a friend of hers has described having pillow fights with the men while working the night shift.[9] At least Dorothy has looked into first aid books and knows that the VADs "do the slogging" (14), yet she tells Topsy, "I feel I am entering on a great adventure, and somehow I think I'm going to meet a M-A-N" (14). Dorothy imagines that the officers will have "crisp fair hair, blue eyes, pretty noses, and a public-school twang" (15). She does not imagine that some of those pretty noses may have been blown off by shells, although she learns soon enough. In an oddly unpropagandistic stroke, however, she does understand the sexual freedom that may await her "after a life of chaperons, and that school training which makes us drop our eyes when meeting men, and refuse to speak unless—*introduced*" (italics Campbell's, 15).

At the beginning of her service in a hospital in England, Dorothy writes to Topsy about the men, including a charming doctor, Captain Vawhan. But Dorothy is transferred to the surgery ward, where she begins to understand the severity of war wounds and the hard work of the surgeons in putting the men back together as well as possible. Indeed, Campbell dedicates the novel to "the doctors, nurses, and VAD's." Describing war wounds to Topsy, Dorothy tells her that the "wounds vary from a scratch from a bully [beef]-tin to a gaping hole caused by a lump of shrapnel. These require varied and constant dressing, which involves much hard work" (25). Here Dorothy suddenly forgets the husband part and becomes devoted to the work. "Somehow I love it," she tells Topsy of the bandage changing. "I feel this is the war, and it is something to ease the pain of these dear boys" (25). Dorothy gradually becomes a fine nurse, although she unabashedly refers to the soldiers as "the cream of the race and the flower of chivalry" and prays that "[God] will punish the monster who has caused the slaughter of those brave boys whose eyes are the eyes of that good man who died on Calvary" (31–32). While we do not see the caricature of the Kaiser here, he is still the devil in a spiked helmet lurking behind the scenes.

As in the story "Twenty-Two," concerts once again play a role in hospital routine. At one such event, Dorothy sees Captain Vawhan with a charming opera singer who is there to perform, and she writes to Topsy that she has gone to her bed and wept. Able nonetheless to quote Ella Wheeler Wilcox after watching a soldier die, Dorothy does change from the flibbertigibbet she was in the opening letter to what Topsy has referred to in one of her responses as "a serious person" (45). In her answer, Dorothy tells Topsy, "Amidst such great suffering, one cannot worship the great god 'I,' or dabble in the mundane frivolities" (45). Commenting on the sturdiness of the professional nurses, Dorothy continues that "nurses have to shed illusions and face realities" (55), yet she still maintains the illusion that "the work develops the instinct for responsibility, and that loving care that we have seen in our own mothers"

(55). During a particularly gruesome scene, the hospital must deal with a convoy of wounded straight from the battlefield, and Vawhan and Dorothy work side by side until all the men are treated, including Vawhan amputating a soldier's leg. During the ordeal, Vawhan begins to refer to Dorothy as "little girl," but the diminutive does not irk Dorothy as Dr. Willie's treatment of Jane proves irksome in the previous story. In fact, Vawhan invites Dorothy to tea with his mother and sister—as we might guess, the beautiful opera singer.

Through her transformation, Dorothy is rewarded finally with the hand of handsome Dr. Vawhan. Dorothy accomplishes the transformation without male tutelage, but Vawhan is watching her as she grows into a strong woman. In the proposal scene, despite British food shortages, Dorothy and her doctor drive into the countryside for tea. Unaware, it would seem, of rationing, Dorothy is concerned with their "first meal," with getting "the right blend of tea, the correct cut off the cake, and the dainty effects of a pretty picnic" (86). The tragedy of amputations and death does not tarnish the moment for them. On the contrary, Dorothy's unquestioning devotion to nursing layered over her "femininity" makes her the perfect wife. As he observes Dorothy's transformation from husband hunter to "one of England's splendid daughters," Vawhan serves as the eyes of the Panopticon, as the food basket from home does in *Not So Quiet*. At the end of their tea as he outlines for Dorothy his plans for the ideal postwar society, Vawhan tells her, "I've been watching you, old girl. I know how you have developed from a careless school-girl into a conscientious nurse." Here, the compliant girl is rewarded for her good behavior with cakes and a husband, an enticing message for young women considering service and for those hoping to marry well, although on a doctor's salary, they will have only "love in a cottage" and a

Ford (96). And, we assume, Dorothy will give up nursing and use that "loving care" as a wife and mother.

Campbell, in his descriptions of Vawhan's ideal postwar society, is climbing on his own soapbox. Earlier as Dorothy sings the praises of nurses, Campbell has put into Dorothy's mouth a tirade against "those half-washed, over-powdered, gaudily dressed things of Oxford Street" who "have the faces of dolls and the brains of a hen" and give birth to "shrieking neurotic babies" (54). Similarly, Vawhan would "burn the slums and all sinks of iniquity" (91). He would also censor literature, including the French naturalists and the movies of Charlie Chaplin. In Vawhan's words, "These vulgar managers handle the Crucifix and the stiletto as you handle sausages and coal. This country permits educated doorkeepers to prostitute Romance and vulgarise the Drama. Why don't we have J. M. Barrie as Controller of Plays?" (92). In response to Dorothy's question, "Bernard Shaw, of course?" Vawhan replies, "Not till they're twenty" (93), a curious exchange since Shaw, a socialist, was criticized for being a pacifist. Vawhan's preference for *Peter Pan* over the works of Balzac, and for Shakespeare over Byron, suggests not only limited literary tastes but a strong desire for social control beyond the war. That is, in Vawhan/Campbell's eyes, propaganda is not enough. In the words of Vawhan, "We must help them to choose" (93). In a way, what Campbell proposes is that the local community, the Gemeinschaft—in this case, doctors—will establish standards for the Gesellschaft, the larger community or the state, an early version of "Community Standards," that vague delineator of pornography put forth by the U.S. Supreme Court. Since the state has been using the standards of the Gemeinschaft to promote war, Campbell's suggestions may seem plausible, if Orwellian. Propaganda not only defines the behavior of our hero and heroine during the war; it continues after the war to regiment undesirable behavior. Such a precedent was established well before the war in movements such as the Purity Crusade, which sought to regulate the lives of the working class, including its procreation, in an almost Nazi-like way. Campbell/Vawhan's diatribe indeed reiterates the dangers of propaganda and blindly following it. Once the propaganda ball gets rolling, there is little incentive for those who initiate it to stop it.

They Also Serve: A Dog's View

While nursing is not involved in Amy Landon Gurlitz's curious and funny story "The Dog of War," which appeared in the April 1918 issue of *Metropolitan,* war service and the marriage plot are, and as with Molly Pollock/Preston of *The White Feather,* the young heroine Evelyn develops under the tutelage of her hero, Captain Brewster. The story shifts inexplicably from the points of view of the five-year-old "twins" Dolly and Susie, youngest of eleven children at the Moorings, and the two dogs, Sheila the collie and Muggsy the bull terrier. A third dog, Nero, is Evelyn's Maltese lap dog, whose point of view is reported by the other two dogs, and whom no one, dog or human, likes. Evelyn is the "Master's" ward and thus is sometimes good-naturedly pursued by Leonard, one of the older children. The twins keep a garter snake in their mother's bottom bureau drawer, but the snake never contributes its observations to the story's conversation.

The point of view also follows Evelyn and Captain Brewster on their walks about the moor and down to the coast. When the story begins, Captain Brewster, a pilot flying for one of the Allies—we are not told which, but we assume Canada—is on leave from the war. Evelyn is doing her patriotic duty by adopting a French soldier, with whom she exchanges letters, and to whom she sends anything that will make his tour of duty easier. Brewster, who does not like the Maltese puppy, casually suggests that she send the dog to her soldier. During a dinner party, the dogs observe as the twins slather themselves with vanishing cream, thinking that true to its name, it will make them invisible. After the ensuing melee, Evelyn and Brewster walk down to the bay, and here, readers learn that Brewster has been in love with Evelyn since she was thirteen. The information unfolds when Evelyn tells Brewster that she has been alone in his house looking for a book and has gone through a drawer in his library. In the drawer, in the manner of a young girl, Brewster has saved mementos from Evelyn's girlhood, including a broken riding whip and a piece of dried Edelweiss from a trip to Lucerne. He later tells her, "Ever since you were thirteen I've been waiting for you to grow up—to be old enough."[10]

Still, Brewster refuses to propose to Evelyn because he does not want her to be bound to him in case he is wounded or killed. Evelyn is sure of his affection and tries to get him to commit himself, but in a very graphic depiction of war wounds, he refuses. "It's a fearful mess, Evelyn," he tells her. "It's awful when they're killed, but usually it's worse when they're not. You knew Harkness, didn't you? There wasn't enough left to bury—just a few ashes under the wreckage of his machine—it burnt, you know." Brewster continues in a more gruesome description of Grimson, who lived but has "both eyes gone and a grin cut across his face from ear to ear, and he'll never talk again, though they've given him a new jaw" (17). Evelyn goes so far as to ask him to marry her before he goes, but Brewster refuses and ships out.

Perhaps as comic relief, although there is a note of cruelty here as well, Leonard contrives as a lark to send the Maltese

Nero with Brewster, so he can hand the dog over to Evelyn's French soldier, Henri. Evelyn knows only that the dog has disappeared until she hears from Henri that "the little dog [is] charming" (68). Surprisingly, Evelyn is not furious with either Leonard or Brewster but instead claims that she has sent the dog herself. Then comes word that the dog is a hero, that on the day America entered the war, he has led Henri's regiment into a German-occupied village the regiment is sent to retake. True, when he gets to the village, the dog runs trembling under the only bed left standing, but his bravery urges on the French regiment, earning Henri's praise as "le brave petit chien" (68). In the next sentence, almost casually, readers are told that "afterward came the report that Captain Brewster had been killed" (68). Evelyn is crushed until "a cable from Brewster denied it indignantly" (68). Brewster returns with the dog, now more insufferable than ever, barking his war stories interminably.

Unfortunately, Brewster is missing an arm and has a twisted leg. He will not be patched up to return to service, as was Seth Braddock of "A Star in the Window," but he will become a war hero whose sweetheart remains faithful, the lesson in the story for young girls. Since Brewster refuses to marry her, Evelyn uses the law and his status as a gentleman to leave him no choice. She tells the twins that Brewster has asked her to marry him and gives them each a dollar; the twins tell everyone else in "systematic" fashion, and according to the code, he "can't go around telling everyone [he's] changed [his] mind" (69). The narrative leaves no doubt that Brewster wants to marry Evelyn, and she uses just the right amount of aggression to see that the deed is accomplished. Brewster may be wounded, but his wounds are not gruesome enough to deter Evelyn in her desire to wed, nor is there the suggestion that his wounds have rendered him impotent, thus he still has value as a potential husband. Everyone here has done his or her bit, including the dog Nero; he gets a special house for doing his duty. Evelyn's duty now will be not to volunteer, at least not beyond the local level, but to mind the home in ways appropriate to a wartime economy. Her reward, an ever-so-slightly maimed husband, is, in a sense, her wartime job. Brewster remains handsome, unlike the blind and horribly disfigured Grimson, and the family unit itself becomes a testament to the state and to war service. Gemeinschaft and Gesellschaft coexist in the permanently public image of the wounded veteran and his devoted wife and, we assume, eventually children.

The use of animals and children in the narrative might lead readers to believe the story is intended for young readers, but the graphic descriptions of war wounds and putting a dog in danger as a joke suggest otherwise. Evelyn's devotion to her long-time sweetheart and her affection for children and dogs make her a perfect role model for the young woman who wants to gain a husband in spite of the war. Evelyn may trick Brewster into marrying her, but his continued refusal is clearly an act of chivalry, which Evelyn's allegiance negates. No devoted woman would accept his refusal, and Evelyn's example offers every young woman the courage to marry a wounded man and to be, as it were, his crutch.

Motion Pictures, the Red Cross, and German Spies: The Ruth Fielding Series

While magazine fiction might reach a more varied audience, novels about the lives of adolescent girls had a much more specific readership: young girls and women who searched for role models of their own age. These novels tended to be published in "series" and were often written by corporate authors to the extent that locating the author of a specific novel can be difficult, if not impossible. The Ruth Fielding series, for instance, includes thirty novels, three of which are set and were published during the First World War. Alice B. Emerson, author of the series, is a pseudonym for a number of writers including Mildred Wirt Benson, who also wrote some of the Nancy Drew novels under the name Carolyn Keene. While Benson did not write the three war novels, they have the same tone as the Nancy Drew books and similar plot characteristics. All portray a spunky, no-nonsense heroine who often finds her girlfriends silly and is willing to get into trouble to get to the bottom of a mystery. Ruth is a smart, independent young woman who comes and goes as she pleases, all characteristics meant to endear her to a young readership. In the war novels, Ruth's charitable acts promote the Red Cross and nursing; her daring makes war service sound exciting and dangerous enough to prove attractive. Still, by the end of *Ruth Fielding Homeward Bound,* readers have an inkling that Ruth will one day marry her best friend, Tom Cameron, who has left Harvard with a number of his classmates to enlist and apply for a commission in the U.S. Army. Ruth does marry Tom, but the mystery novels and her film career continue, even after she becomes a mother. The final novel in the series, *Ruth Fielding and Her Crowning Victory,* was not published until 1934, fifteen years after the final World War I novel.

In spots these novels are awkwardly written, especially in the area of filling in readers on Ruth's past and her previous adventures. The girl of the Red Mill, as Ruth is known, lives with her Uncle Jabez Potter, a surly old miller who gradually takes to the orphan because of her independence. Ruth's wealthy friends, twins Tom and Helen Cameron, live on the land next to the Red Mill. Ruth and Helen attend boarding school then college together. Grudgingly, Uncle Jabez acknowledges Ruth's success and the benefits of her education. We are told of the old New Englander, "he had begun to realize that all this education Ruth had been getting (quite unnecessary he had first believed) had led her into a position where she was 'making good.'"[11] In the first of the 1918 war novels, *Ruth Fielding in the Red Cross*, Ruth and Helen have come home halfway into their sophomore year to do war work, but Ruth has already ventured far from home to become involved in writing "moving-picture scenarios of the better class," and she now owns an interest in the "Alectrion Film Corporation" (12–13). Through her exploits, Ruth has become quite wealthy, with "bank accounts and investments [that] now ran well into five figures" (13). While "five figures" does not demonstrate great wealth in the twenty-first century, it was a substantial figure in 1918, and Ruth is a single woman; to Ruth, the money and her interest in the film studio mean she is her own woman.

The first of the three war novels opens with Uncle Jabez and Aunt Alvirah, his aging housekeeper, providing comic relief and with Helen Cameron demonstrating a tendency to tearfulness that offers a contrast to Ruth's toughness. Helen weeps as she reads the letter saying that Tom has enlisted, and Uncle Jabez declares that if he were younger, he would take Old Betsey, his Civil War rifle, and go along. Fired up about the war, Uncle Jabez discharges the rifle out the back door, only to have it blow up in his face because Aunt Alvirah has poured concrete into the barrel as a safety measure. But the novel quickly moves into the mystery plot with the introduction of the "woman in black," Mrs. Mantel, who speaks ill of the Red Cross in an attempt to prevent the women of Cheslow, the nearby town, from joining. According to U.S. Government propaganda, spreading rumors about the Red Cross was a German tactic designed to undermine American patriotism. George Creel's ubiquitous agency the Committee on Public Information published the ad "Spies and Lies" in *Pictorial Review* for July 1918, warning Americans not to "become a tool of the Hun by passing on the malicious, disheartening rumors which he so eagerly sows," including those of "gross scandals in the Red Cross."[12] Mirroring Creel's warning, the novel right away casts Mrs. Mantel as a potential spy whose goal, in addition to embezzling money from the organization, is to cast aspersions on the Red Cross and damage its ability to recruit volunteers.

While Mrs. Mantel is never quite as sinister as Fräulein Schroeder from *The White Feather*, she is bent on undermining the Allied cause. Readers first observe Mrs. Mantel at a meeting of the Methodist Ladies' Aid Society in Cheslow, where Ruth and Helen go to recruit. The meeting is hosted by the mother of one of Ruth's school chums, and Ruth plans to address the women to drum up support for the war effort. Ruth catches Mrs. Mantel in a lie when she declares that she has seen a local girl wearing a sweater Mrs. Mantel claims she knitted for the Red Cross. According to Mrs. Mantel, the girl said she bought the sweater in a store, but Mrs. Mantel cannot say what store. Clever Ruth prompts her friend Mercy to ask Mrs. Mantel for advice on her knitting, and Mrs. Mantel remembers suddenly that she has to be somewhere else—that is, she does not really know how to knit. Mrs. Mantel disappears from Cheslow but reappears at the state headquarters in Robinsburg, where Ruth goes to volunteer after making a highly successful film about the war and the Red Cross, "The Boys of the Draft," which she has convinced even the well-off but parsimonious Uncle Jabez to invest in. Ruth's job is in the supply department at Red Cross headquarters, and she notices suspicious behavior when she observes Mrs. Mantel dining with two other Red Cross workers: Mr. Legrand, whom Ruth does not like, and José, a Mexican. Ruth fails to suspect José until she sees him "doing something" to the fire extinguishers in the business office where Mrs. Mantel does the bookkeeping (62). As astute readers will guess, Mrs. Mantel is embezzling money, and when her desk conveniently catches fire with all the ledger books on it, the fire extinguishers fail. José and Legrand disappear for the time being, and Ruth decides to keep the matter to herself because she has been reassigned to a supply unit in France. The mystery deepens as Ruth sees a man she believes to be Legrand on the ship over and hears him speaking German. We learn that in fact "Legrand" and Mrs. Mantel are German spies, whom Ruth is eventually responsible for catching. José is also a spy, a Mexican, and the nephew of an employee of the Countess Marchand, whose estate in France is near the hospital where Ruth is stationed, and whom Ruth also incorrectly suspects of spying for the Germans.

The plots of the three novels overlap and are linked by several elements introduced in *Ruth Fielding in the Red Cross*—Ruth's capacity for sniffing out spies—sleuthing, in Nancy Drew parlance—as well as her fearlessness, and Ruth's "friendship" with Tom Cameron. The details reveal Ruth's capacity for observation and speak to Creel's propaganda claim that spies are everywhere, even in rural Cheslow at the Ladies' Aid meeting. The unity of the small-town community, the Gemeinschaft, represented by the Methodist Ladies' Aid and the gruff kindness of Uncle Jabez and Aunt Alvirah, is endangered by German autocracy and its Kultur. But Ruth's vigilance keeps the community intact. In France, Ruth develops a working relationship with Monsieur Lefranc of the French Secret Service, whom she periodically contacts with information about spy suspects. Ruth is human and her suspicions misfire when she suspects the Countess Marchand and her two sons of being German spies; in reality, they and their greyhound Bubu, which freely delivers messages beyond the front lines because the peasants believe he is a werewolf, are actually French spies and help Ruth save Tom Cameron's life.

More than once, Ruth reveals a heroism and selflessness that is universally admired and respected. After declaring "honestly" to Helen that "men and women are not equal . . . and they never will be" (50), Ruth receives praise from the French Secret Service agent Monsieur Joilette, who has told Monsieur Lefranc that Ruth has "the logic of a man—and a man's courage" (192). While Ruth may claim to yield to the ideology that she is inferior to Tom, her actions and Joilette's words belie that claim. In fact, the novel suggests that logic and courage are not solely a man's domain, that all women should be capable of Ruth's courage and logic, and if they are not, they deserve the epithet "silly," which Helen often deserves. Even though Ruth lives by a feminist doctrine, her refusal to espouse it allows Ruth to remain an essential part of the Gemeinschaft, to remain a brave woman who never loses sight of her role in the community.

In *Ruth Fielding at the War Front*, Ruth displays courage when she goes with American ambulance driver Charlie Bragg, who is writing books about his war experiences, to take supplies to a field hospital that has been bombed. Ruth knows that the worker who previously ran the supply depot has been killed by a bomb, but she tells the doctor there that while she is frightened, she has experienced "night air raids . . . [and] as Charlie Bragg says, 'I have not been killed yet.'"[13] In spite of the distinct possibility that she may be killed, Ruth is willing to go where she is needed most. Her bravery parallels Charlie's, as Monsieur Lefranc has pointed out; wounded soldiers depend on Ruth as much as they depend on Charlie, a truth of which Ruth is well aware. Yet Ruth is completely unassuming, a quality reaffirming the idea that she believes any woman can do what is necessary under the pressures of war. Unlike Helen, Ruth is not in the war for the fun of it, and her actions repeatedly verify her intentions.

In the most crucial scene in the second novel, Ruth agrees to go with Major Henri Marchand, the Countess's older son, across the front lines into Germany to pose as Tom's sister and get him out of Germany, where he has been impersonating a German officer. Tom, using the identity of a Bavarian, Captain Von Brenner, has supposedly been waiting for the arrival of his sister at the hotel in Merz near the summer estate of the Marchands, which of course is now billeting German officers. Rumors have had it that Tom has defected, and while she denies the possibility, Ruth does not know the truth until the Marchands receive a message in Bubu's hollow tooth that Tom is under house arrest at the summer estate and is in danger of having his true identity discovered. Under cover of darkness, Ruth, dressed as a soldier, follows Marchand through trenches and a marsh to the gardener's cottage on the estate where the younger Marchand brother is hiding. Tom's German is flawless because he had a German nanny, but Ruth's is only adequate, and she risks being caught and, of course, shot. Still Ruth is the better candidate for the mission because Tom's real sister Helen could not possibly perform the tasks Ruth performs.

The Marchands have upper-class German clothing for Ruth at the cottage and, dressed in it, she leaves the cottage by the back way and arrives at the hotel, where she demands that her brother be brought to her. The Marchands have coached her, but she has to be careful not to say enough for her American accent to be detected. Ruth's behavior here employs German stereotypes—she is very precise and demanding, barking commands at the hotel staff when she finds her brother is not there. She sends a letter, signed by Mina von Brenner, the agreed-upon name of the awaited sister, and Tom is allowed to go to the hotel, where he is astonished to find Ruth. The Marchands spirit them back across the lines and Tom's life is saved, at least for the moment. When Major Henri Marchand drops Ruth off back at the Red Cross hospital, he tells her, "I approve of you—I admire you. Your courage is sublime—and your modesty and goodness equally so" (201). Once again, Ruth's heroism is matched by her circumspect behavior. While she risks her life crossing the front lines and learns to swagger like a German officer while in this guise until she dons the dress, she never loses sight of her gender. She may for a moment allow herself to be re-imagined in military terms as she wades through the trenches alongside Tom, but she is still at heart the girl of the Red Mill.

Ruth's final act in *Ruth Fielding at the War Front* is to stave off questions from Helen and Jennie Stone, their school friend, who have come to the field hospital from Paris for excitement. Jennie believes Ruth has been missing for two days in order to be married, and she asks Ruth, "Are you really wedded?" Ruth, who has not slept for the two days she has spent rescuing Tom, replies, "I am wedded to my work" (202). Helen and Jennie cannot imagine the exertion of strength and will involved in Ruth's escapade across the lines; they can only imagine her truancy in terms of romance. The frivolity of the two girls contrasts to Ruth's exhaustion and to what she has seen crossing the trenches. When Ruth tells Helen that she has spoken to Tom and he will arrive shortly to see her, Helen, very nearly giddy, says, "Goody! Dear old Tom will take us around and show us the big shell holes—and all" (203). Having just risked her life crawling through shell holes to save Tom, whose intelligence gathering on the current German attack is saving Allied lives, Ruth might be fed up with her friends, but she merely sends then away to perform her duties in the supply room so that she can rest.

Restrained but brave, Ruth's actions on the front contradict the idea of the foolish girl who gets into trouble and must be saved by the hero of the story. Indeed, in the Martha Trent "Somewhere" series discussed later, we again see the heroine saving the hero and doing so not in spite of herself but because of her wit and strength. Ruth is a real trooper. There should be no surprise at the popularity of the entire series. The war aside, young girls were looking for examples of brave independent women, and they found them in Ruth Fielding and Nancy Drew. I must admit that as a young girl I devoured the Nancy Drew novels, and even though no one was still using the term *roadster*, I found the idea that Nancy had her own car invigorating. I was disappointed when the Nancy Drew spin-off TV series *Veronica Mars* was canceled.

The third Ruth Fielding war volume, *Ruth Fielding Homeward Bound*, published just after the war, begins with Ruth, Helen, and Jennie celebrating Jennie's engagement to the newly promoted Colonel Henri Marchand—a surprising twist, since at the end of the previous novel, Jennie and Henri had not met, and Jennie is a very large girl, nicknamed "Heavy" Stone at school. As they chat and drink their tea, the hospital is shelled, and almost immediately Ruth is wounded when the window she is standing near implodes. As it turns out, Ruth has minor cuts but also a broken shoulder, a wound serious enough to send her home on a ship, the location of her final heroic adventures during the war. First, Ruth is told before she boards that Tom Cameron has gone down in a plane and is believed dead. Through point of view shifts, absent from the other two books, we learn that

Tom's pilot friend has taken him up on a lark, and in the course of the joyride they encounter Germans. In spite of Tom manning the plane's machine gun, the Germans shoot them down over the very waters through which Ruth is traveling.

On board ship, distraught but ever vigilant, Ruth overhears conversations that make her believe German spies are planning to blow up the vessel. She speaks to the ship's first officer, Mr. Dowd, who believes Ruth's story in spite of the captain's scorn. Actually, the plot is not to blow up the ship but to commandeer it for the German cause. Because Ruth and Dowd suspect a plot of some sort, they are left on the ship with Rollife, the radio operator, when the ship is abandoned after a superficial explosion causes a panic. The Germans could just shoot the passengers, but the "explosion" offers an explanation for the absence of the ship. When the conspirators return to claim the ship, Dowd goes for pistols and Ruth tells him, "Bring one for me, . . . I can shoot a pistol. Three of us might hold off a small boarding party, I should think."[14] Unfortunately Dowd brings the wrong pistols, ones that are not loaded, and the three are taken prisoner. Ruth is locked up in her cabin until she offers to cook for the Germans, an offer they accept, freeing Ruth to go about the ship and observe what is going on.

Different from the other two war novels, the third employs point of view shifts to allow readers to follow Tom's adventures as well and to let us know that Tom is very much alive. Like Ruth, Tom is also taken prisoner on a Zeppelin until he manages to bring it down and escape on a part of the gondola that serves as a raft. Needless to say, Tom and Ruth meet at sea and subdue the pirates with the aid of Dowd, who this time brings the loaded pistols. Predictable as the plot may be, Ruth's courage when she offers to shoot the Germans, and her ingenuity when she contrives to gain her freedom by becoming cook, all with a broken shoulder, reiterate her willingness to respond to the German menace with bravery and logic.

For American girls who read these books during the war, Ruth Fielding must have seemed a superwoman, an alternative to the sweater-knitting girl-next-door who declined to venture beyond her home town. At the same time, as Henri Marchand insists, Ruth's "modesty and goodness" recommend her as an admirable role model, and her insistence on gender inequality in spite of her actions must have allowed parents to see Ruth as a harmless image to offer their daughters. Like Edith Cavell, Ruth is brave but virginal, and devoted to family. With her money and script-writing skills, Ruth could live in New York or Hollywood, but she returns to the Red Mill to nurse Aunt Alvirah, who has temporarily become ill in Ruth's absence. And although we do not see a marriage proposal by novel's end, we do see Tom and Ruth ride off together in Tom's car. When Ruth points out that they have the whole afternoon together, Tom replies, "I wish it was going to continue forever—just for you and me, Ruth! . . . A life trip, dear!" (210). Once again, the marriage plot triumphs and the family unit remains intact, in spite of the German threat. Ruth fights for her man and her home, and even risks her life to save his, but she remains in the service of family members as traditional caretaker. The Gemeinschaft has served the state and preserved it as well as preserving itself. As propaganda, these novels are rousing. The image of the strong but unassuming woman, who not only takes care of herself but when necessary puts her life on the line for those she loves, tenders for all women the notion that anything is possible with effort. Culturally, if incidentally, the Ruth Fielding and Nancy Drew novels paved the way for other popular female icons, including Emma Peel and Buffy Summers, among many others.

Lassos, Omelets, and Machine Guns: The Martha Trent "Somewhere" Series

Like the Ruth Fielding series, the Martha Trent novels offer young female readers a glimpse into the lives of "special" women, in this case from around the world. With the exception of *Phoebe Marshall Somewhere in Canada,* which was released in 1919, the novels were all published in 1918 and are all linked, if in highly coincidental ways. Beginning with the third novel, advertisements in the backs of the books proclaim that

> Around a central figure "half girl, half boy, and the better part of each" the author has written a fascinating story layering the plot first in America and subsequently, in the other stories, in other countries. The author's intimate knowledge and deep insight into the life and surroundings of the young heroines in the various countries add distinct educational value to the pronounced charm and quaintness of the stories.[15]

The copy goes on to call the novels a "particularly timely series of books for young readers who have been following the progress of the war."[16] The description "half girl, half boy, and the better half of each"—(*half* is the word used in the novel)—comes from *Helen Carey Somewhere in America,* the first novel in the series.[17] Like Ruth Fielding, each of the young women exhibits bravery that is most often thought of as masculine. Each of the heroines, at least for the duration of the war, dispenses with the expectations of frailty and dependence that surrounded young girls. These women are nothing at all like Molly Pollock of *The White Feather* or Mary Hamilton of "One of Ten Million" before her nightmare about the cannibal Kaiser. These young women do not need male direction in their bravery, although they all have or find male presences in their lives.

The idea that the novels have educational value alludes to the cultural differences in the lives of the women and their home countries but also to the singleness of their goal—defeating German Kultur. Readers can learn about life in a Belgian inn and about life as an Italian goatherd. Crucial to the "educational value" is the assertion that the novels can help young women follow the progress of the war, and therein lies the propaganda value of the stories. All six heroines, like Ruth Fielding, risk their lives without hesitation to save the lives of others. In each case either a loved one is in danger or Allied troops are at risk, or in some cases both. Each young woman has close family ties, and like Ruth Fielding, each maintains those ties in the face of war and separation. The family unit, even if it is not a typical nuclear family in every case, provides strength and inspiration. And if the family unit is not enough, the state, in its various Allied guises, provides the final impetus for bravery. Once again the state calls on the local community, the Gemeinschaft, to sacrifice its members for the larger society. Nowhere in any of the six novels is the war questioned. Only negative characters, German sympathizers, seek to undermine the cause of the Allies.

Even Cowgirls Go to War

Helen Carey Somewhere in America is set in Wyoming. Helen, or Missy as she is called, lives on a ranch with her father and, since the death of her mother, her aunt Tabitha. Like Ruth Fielding's "family," the Careys are wealthy but do not live as if they are. Helen rides and ropes with the best of the ranch hands, but she goes to school in Philadelphia at the request of Aunt Tab. When the novel opens, Helen is back home for the summer and awaiting a letter from her adopted Belgian soldier, Henri, who turns out to be the brother of Marieken De Bruin, of the second Somewhere novel. America has not yet entered the war, and even the ranch hands look forward to Henri's letters. After learning that he lacks tobacco much of the time, Helen and the hands take up a collection and send him a large tin of it.

"Half boy, half girl and the better half of each" (11), Helen is not a traditional girl by any means. Although she is only sixteen, there is "an expression of courage and self-reliance in her whole manner" (12). Without dwelling on the fate of his herd at the war front, Helen's father has arranged to sell some horses to an English officer for the British Army, and trouble appears to be brewing in connection with a neighboring rancher of questionable ethics, who plans to switch his own inferior herd for the Carey horses, a plot Helen has discovered. Helen demands to go along with the hands to prevent the switch. When she is told she cannot go and complains about the restriction, her father tells her, "You ought to have been a boy, Missy. . . . You certainly are material wasted, but you're not one, and you can't expect us to let you ride into possible danger" (74). Resentful, Helen is sent off to visit her girlfriends, and we are told that "some of the old natural fellowship [with the hands is] gone and a new consideration [has taken] its place" (75).

Helen may be expected to behave like a girl, but she cannot stay out of trouble; when she tries, trouble finds her. One of the ranch hands, nicknamed "Shoulders" because of his physique, tells her there might "be a little shooting," but Helen ignores him and rides out on the day the horse switching is supposed to occur. Responding to her horse, which suddenly appears nervous after riding through a deep draw, Helen dismounts and stumbles on a revolver with one chamber empty. Finally taking care, Helen creeps forward toward a pile of rocks and overhears the despised rancher and one of his associates plotting to throw Shoulders, who lies unconscious in front of them, into the draw where he will fall to his death. Using the gun that the unfortunate Shoulders has dropped, Helen holds the two men at gunpoint until Shoulders revives and rides off to get help. Helen is credited with saving Shoulders's life, in what proves to be the first of two incidents.

A further complication of the horse deal has to do with a young American who accompanies the British soldier to purchase horses. Allan Webb turns out to be the cousin of one of Helen's schoolmates, and even though he has overheard Helen call him a tenderfoot, he falls for her. When the United States enters the war, Allan, Helen's brother Tom, and Shoulders all enlist. At Allan's urging, Helen goes to stay with his cousin Violet in Indiana to participate in a fair to raise money for the war effort, and to see him off.

Helen's second courageous act occurs on the evening of the fair, after she has given a demonstration with her lariat by roping anything anyone asks her to for twenty-five cents a request. Helen learns, by way of a rude German child she has met on the train, that the child's father is going to sabotage the railroad bridge over which the train carrying troops, including Tom Carey and Shoulders Fielding, is shortly scheduled to pass. Allan and Helen race to the bridge in Allan's car, and as they speed toward the site, Helen realizes that she has not put down the lariat. Allan and the German saboteur, who has already removed a large section of rail, fall into the water in a struggle, and Helen must act on her own. She drives Allan's car in the direction of the troop train, and when she spots it, she lassos a switching sign on the other side of the tracks, so that it breaks the window of the locomotive and the engineer stops the train. Like Ruth Fielding, Helen breaks her shoulder, but she saves Tom and Shoulders. By the end of the novel, Helen is engaged to Allan and wondering, as she reads Henri De Bruin's last letter, if she will ever get to meet his brave sister, Marieken. She does in the third novel, *Valerie Duval Somewhere in France*.

While Helen's courageous acts occur in the United States and outside the realm of war, she saves Shoulders's life twice and prevents a trainload of soldiers from going into the river. Shoulders is not Helen's love interest, but as a loyal hand on the ranch, he is deserving of Helen's sisterly affection. Helen is not so different from the other ranch girls who can also ride and rope, but she beats them all in a series of games at a farewell picnic for the hands before they ship out for war. As Shoulders and Tom are riding home after the picnic, Shoulders remarks that it's "too bad she isn't a boy" (155), a remark he has also made earlier at the picnic, and , as we have seen, that her father has made as well. But Helen reminds readers that she need not be a boy, that girls are tough too. Helen in fact does it all; she is smart enough to go to school in Philadelphia and pretty enough to wear a dress copied from a pattern her Aunt Tabitha once wore, features that make her a character for adolescent girls to emulate. Like Ruth Fielding, Helen does it all with decency and verve, and her reward is the dashing Allan Webb, who becomes Captain Webb in *Valerie Duval Somewhere in France*. Nowhere in these novels does a heroine decide she will strike out on her own and thus become a threat to the Gemeinschaft—a dangerous, albeit valuable, woman like Miriam Lee of *The White Feather*. Each young girl acts out of necessity, and to each applies the compliment Henri Marchand pays to Ruth Fielding regarding her "modesty and goodness." All serve the family on behalf of the state, and all are triumphant.

Female bravery escalates in the next four of the Somewhere novels, which place all of the heroines, including Helen Carey, at or near the front lines. As the girls meet under sometimes troubling circumstances, their heroism forms bonds among them, bonds that transcend international boundaries. In the second novel readers are situated "Somewhere in Belgium," in territory occupied by German invaders. Marieken De Bruin, our second heroine, is the fourteen-year-old daughter of an innkeeper, his favorite, who "had grown up with more independence of thought and action than is usually permitted to the average village girl."[18] When the Germans march through Belgium, Monsieur De Bruin is killed. The sly Marieken makes a proposition to the German general who occupies what has become her inn because her mother is shell-shocked and her brother Henri, Helen Carey's pen pal, has not been heard from in a while. If Herr General will not molest her chickens and cows, she will house and feed the Germans lavishly. The general, who could demand Marieken's acquiescence regardless, accepts her proposition, and thus Marieken gains the upper hand with the invaders. She saves the best eggs for the village priest and digs a tunnel between the basement in the house and the dairy. When she wants to accomplish something during the night, she gives the general a bottle of rich wine that puts him to sleep.

Among Marieken's acts of bravery are helping a group of English prisoners of war escape when she overhears the general order their execution, the same act for which Edith Cavell was shot. Marieken puts the general to sleep with wine and leaves the pantry door open so that the German soldier guarding the cellar will also appear to get drunk. Then she leads the British soldiers out through the tunnel to the dairy so that they can escape, and the sentry is blamed. Coincidentally, Alice Blythe's brother Gilbert is posing as a German officer, and Marieken discovers his true identity. She delivers a dispatch from him to the British front line herself and later steals a map and plans for an attack from under the sleeping general's head, so that a wounded British soldier who was unable to escape earlier can take the map to the British. Finally, Marieken warns advancing Belgian and British troops that the Germans have a machine gun hidden in the town hall to thwart their advance. Here Marieken is wounded in the shoulder by shrapnel—the third shoulder wound in the two series—but the Germans are driven out of town.

Although Marieken is only fourteen, she appears to be in love with Captain Blythe and he with her. He does not overtly act on his affection, but he does have Alice buy Marieken a white dress with blue ribbons, a garment she has longed for. And in two scenes toward the end of the book, Marieken and Gilbert Blythe are together. The first of the two scenes occurs at the inn shortly after Marieken has been wounded. After being convinced that she is not in condition to cook dinner, Marieken agrees to cook only the omelets, her specialty, and when dinner is over, the soldiers around the table show their admiration for her by giving her their medals. As the scene ends, she falls asleep curled up on Captain Blythe's shoulder, a surprising intimacy in view of the historical precedent of marrying off young girls to "older" men. In the final scene, a week after Henri shows up wounded at the hospital in Fleurette where Marieken has healed and is now working, Blythe shows up with the white dress, and he and Marieken, wearing the dress, walk off together on the green lawn of the converted chateau.

While Marieken is too young by American standards for a proposal from Captain Blythe, we might suppose he will wait for her, as Captain Brewster has waited for Evelyn in "The Dog of War" and as Shoulders promises he will wait for Valerie Duval at the end of her story. As American propaganda, these novels could not suggest that marriage at fourteen is acceptable, and Captain Blythe and Shoulders are honorable men who will wait. Although Shoulders is a ranch hand, he is more or less part of the Carey family and he understands, perhaps through his relationship with Helen, how to behave as a gentleman. And he is an American, after all; the savage Huns are the ones who take advantage of women. While some class differences might exist between the Blythes and the De Bruins, that does not appear to be the source of Gilbert's delay in proposing to Marieken. Monsieur De Bruin was a substantial member of their Belgian community before he lost his life during the German invasion, and of course war is a great leveler.

A young American girl reading the novel must feel nothing but admiration for Marieken, and her heroic deeds will serve their purpose as war propaganda. Marieken is cunning enough to get the German general drunk when she needs him to be and fearless enough to approach the front lines alone. In addition, if the end really does foreshadow a marriage plot—and readers are free to imagine that it does—the romance of war also contributes to the story's propaganda appeal. The plucky girl is rewarded with a husband and the family survives, more or less intact. Only Monsieur De Bruin, the family patriarch, does not survive the war. His death conveniently paves the way for the fourteen-year-old Marieken to become, at least for the duration of the war, the head of the household. Henri does recover from his wounds, and Madame De Bruin regains her strength when she sees her daughter wounded and in need of her help. Repeatedly in the novels, the family and the local community serve the state. In this second novel in the series, the family and local community are Belgian and Marieken makes omelets instead of riding and roping, and keeps chickens and cows, not horses, but the values of family loyalty and duty to the community remain the same. We might note at this point that in depriving the Germans of the best eggs, which

Marieken delivers to the village priest, she also risks her life and property. Yet in the prospect of marriage between Captain Blythe and Marieken lies the hope of international relations, and the family will continue to serve the larger community, both states, by maintaining the connection between the local community and the state and by producing sons and daughters who will perform acts of valor on behalf of the state, one that is becoming international.

Machine Guns and Family Honor: *Valerie Duval Somewhere in France*

The most violent of the Somewhere novels, *Valerie Duval Somewhere in France,* begins with Captain Allan Webb, Helen Carey's fiancé, and her brother Lieutenant Tom Carey arriving on the Duval farm ahead of the advancing American troops to make arrangements for quarters. Madame Duval, who has run the farm since her husband died ten years before, offers her three extra bedrooms to the officers, the third of whom is Lieutenant Shoulders Fielding, and offers her barn to the privates. Like Helen Carey, Valerie is compared to a boy. Valerie's crippled brother Pierre, on the other hand, is "feminine." The villagers near the Duval farm are puzzled that "the good God had seen fit to give the girl the looks of a boy, and the boy the wistful eyes and sensitive features of a girl."[19] The Duvals are a fighting family, and Pierre is very sensitive about his condition, especially when their grandfather makes patriotic speeches at dinner, as he does on the first evening the Americans spend at the Duval farm. The speech so disturbs Pierre that Valerie decides to enlist in her brother's place. Even though she dresses like a boy, she is found out, but her bravery impresses the corporal, who agrees not to send her home. She salutes him "in a spirit of mischief" (60) as he leaves her, and the corporal admits to himself that "she does it better than any of the new recruits, . . . I almost wish I had held my old tongue" (60).

Even though she cannot go as a soldier, Valerie does get to fight. The corporal sends her to the inn the French soldiers use as a canteen to help Madame Lefevre. Valerie's chance occurs one evening when, unable to sleep during a German bombardment of the French lines, she goes outside to find an American ambulance driver who is lost and has six wounded men in his car. Valerie takes him to French headquarters, and the officers make the decision to convert the inn to a field hospital with the aid of some medical students to whom Valerie has served wine the previous evening. Two other ambulances arrive, and among the wounded is a gunner who tells Valerie before he dies that he has the location of the hidden German gun, one Valerie has heard about, and he gives her the coordinates he was about to use when he was hit. The American driver Billy Lathrop, the fiancé of Miss Brooks, head nurse at Fleurette, tells Valerie he is going back to the dressing station at the front to get supplies, and as he pulls out, Valerie jumps in the back of the ambulance with the idea of getting to gun number five so that she can use the coordinates given her by the dying gunner and take out the big German gun.

Since the gun is doing a great deal of damage, killing Allied soldiers, Valerie never considers failing to act on the information. Of course, she locates the appropriate gun, gives the remaining gunners the coordinates, and with their last shell, they take out the hidden German gun. One of the gunners is wounded, and Valerie tricks the other to drive the ambulance back to headquarters, then goes looking for Lathrop because she is afraid he has been caught in the firing. She finds him in a cellar, buried under the collapsed roof but relatively unharmed. The two hide as the advancing Germans set up a machine gun

Without thinking what she did she picked up Lathrop's
revolver and fired at once

Page 111

FIG. 16. An illustration showing Valerie Duval shooting a German soldier, in *Valerie Duval Somewhere in France*.

in their cellar to attack retreating French soldiers. Lathrop kills two of the Germans and turns the machine gun against the enemy troops instead of the French. Before he can fire, a third German appears and wings Lathrop. Infuriated, Valerie picks up Lathrop's gun and kills the German soldier (fig. 16). Lathrop can still fire the machine gun and does so until he is hit again by a shell. Valerie, also knocked unconscious, revives first and takes over the machine gun firing as she has seen Lathrop do.

In effect, Valerie mows down the Germans until they scatter and she runs out of ammunition. When they are back at the inn, Valerie tells the wounded Lathrop, "I killed that big man with your gun—do you remember?—I Valerie Duval killed a man" (125). Lathrop replies offhandedly, "You bet you did, . . . you're a good shot, too. If you hadn't been, well, neither of us would be sitting here quietly discussing the price of potatoes. You saved my life twice within a couple of hours" (125). Before running away from the farm to enlist, Valerie has heard from Shoulders how Helen Carey twice saved his life, and she feels she has lived up to those high standards. Here female bravery is matched by further female bravery; although they have not yet met, the two women bond through mutual acquaintances and prove that valor is not limited by either gender or nationality. Nor are the rescued males reluctant to admit they have been saved by female valor. While Helen receives only praise from her friends, especially Shoulders, Valerie receives a Croix de Guerre for her exploits, and as the French general pins the medal on her dress, he compares her to Joan of Arc. Valerie's ultimate reward, however, is that her grandfather Duval honors her by hanging the sword of the Duval family over her bed. She has joined up to extend the fighting tradition of the Duval name, and the gift of the sword validates that family tie.

Valerie accepts a position at the hospital in Fleurette when

Janet Brooks, Lathrop's fiancée, writes to her and asks for her help. When Valerie steps off the train, she finds herself face to face with Helen Carey and is escorted to her room by Marieken De Bruin. Alice Blythe is only a few miles away, and Lathrop has gone to Italy, where he meets Lucia Rudini. Allan Webb and Shoulders also show up at Fleurette and Shoulders proposes to Valerie, agreeing to wait until she is old enough to wed. Like Helen Carey and Marieken De Bruin, Valerie is rewarded for her war service with male protection, although it is clear she does not need it. The only one of the six actually to kill enemy soldiers, one face to face, Valerie remains a girl at heart. She has been touched by what she has seen and done, as has Marieken, but she does not become cynical like the women in the realistic novel *Not So Quiet* by Helen Zenna Smith. Valerie has fought on her own terms to save her home and family, and she will eagerly return to her family with the knowledge that she and Shoulders will keep it going, whether in France or in the United States. She is proud to have served France and to have upheld the fighting reputation of the Duval family. Along with Marieken, she also hates the Germans, an ethnic hatred that long predates the war and incidentally adds to the propaganda value of the stories.

Secret Dungeons, Goats, and Tanks: The Final Three Somewhere Novels

The first three Somewhere novels establish the tone and plot structure of the last three. All in their teens, Alice Blythe, Lucia Rudini, and Phoebe Marshall are no-nonsense girls who are determined to serve the Allied cause to protect their families and preserve the state. Alice is already unofficially engaged to her distant cousin Peter St. John, who secretly teaches her to fly his airplane. Peter is in the Royal Flying Corps training near his aunt's house where Alice is staying, so he can take Alice up often. Alice's father is an important London doctor, and we have already seen her brother Gilbert and his admiration for Marieken De Bruin. Alice insists on going to France to work at a hospital run by family friend Michael Jepson, also a physician. Helen Carey is there before she transfers to Fleurette, and the two hit it off immediately. But Alice is not at the hospital for long. When an ambulance wrecks in front of her as she and Helen wait for the wounded, Alice decides to drive it.

In spite of her superior driving skills, the rough roads get the best of her, and she skids into a shell hole. There she finds a downed pilot who needs to get a message back to headquarters, coincidentally the headquarters of Peter's unit. Since Alice can fly, she drags the wounded pilot to the road and takes off at dawn with the message in her pocket. The flight goes well until she slightly misjudges the landing, but she has only a broken ankle and delivers the message, to the surprise of all the men. Alice returns to her aunt's to recuperate, but once again she must perform a heroic deed. Peter is missing, and when she hears a plane land on the field where he gave her flying lessons, she goes to investigate. The pilot is in a British uniform, but Alice realizes it is Peter's uniform when she sees a blue forget-me-not she has embroidered on the underside of the collar. Obviously a German spy, the soldier agrees to go home with Alice, and she and the Scottish gardener trap him in the hidden passageway of the old house, where they keep him imprisoned for days, feeding him by way of a second entrance. It never occurs to either Alice or the gardener to mistreat the German, beyond locking him up in the dungeon. Through him, they are able to locate Peter and a missing village boy as well.

Unlike the other heroines, Alice does not quite get the respect she deserves. When Peter returns and Alice offers up the German prisoner, he tells her she cannot go into town with him to deliver the German to the authorities. "'This is a man's job,'" Peter declares "with a condescension that infuriated Alice."[20] Instead of reminding Peter that she was the one who captured the German in the first place, Alice agrees to marry Peter when the war is over. Until then, despite Peter's haughty attitude, she continues to do her war work. She returns to Dr. Jepson's hospital, where we see her at the end of *Phoebe Marshall Somewhere in Canada* getting another broken ankle in a train wreck, but continuing nonetheless to aid the injured. Thus she remains faithful to her family and to Peter as well as to the state.

In addition to Peter's hubris at the end of *Alice Blythe*, evidence of the hasty composition of the novels (and most likely of their corporate authorship) shows up more than once in *Alice Blythe*. In the earlier novels and in *Phoebe Marshall*, we are told Alice's ankle was broken, but in *Alice Blythe* the injury is a sprain; and the name of Helen Carey's fiancé, spelled Allan in the earlier novel, now is spelled Allen. Still, the novel presents a heroine who makes herself useful to the Allied cause, even in the face of initial parental objections. In the opening scene we observe Alice trying to knit, and we learn she is a miserable failure at that feminine undertaking, although she does embroider the flower on Peter's uniform. Yet she can drive an automobile and pilot an airplane, and she has the no-nonsense attitude required for war service, qualities young readers might wish to emulate. In one scene early in the novel, Alice makes an impassioned speech in favor of the war while standing on the seat of her roadster. She is never deterred by the suggestion that her behavior is unladylike, and while Peter is the only male character in the series who fails to acknowledge female endeavor, Alice ignores this.

Underscoring the "educational value" of the novels, the Italian Lucia Rudini is the only one of the six girls who is not financially well-off, although the Rudinis do own a farm. A goatherd who lives with her grandmother in a modest cottage, Lucia looks after her little brother and the goats, including the mischievous Garibaldi, a nanny goat in spite of the name, and Lucia's favorite. Lucia has been leaving milk for a soldier whom she has never seen but who places pennies on a rock in return for the milk. Lucia and the goat are temporarily captured by Austrians who are attempting to invade her village, but she escapes and overhears a spy dressed as a peasant discussing battle plans with Austrian soldiers. Running to tell anyone she can find, Lucia falls, and when she wakes, she is looking into the face of her "soldier of the pennies," as she calls him. He tells Lucia that he must blow up the bridge into town, that it is in fact already mined. When Lucia's soldier is hit by a shell, Lucia runs to the convent where the sisters are tending the wounded. Together with her cousin Maria's wounded and still weakened soldier-beau, Lucia blows up the bridge and then drags the soldier-beau, who has passed out, back to the convent. Garibaldi in tow, she goes back into the shelling looking for her own soldier of the pennies. He cannot walk, but he is alive, so Lucia rigs up a stretcher which she and the goat pull toward town until she runs into the American Lathrop of Valerie Duval's story. With Lucia and the goat at his heels, Lathrop carries the Italian the rest of the way to the hospital.

Lucia's soldier turns out to be a very important captain in the Italian army.[21] For her bravery in blowing up the bridge and saving the life of her soldier, Lucia, like Valerie Duval, is awarded the favor of her soldier of the pennies, Captain Riccardi, and a medal from the king of Italy. Captain Riccardi is bewitched by Lucia even before he calls down to her for milk from his observation post in a tree high in the mountains. Riccardi shows his gratitude by moving Lucia, her brother, her grandmother, who is skilled at making lace, and the goat Garibaldi to his villa in southern Italy, we presume Naples. Riccardi tells Lucia that he wants her to take the place of his little sister who has passed away, but once again there is the hint of romance in Riccardi's description of first seeing Lucia. He explains, "I thought you were a fairy when I first saw you. . . . You were with your goats. I looked at you through my glass, and your pretty flowered dress, and the kerchief you wore over your hair, made me think of the little girls at home."[22] Like Gilbert Blythe and Marieken De Bruin, Lucia and Riccardi offer readers the promise of love when Lucia grows up. Once again by American standards, Lucia is too young to wed, so she remains in her own extended family, caring for her small brother and her aging grandmother as well as the goat Garibaldi, a bona fide character in the novel. All become Riccardi's adopted family until marriage can further the family bond, a bond he desires. Italy, like France and Belgium, will survive because family ties survive in spite of the ravages of war. Each girl has proven necessary to the survival of the state through her actions in war and her devotion to family. While each girl may exceed the cultural expectations of girlhood, may in fact ignore the gender boundaries that would apply under peaceful circumstances, none presumes male liberties. All remain chaste, earnest, circumspect, and all remain unquestioningly loyal to state and family.

The last of the novels and the only Somewhere novel published after the war's end, *Phoebe Marshall Somewhere in Canada,* does not offer either the romance or the excitement of the other five. At the onset of the novel, Phoebe is nursing convalescent soldiers in a trading post that has been converted to a hospital. While performing her duties, Phoebe falls in love with the dashing Canadian officer Captain "Lucky" Struthers of the tank corps, even though she pines for her missing brother Phil, who has gone down in an airplane in France and never been found. Phoebe's adventures involve riding in a tank to direct the driver toward the Canadian coast where a German submarine is about to land and, once she is in France looking for Phil, taking to British headquarters a document pulled from the shoe of a German spy Phoebe knew in Canada. Phoebe's vigilance in Canada has allowed her to ferret out the spies and foil their plan to land the submarine, although one spy escapes. Phoebe discovers the spy dead after the train she is on with Alice Blythe and Dr. Jepson crashes. Lucky finds Phil nearly dead of starvation in a German prison camp and brings him and a number of other soldiers out of the camp on the tank in which Phoebe has ridden earlier.

Like Peter St. John, who insults Alice, Captain Struthers at one point insults Phoebe, but with a different result. When Phoebe leads the tanks to the German submarine back in Canada, Struthers tells Phoebe she has no right to be in that tank. Phoebe retorts, "If you would take time to think you would realize that I have quite as much right to be here as you have." Lucky's response is to "[look] at her in amazement. He had never had a girl defy him before and, contrary to all expectations, he found himself rather enjoying the sensation."[23] Struthers does not need to dampen Phoebe's spirit and learns to respect her bravery, which is similar to his own. Lucky, his lieutenant Tommy Bunce, Phoebe, and Phil show up on November 11 at the Canadian trading post where the novel began, and Lucky and Phoebe announce their engagement to the old Scottish factor, the novel's father figure, who is beside himself that the war is over, Phil is alive, and they are all reunited. While the family here is a slightly unorthodox one, it survives the threat of war and of German spies. Even if the final novel lacks the bravado of the earlier ones, Phoebe, like all the heroines, is very much a role model for British or American girls who wanted to volunteer as nurses' aides or VADS or to work for the YMCA or the YWCA. She fearlessly rides in a tank—in World War I these were very small—and she must convince British officers that the document she carries really did come out of the shoe of a dead spy. As the last novel in the series and one celebrating the war's end, *Phoebe Marshall Somewhere in Canada* serves as a suitable conclusion to a series foreshadowing a new woman of sorts, one who can stand on her own but who will remain a staunch defender of home and hearth.

Khaki Girls and the Wizard of Oz

Other series beyond Ruth Fielding and the Somewhere books proliferated during the war. Cupples and Leon, publisher of the Ruth Fielding series, also published the Khaki Girls series, two of which came out after the war. Similar in tone to the Ruth Fielding novels, the Khaki Girls stories offer strong role models for young readers. The Aunt Jane's Nieces series by Edith Van Dyne, however, differ in that the women in these novels are more consistently and visibly dependent on male authority. Edith Van Dyne is a pseudonym for L. Frank Baum, author of *The Wizard of Oz*. And not surprisingly, the war novel *Aunt Jane's Nieces in the Red Cross*, focuses as much on the wealthy patriarch John Merrick as it does on the "nieces."[24] Set only a few months into the war when the United States still maintained neutrality, the novel presents Aunt Jane's niece Maud Stanton, a silent film star, arriving at "Uncle John's" apartment in New York declaring that she intends to go to France as a Red Cross nurse. Maud has had nurse's training and is thus qualified to make good on her threat. But when Patsy and Beth, who live with Uncle John, decide to go along, Uncle John takes over a yacht belonging to A. Jones, a young man who actually owns an island and is independently wealthy, and with the blessing of the Red Cross turns the yacht into a hospital ship. Patsy, Beth, and Maud thus go to war with the protection of Uncle John and Ajo, as A. Jones is called. While moments of tension arise, the girls are largely kept to the ship and later a French chateau, nursing. With the possible exception of Maud, who is a real nurse, the girls are more or less interchangeable and much less exceptional than Ruth Fielding or the heroines of the "Somewhere" series. By novel's end, Maud has fallen for a photographer she knew before the war; he has been wounded filming battle scenes, and when he recuperates, he makes a great deal of money on the films. Beth hooks up with Dr. Gys, who at the beginning of the book is horribly disfigured by injuries incurred on various dangerous travels. When Gys is himself wounded and treated by a depressed but excellent French surgeon, the Frenchman performs plastic surgery so that Gys looks exactly like his former self. And Patsy has an understanding with Ajo that they will wed at the end of the war. Although readers of earlier Aunt Jane's Nieces novels may have appreciated the exploits of the three girls, a wicked witch or a pair of red shoes might have spiced up the story; it lacks the narrative vigor of other novels discussed. Nancy Drew would never have been a teenage icon had she been created by Edith Van Dyne.

Black Cat Cigarettes and American Girl War Workers: Advertising Celebrates the War

Portrayals of women's wartime roles turned up in one seemingly unlikely popular medium. In 1916, Carreras Limited of London issued in packages of its Black Cat Cigarettes a series of fifty cigarette cards devoted to "Women on War Work." Like the American baseball cards issued in packs of bubble gum, cigarette cards were a common feature in cigarette packages before the war. But the War Work cards brought home to both men and women that the war would require special sacrifices of British women. Numbered in order, each card shows a willing woman performing a task that men would have performed prior to the war. Like many war posters, the Black Cat Cigarette Cards are informed by social class. Card number 1, for instance, Motor Driving, depicts a woman driving (fig. 17). The copy on the back of the card reminds us that "before the war, it was rather an unusual thing to see a woman driving a motor car in a big town." On opposite sides of the Atlantic, Ruth Fielding, Helen Carey, and Alice Blythe drive cars, which suggests that the activity is one largely reserved for the middle and upper classes. It was, after all, upper middle-class women who drove ambulances in France because they already knew how to drive. The card suggests that women can also drive lorries and vans, but the woman depicted in card number 1 wears the same uniform and drives the same vehicle as the woman in card number 13, Ambulance Service (fig. 17). The card alludes to Red Cross service, as does card number 32, Red Cross Nurse (fig. 18). According to the copy on the nursing card, nursing is women's work anyway, but the war makes the job dangerous and much more distressing. Card number 43 shows a smartly uniformed VAD Woman (fig. 18), but many of the other cards are devoted to working-class tasks such as street sweeping, gardening, and stoking a furnace (fig. 19). While Lucia Rudini herds goats and Valerie Duval cooks, they are both still of propertied families. Neither would give up her family position to work in a flour mill or wash windows, jobs suggested on other cards.

Even though the cards rely on class stereotypes, they suggest

FIG. 17. Black Cat Cigarette cards, nos. 1 and 13.

BLACK CAT
CIGARETTES
AMBULANCE SERVICE.

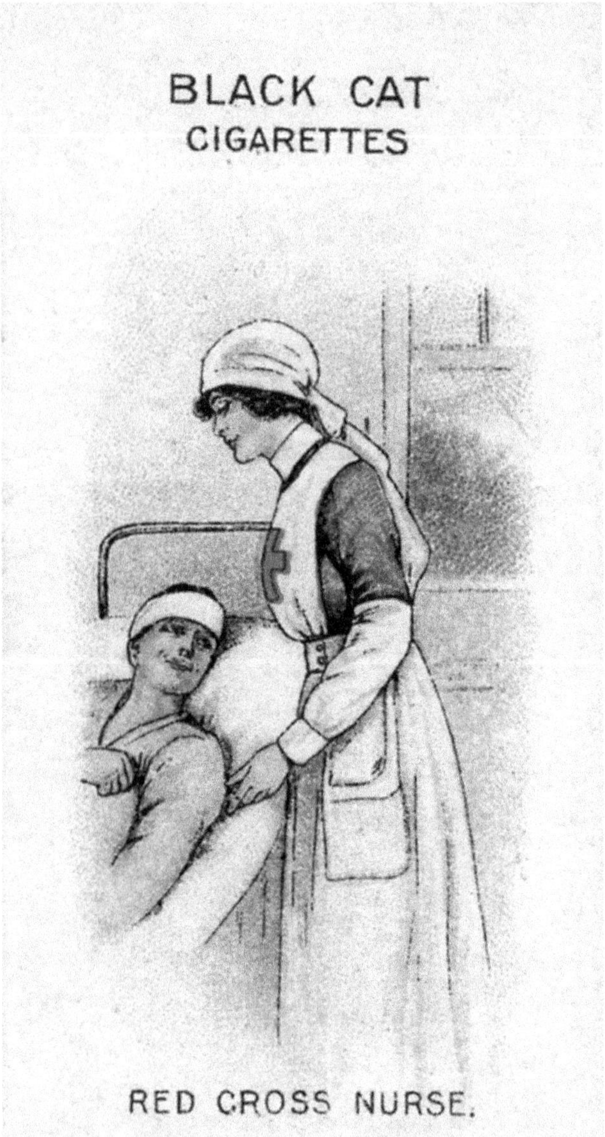

FIG. 18. Black Cat Cigarette cards, nos. 32 and 43.

BLACK CAT
CIGARETTES
V.A.D. WOMAN

FIG. 19. Black Cat Cigarette cards, nos. 26 and 24.

BLACK CAT
CIGARETTES
GARDENING.

some kind of work for every able-bodied woman to do during the war. In addition, each card also shows a beautiful, neatly dressed, circumspect woman; even the Woman Stoker, although she wears khaki work pants and vest, has her hair vampishly tied in a turban. The gardener sports a stylish hat and a smart midi under her gardening apron. By 1920 Black Cat was advertising its cigarettes to women, a nod to the liberating influence of the war work women of all classes performed. One such ad, a photograph on a postcard printed in London but labeled "U.S.A. Postcard" on the address side, pictures a woman smoking a cigarette (fig. 20). Wearing a cap and an aproned dress, the woman appears to be a parlor maid, although the Black Cat logo and cigarette packages attached to the apron render the dress inappropriate for anything but an advertisement. The dress also suggests that smoking is still a working-class pursuit. But the cards themselves and references to smoking in Helen Zenna Smith's *Not So Quiet* suggest that upper middle-class women had taken up the habit of smoking, and taken it up much earlier. Indeed, Sally Seton of Virginia Woolf's *Mrs. Dalloway* shocks the household at Bourton late in the nineteenth century because, among other things, she smokes. Nevertheless, the young heroines from the pages of propaganda novels did not smoke. Except for the flirtatious kiss doled out to keep up soldiers' morale, these girls are beyond virtuous; they are cheerful and willing to serve the state to preserve the ideals of home and family, and they are celebrated in American ladies' magazines as well as on cigarette cards.

The cover of the October 1918 issue of the *Ladies' Home Journal* depicts an American canteen staffed by YMCA workers, one of whom mends a soldier's uniform while others pass out sandwiches and coffee. Through the open door, an airplane is visible, and a sign on the canteen wall reminds the soldiers,

FIG. 20. Black Cat Cigarette postcard.

"Don't Forget to Write Home."[25] Inside the magazine, a tribute "To You: The American Girl War Worker," maintains:

> Already you have won the war cross of selflessness, the golden ribbon of endurance, the holy order of devotion and loyalty, and of bravery under daily fire of innumerable harassing tests. There is no respite for you now; but in the day which is to come, we see you no longer pale and anxious and the least bit shabby in your scrupulously pressed working frock; but tall and radiant and transfigured, clad in the glorious garments of achievement completed, over your breast the decoration of the kept faith, the race well run—in your eyes the light of victory.[26]

Worthy of photos of a young Edith Cavell, the paragraph idealizes war service in hyperbolic language absent in the novels, yet the "decoration of the kept faith" becomes a reality for the three European heroines, Valerie, Marieken, and Lucia. As we have also noted, the marriage plot promises husbands for all three, a reward perhaps more significant than a medal, a reward the novels promise young American readers.

A month before the end of the war, the magazine devotes a great deal of space to female war service. An article on the YWCA, "The Girls behind the Men behind the Guns," follows. Two of the accompanying photos show uniformed women in drill formations—one group destined for the Army Signal Corps in France, the other a shift of munitions workers. The caption under the photo of the munitions workers declares "Go to It! Let's Show Them That Women Can March and Salute and Drill as Well as Soldiers," a skill we have seen in Valerie Duval.[27]

A third feature in this issue, "The American Girl 'Over There,'" in many ways contradicts the message in the Somewhere novels. The author speaks of the women's "ENDURANCE:

splendid endurance!"[28] But she goes on to say: "Our American girls in France are rarely in the limelight. They are not Deborahs, nor Joans of Arc. Did it ever occur to you that if women should suddenly turn into exceptional women the race would cease? It is the normal, not the unusual, women who keep us steady."[29] Perhaps, but when the safety of the family and the state is at issue, women become exceptional, become Joans of Arc—with one obvious exception. As we have observed, all the propaganda heroines survive to accept either marriage proposals or male protection if they are too young for matrimony. While Valerie Duval kills for France and is compared to Joan of Arc, she still accepts Shoulders Fielding as her future husband, and she remains loyal to the Duval name. Lucia is of course compared to the saint of the same name, and while she may be saintly at war, she remains a flesh and blood girl who is in touch with nature in the beauty of southern Italy and her instinctive knowledge as a goatherd.

Family and the state survive together, but it is the Gemeinschaft that triumphs in each story and provides the impetus for propaganda. Young girls with exceptional—but not too exceptional—talents step forward at the call of the state, excel at war service, and at war's end, retreat into the arms of husbands and family. While the plots are exciting and potentially edifying, they are also unrealistic, not in the assertion of female bravery and family loyalty but in the naive plots in which all major characters survive and our heroines receive only shoulder or ankle wounds. We see no rapes, and while the Austrians threaten to shoot Lucia's goat Garibaldi, they refrain on the grounds that they may be able to milk her. Rape and pillage are among the most prominent elements of propaganda, and as emerges in chapter 5, these deeds inspire men to protect their women, not the other way around. Even Phoebe Marshall, who really does not risk her own life, saves other lives as she leads the tanks to the location she has overheard the German spy describe while she lay drowsing in a hammock in the woods beyond the trading-post-turned-convalescent-hospital where she works. These novels are not meant to enlist soldiers; they are meant to suggest to adolescent girls that they too can for a time be exceptional, that they should serve the Allied cause, and serve it in ways that leave them attractive and available for marriage.

And they did volunteer to serve the Allied cause. Efforts to recruit single women as nurses and in other capacities were incredibly successful. In his 2006 history of the First World War, *A World Undone*, G. J. Meyer, after acknowledging the "affront to truth" involved in recruiting materials for nurses, cites telling statistics detailing the numbers of young women who volunteered as nurses, nurses' aides, and other kinds of war workers. Between 1914 and the fall of 1918, fifteen thousand American women volunteered for service in the Red Cross and similar organizations, an astonishing statistic when the United States did not officially become involved in the war until the spring of 1917. British volunteers as nurses and nurses' aides numbered in the vicinity of thirty-eight thousand, French volunteers about sixty-three thousand, and German women signed on in numbers at about ninety-one thousand. As Meyer puts it, "the start of the conflict, and the outburst of patriotism to which it gave rise, had brought out masses of women volunteers in all the belligerent nations."[30] Those who were not involved in nursing became clerical workers and telephone operators and served, as Meyer explains, "in nearly any job . . . where they could free a man for combat. The British would ultimately have a hundred thousand women in service in this way."[31]

The women Meyer speaks of here are upper middle-class

women, and to that number could be added the working-class women who performed the dangerous service of toiling in munitions factories—the yellow girls, or girls with yellow hair, a reference to the side effects of working with TNT. In addition, both Great Britain and the United States recruited women to serve in the armed forces. Female recruits in Great Britain were not awarded military rank, but women recruited as "yeomanettes" in the U.S. Navy were given military rank, although they did not see combat. When the U.S. Marine Corps asked for female volunteers, it received two thousand applications in New York City alone, of which the corps accepted around three hundred.[32] While authors such as Jane Marcus may view the VADs, at least those depicted in Helen Zenna Smith's *Not So Quiet*, as women who are resistant to middle-class values, the women's cynicism develops only when the "affront to truth" of propaganda becomes apparent, revealing the hypocrisy of those at home.[33] And of course we see the same cynicism in the male counterparts of these volunteers. Certainly we must acknowledge the novels and short stories of Ernest Hemingway, e. e. cummings, and John Dos Passos. Both men and women volunteered for service on the basis of lies, and resentment against those at home is the logical response, a point Jennifer Haytock establishes in *At Home, at War*.[34] But many volunteers never acquired that cynicism, never became disillusioned; they remained focused on home and family, which they felt they had served in the name of the state.

While young women volunteering for service may not have planned to die serving the cause, they still emulated Joan of Arc and Edith Cavell, both of whom did pay the ultimate price of their lives. The memories of Joan of Arc and St. Lucia echo in the novels, but Cavell is never referred to directly, perhaps because she became one of the millions of noncombatants, if we can consider her a noncombatant, to die in the war over four years. Yet her example is there nonetheless, in the selflessness and chastity of the Somewhere girls. Possibly she remains unnamed because the point of these novels after all is to celebrate the girl hero who survives, the one who lives to protect the community and the family and ultimately to carry on its traditions.

FOUR

"Learning to Hate the German Beast"

Children as War Mongers

Perhaps one of the most insidious forms of propaganda is that directed at children. Much propaganda from the First World War is meant to enlist even the smallest citizens in the war effort. Children wore the uniforms of soldiers and Red Cross nurses and carried toy weapons. Two of the three primary relationships of the Gemeinschaft are tapped here: that between mother and child and that between siblings, and in this case also peers. In *Falsehood in War-Time,* Arthur Ponsonby argues that one of the reasons nations resort to propaganda is to "inflame popular passion sufficiently to secure recruits for the continuance of the struggle."[1] But World War I propaganda went beyond the goal of securing recruits for the future. Propaganda in the United States, Great Britain, and France urged children to fall in line, so to speak, to save their pennies, inform on slackers, eat oatmeal rather than wheat, and above all to hate everything German.

In the face of global conflict, it might seem psychologically sound to protect the young from violence, to grant them whenever possible the liberties childhood normally offers. Instead, children were expected to go along with the group and play war games in which hating the enemy became great fun. Posters, picture books, and pamphlets made war part of childhood experience, using details sometimes linked to fairy tales that would have been familiar to most children. A United States School Garden Army poster shows a flute-playing Uncle Sam

FIG. 21. "Follow the Pied Piper," poster by Macinel Wright Enright.

leading a group of small children armed with rakes and hoes, an innocent enough image were it not for the caption that instructs children to "Follow the Pied Piper" (fig. 21). The allusion to the thirteenth-century fairy tale "The Pied Piper of Hamelin" is a frightening one. In the story the children of Hamelin are lured away from their homes because the village fails to "pay the piper" for ridding the town of its rat problem. The moral of the tale is not to renege on promises, but the message of the poster is mixed. Children must follow Uncle Sam, but in view of the fairy tale, they may never be heard from again. The image also illustrates the power of propaganda, like that of the Pied Piper, over guileless children. In spite of the implied threat to the young, the image suggests that following Uncle Sam with your garden tools is less dangerous than falling victim to the German menace. Children were thus recruited, with the hope that they would not only become warlike themselves but would pressure their parents to do the same, thereby becoming an important part of the propaganda machine.

In her study of French children's literature, "War Games," Margaret Higonnet aptly argues that "through propaganda in school and at home, children were mobilized as patriotic citizens."[2] But in the literature itself, Higonnet finds moments of pacifism, moments which in her words "question the inevitability of war."[3] And it would seem the works she examines do exhibit a complexity of sentiment totally lacking in the jingoistic propaganda materials routinely distributed to children. Far from encouraging a rational view of war, these books and pamphlets seek only to light patriotic fires and to undermine the socialization process that normally keeps in check the childhood cruelty lurking beneath the surface of those ubiquitous blonde curls. Indeed much literature before and after the war focuses on the barely submerged shadow, to use the Jungian term, in the child's psyche. Henry James's *The Turn of the Screw*, which predates World War I, and the more recent *Lord of the Flies* by William Goldman come to mind, as does *1984*, in which young children belong to an organization called the "Spies," after which they graduate to the "Youth League." Both organizations in this case help Big Brother catch Thought Criminals, paralleling children's activities in the World War I Tick-Mouse series, to which we turn shortly. Playing to the idea that children are not fully socialized, propagandists find easy targets in the young.

World War I propaganda uses those "blonde curls" to motivate adult behavior as well, and the shameless sentimentality of some of these images is discussed in chapter 5. For the moment, our focus is on children's literature, toys, and games, materials intended for consumption by children and created with the intention of teaching them warlike behavior, of encouraging them to follow the Pied Piper and become little soldiers, little nurses, and little spies. In the same way those adolescent novels motivated young women to become nurses and VADs, children's propaganda motivates the young to focus on the war, to help finance it with their allowances, and to prepare themselves for signing up when they come of age, provided the war is still going on.

Financing the War with Cultural Stereotypes

In the United States, the Food Administration and Liberty Loan Committee printed materials that attracted the attention of children. Porter Emerson Browne, creator of the highly sentimental story "Mary and Marie," authored the small pamphlet "A Liberty Loan Primer," illustrated by James Montgomery Flagg, one of the most popular and recognizable of the American poster artists. Crude in comparison to Flagg's posters, the illustrations thoroughly demonize the German soldier, giving him a tail, a Kaiser-like moustache, and a spike resembling those on the German helmet growing directly out of his head. Black boots, the soldier's only garment, give the drawing a truly perverse nature (fig. 22). With spelling-book hyphenation of words, the

FIG. 22. Illustration by James Montgomery Flagg of the Kaiser as monster, from Browne's "A Liberty Loan Primer."

accompanying text declares: "Uncle Sam . . . is Fight-ing the Ger-man Beast to Keep the Ger-man Beast from Kil-ling Am-er-i-can Wo-men and Child-ren. Shall We Help Him? What Do You Think?" The reply is an illustration of the Kaiser wielding a bloody bayonet and a definition of the Kaiser as a "blood-thirsty old anachronism" that Uncle Sam is about to render extinct. The Crown Prince, or "Clown Prince," is rendered as a limp-wristed, female-hipped dandy who is "things" that are "Not Nice Things for Lit-tle Children to Hear." Clearly these references are intended for parents reading to their children; curious children must have wondered what special evil possessed the Kaiser's son. Overall, the message is that in order to defeat the enslaving German autocracy, Americans, "Grand-pa and Grand-ma" included, must buy Liberty Bonds or end up "Work-ing for the Kai-ser for Sev-en Cents a Week and Wish-ing They Were Dead."[4] The implication is that both the young and the old will fall victim to the evils of the Hun unless the entire family contributes to the Allied effort, a message Browne thoroughly embraced, and one that places the family at the service of the state, this time via the child. Like young girls, children must rise to the occasion to save the family or risk becoming orphans at the mercy of Germans.

A master of hyperbole and jingoistic sentiments, Browne published numerous "articles" in *McClure's* during the war. Two of these pieces, which are formatted in a way similar to the "Liberty Loan Primer," appeared in the May and June 1917 issues. "A Primer for Pacifists" and "Another Primer for Pacifists," illustrated with "Old Woodcuts" by Rhea Irvin, both lambaste slackers and pacifists who, in their resistance to war, only serve the cause of the evil Kaiser. "A Primer for Pacifists," for instance, beside a woodcut of a battleship that is not old, announces:

> This is a new Bat-tle-ship.
> It is a ver-y nice new Bat-tle-ship.
> Has it a Crew?
> Oh, yes it has a Crew.
> Where did it get its Crew?
> They laid up three oth-er good Ves-sels
> and took the crews from them.[5]

In response to the question why, Browne continues, "Because men won't en-list in the Nav-y un-der pre-sent con-di-tions. . . . Be-cause there is too much Pol-i-tics and not e-nough Pa-tri-ot-ism."[6] Only by supporting the war effort wholeheartedly can the United States prevail against Germany. "Another Primer" continues in the same vein. The format, including the spelling-book hyphenation of words, parallels the "Liberty Loan Primer," yet the message is intended for adult "slackers" who in their reluctance to enlist aid the enemy.

While the intention of the "Liberty Loan Primer" may seem debatable, several points are certain. First, much war propaganda encouraged children to earn money so that they could buy War Savings Stamps and to suggest to the adults in their lives that they too should contribute financially to the war effort. In effect, the War Savings Stamp was the child's version of the Liberty Bond, and the Liberty Loan Committee made strong appeals to sell both. Second, the size and format of the little book makes it ideal for children to read and to draw on themselves. In fact, the black and white drawings invite the application of crayons. Finally, the drawings themselves, aberrant partly because they are stylized or simplified, are nothing like the more sophisticated drawings in the *McClure's* "articles" and nothing like the rest of Flagg's work. Childlike humor would find it funny that the foul old German soldier has a tail, and horns grow out of his head.

As we have seen in references to his drama and to the story "Mary and Marie," Browne is given to melodrama. The "Liberty Loan Primer" allows Browne to perform without restraint, although as we have also seen, the war issues of *McClure's* tend to jingoism and sentimentality as well. "A Primer for Pacifists" appears only a few pages from a poem by Ella Wheeler Wilcox, "One Night in May," which ends with the lines:

> The woes of earth fall dully on mine ear,
> Nor am I moved by its appalling plight.
> For all these things seem trivial beside
> This monstrous fact that *one night in May you died.*[7]

An unquestioned master of sentimental verse, Wilcox does not disappoint in the above lines. Playing on the emotions of those who have lost loved ones, Wilcox continues the theme of the "Win-the-War" issue—the Allied nations must sacrifice and die to defeat the "shameless Hun."

Not as violent as the Liberty Loan Primer, "ABC for Little Willie and Others" pokes fun at the German Crown Prince William at the same time as instructing children that "all should help with might and main."[8] The title page, illustrated by G. A. Stevens, depicts the Crown Prince in short pants and a dunce's cap, but the poem on the next page concludes with the thought that "Each boy and girl can say with pride / 'I helped—or, anyhow, I tried.'" Like later Bugs Bunny and other Warner Brothers cartoons, the "Liberty Loan Primer" and "ABC for Little Willie" employ adult humor at the same time they entertain and, in the case of propaganda, instruct children. The letter *Q* shows "Queen Mary to duty a slave," and "R's the Red Cross with its nurses so brave." But the letter *L* refers to the Crown Prince's looting. The prince is drawn as a foppish character smoking a cigarette in a long holder. This juxtaposition of images that celebrate the Allies and images that demonize Germany instills in children national stereotypes, the differences between "us" and "them," and endorses the idea that hatred and bigotry are acceptable, that soon enough they will be able to kill the enemy. Until that time, they must laugh about the evil Germans, play war games, and keep watch for slackers.

The cartoonish appeal for children to save their grandparents from the Kaiser in the "ABC for Little Willie" and the "Liberty Loan Primer" and the banal rendering of the loss of a spouse invoke images of the primary relationships that war demolishes. Propaganda instructs us in the concept of us versus them using the most basic concern—love of home and family and fear of the different and the perverse. To save itself, the Gemeinschaft must act in the service of the Gesellschaft, the family must act in the service of the state. Since the state representing home in this case is the United States, Uncle Sam must have his way. The drawings and admonitions in the "Liberty Loan Primer" sought out patriotic impulses in children who believed it was their responsibility to buy War Savings Stamps and to pressure the adults in their lives to buy Liberty Bonds, all for Uncle Sam. And the ensuing paranoia pertaining to the ubiquity and evil of the enemy undoubtedly paved the way for the Orwellian impulse to spy on other children who did not "do their bit," an impulse dramatized in the Captain Tick-Mouse series, published by the Elgin Watch Company and distributed in jewelry stores carrying Elgin watches.

Following Orders, Catching Slackers and Rewarding Thrift: Captain Tick-Mouse and Happy Jack

Captain Tick-Mouse, the creation of Roy Rutherford Bailey, author of other government and corporate publications, appeared in prewar stories as Mr. Tick-Mouse, but when the United States entered the war, the character joined up to become "Uncle Sam's New Helper." In the first of the war stories, *Captain Tick-Mouse and His Adventures in Secret Service*, Tick-Mouse's human friends, fraternal twins Davy and Dorfy, are burying a dead bird in the back yard when the uniformed mouse approaches. Tick-Mouse's companions, Peter Rabbit and Reddy Fox, want to arrest Davy and Dorfy on the spot for being slackers—that is, for violating Scout Laws number 7 and number 9. Scout Law number 7, which Davy recites, is "Obey Orders." The children, in their desire to bury the bird, have ignored their mother's call three times. Law number 9 has to do with waste, a concept Dorfy, the little girl twin, tearfully associates with time. To rectify the

FIG. 23. Davy and Dorfy with their animal friends, from Bailey's *Captain Tick-Mouse and His Adventures in Secret Service.*

situation, and we assume to avoid jail, Davy and Dorfy must live up to their potential as members of the Secret Service. Captain Tick-Mouse explains that Uncle Sam has told him, "The most precious thing Miss Columbia and I have is our boys and girls. We are looking a long way ahead, now that we're in this war for keeps, and we need someone who *knows* young America"; that is, Captain Tick-Mouse.[9]

Tick-Mouse becomes Uncle Sam's helper by spotting slackers, "not grown-up slackers, to be dragged off to jail; but finding the soft spots in our boys and girls—spots in their character that might grow to be rotten spots in the nation."[10] Once again Davy and Dorfy are presented with the possibility of jail time for those who fail to support the war effort. The twins are depicted in drawings as round-cheeked little tykes for whom the threat of jail, improbable though it is, must fall only just short of the threat of Hell, a punishment with which the children are surely familiar. Of course, the twins can avoid jail if they help the Captain catch the slackers—children who need to be corrected of any behavior that might not be appropriately patriotic—which Davy and Dorfy immediately do by turning in a boy who wants to quit school. But the children will ultimately do more than inform on their classmates. On both front and back covers, the twins and all the animal characters carry rifles with fixed bayonets (fig. 23). The kind of indoctrination condoned in these books and the suggestion that Davy and Dorfy will grow up to be soldiers because the war is likely to go on are disturbing. If Uncle Sam can get to children early enough and eliminate those soft spots, he will have loyal citizens who will follow the Pied Piper; they will inform and they will kill without asking questions. And as they fight, they will wear Elgin watches.

The second of the Captain Tick-Mouse stories, like the "Liberty Loan Primer," focuses on buying Thrift Stamps or War Savings Stamps to raise money for Uncle Sam. Inside the little book is a fold-out window poster of Lady Liberty's torch (fig. 24).[11] Children can keep the torch in the front windows of their homes as long as everyone in the house saves at least

FIG. 24. Window poster of Lady Liberty's torch, from Bailey's *Captain Tick-Mouse and His Adventures with the Torch Bearers.*

one Thrift Stamp a week. This campaign places a portion of the burden of financing the war on children. If anyone in the household fails to save, the window poster must come down, a potential source of shame for children who want to "Serve America First."

Another little book designed to promote War Savings Stamps, "Happy Jack's Thrift Club," also employs animal characters, and like the "Liberty Loan Primer," uses hyphenation to help children pronounce words outside the realm of their ordinary vocabulary. At the beginning of the story, Peter Rabbit is "dis-conso-late." Instructive as well as entertaining, the text continues, "That looks like a big word, but say it quickly and you won't find it so big after all."[12] Peter is disconsolate because all of his animal friends are joining a club and he has been excluded. According to Striped Chipmunk, Peter is excluded because the club is "'Happy Jack's Thrift Club,' and no one can join it unless he is thrifty."[13] Peter, who literally does not know the meaning of the word thrift, tries his best to store up clover, but of course grass is not conducive to storage, so Peter fails miserably. He finally earns the right to join the club when he begins to locate chestnuts, which he does not eat, for the rest of the club. Happy Jack Squirrel then turns to Farmer Brown's boy to scold, and the child gets the idea to start his own club for children to save their pennies for War Savings Stamps. The upshot of the story is that children who have not learned to save, or will not learn, will be ostracized by their peers. A short paragraph at the end of the book explains that children and adults can join the club, but all must buy Thrift Stamps or War Savings Stamps to wear the Thrift Club button. Like the window poster from the second Captain Tick-Mouse book, the button is a visible proof of "patriotic thrift."[14]

Captain Tick-Mouse and Happy Jack clearly illustrate the idea that thrift formed an important part of the propaganda campaign aimed at children. War Savings Stamps and Thrift Stamps fed the starving children of France and Belgium and paid for the bullets to kill the Kaiser. The pamphlets, posters, and story books we have examined all implore children to work hard and save to pay for the war effort. Additional materials, some of them employed directly in schools, sustain the message of thrift. A one-page flier sponsored by the Division on Women's War Work, Committee on Public Information, Creel's committee, relies on both guilt and fear to motivate hard work and thrift for children. "School children of America," the text begins, "do you realize you are enjoying security and comfort unknown to those of your age across the sea?"[15] The text goes on to describe French children living in dark cellars who cannot "smile because of the cruelty of the German invader." Belgian children are forced to beg for food, and even worse, Polish and Turkish children "have seen their mothers shot down beside them." Children reading this flier might well have been terrified that their lack of cooperation could result in a German invasion of their own territory or even to their own orphaning. One of the four photographs on the flier shows two young boys guarding the Liberty Bell with rifles. Another shows "The Hungry Children of France," who, school children are told, are "stretching out their arms for help. To whom? To you children of America." As the starving children in China guilted me to clean my plate as a child, the children of France serve the purpose here. To answer the call, children must clean their plates, buy Thrift Stamps instead of candy, and work on farms or in vegetable gardens. Like the Captain Tick-Mouse books, the flier also declares that children are responsible for persuading adults to buy Thrift Stamps. And school children are expected to guard the home front; they are the "home army that is backing up our Army in France. . . . There must be no slackers." Slackers, we must presume, will be at the mercy of Davy and Dorfy and their helpers in the Secret Service, who under the right circumstances will recommend jail time.

A similar four-page flier, "The Junior Four Minute Men War Savings Contest," invites schools to have speech contests based on monthly bulletins prepared by the ever-present Committee on Public Information. "Pupils" are to "prepare four-minute speeches or essays," which they present to their schools and on which they are judged.[16] The winner is awarded a certificate, and his or her name is sent to Washington. The issue for March 11, 1918, explains the difference between Thrift Stamps and War Savings Stamps, which can be obtained by filling a card with Thrift Stamps and trading it in for the more valuable item. Children who do not contribute to the war chest are called slackers or even traitors for spending money on useless or wasteful items. The back of the pamphlet lists chores children can do to earn money for Uncle Sam, such as "beating carpets, waxing floors, . . . caring for neighbor's baby, and selling magazines."[17] A similar text poster for War Savings Stamps urges children to use their summer vacations to earn money to fund the war. Above a picture of a "Vacation Thrift Bank," available for the purpose of saving coins, the poster lists chores children can perform for quarters with which to buy savings stamps. In addition to beating rugs, children can tend chickens, cut grass, and even caddy. Given the dire tone of the poster, it is hard to imagine an adult out playing golf, but the poster, inked by Stacy H. Wood, does show a young boy carrying a golf bag.

A text poster published by the National Security League was intended for teachers to use as a tool for teaching patriotism.

Featured prominently top center is a picture, printed by courtesy of the *Red Cross Magazine*, of Belgian boys carrying the flags of Italy, France, and the United States. The copy also describes the Union Jack and the Belgian flag, which are pictured in the top corners of the poster. The boys march beneath an arch while a Red Cross nurse, clad in solid white, looks on. The copy on the front of the poster, meant to be displayed to children, first praises each flag, especially that of the United States. A poem declares:

> We shall always love the Stars and Stripes,
> And we mean to be ever true
> To this land of ours and the dear old flag,
> The Red, the White, and the Blue.

The poster goes on to advocate "Universal Military Training" and to include quotations from George Washington, Robert E. Lee, and the Bible. In the bottom corner, a pledge meant to be signed promises to "do nothing to desecrate her soil, pollute her air, or degrade her children." But the most important element of the poster is printed on the back as instructions "To Teachers," who are directed to "Use the splendid picture of the child Flag Bearers for: Oral Language. / Basis of Blackboard Reading Lesson. / Number Lessons. / Story Telling—Imagine what the R. C. Nurse thinks." The instructions suggest that the children "tell a story for each of the flag bearers. The children can play this game. Let them pantomime the picture. Let them know that when working for the Red Cross, they help the fathers of such children as these in the picture." The propaganda message of the poster is quite clear. School children must be patriotic, and their education is meant to prepare them for service either in the military or in nursing. The directions even break down the use of the poster according to grade level. And if teachers have any doubts about the function of the poster, they are told, "For further information concerning patriotism or Americanization, apply to ETTA V. LEIGHTON," Civic Secretary of the National Security League. Orwellian in tone, the instructions to teachers make patriotism not only a valid subject for study in the classroom but a game children can play and pantomime. The stark reality of war, to an extent present in the smaller flier and used to inspire guilt, is absent from the poster. This lesson is designed to produce, in the words of Wilfred Owen, "children ardent for some desperate glory."[18] It is in fact part of the "old Lie: *Dulce et decorum est / Pro patria mori.*"[19]

Other posters conveying the same message were directed at children and adults alike. Bond and thrift stamp posters make use of pleading, patriotic children (figs. 25, 26, and 27). Canadian artist Samson's poster "Oh please do! Daddy, Buy Me a Victory Bond" mirrors the anonymous American poster "My Daddy Bought Me a Government Bond of the Third Liberty Loan: Did Yours?" Both posters depict rosy-cheeked little blonde girls with red bows in their hair. The Canadian poster admonishes adults to buy bonds, but the American poster places the burden of persuasion on other children. Another Liberty Bond poster by artist Dewey pictures a small boy and girl, both blonde and rosy-cheeked, waving an American flag and proclaiming, "Our Daddy is fighting at the Front for *You*—Back him up—Buy a United States Gov't Bond of the 2nd Liberty Loan of 1917." Again the little girl's blonde hair sports a red bow. Two War Savings Stamps posters place the boy and girl hand in hand, either with General Pershing or with Uncle Sam (fig. 28). The Uncle Sam poster, drawn by James Montgomery Flagg, declares "Boys and Girls! You can help your Uncle Sam Win the War: Save your Quarters, Buy War Savings Stamps." Possibly the most perverse poster employing the image of a child is the Herbert

FIG. 25. "Oh please do! Daddy, Buy Me a Victory Bond," poster by Joseph Ernest Samson.

FIG. 26. "My Daddy Bought Me a Government Bond of the Third Liberty Loan: Did Yours?" poster, anonymous.

FIG. 27. "Our Daddy is fighting at the Front for *You*—Back him up—Buy a United States Gov't Bond of the 2nd Liberty Loan of 1917," poster by Dewey.

FIG. 28. "Boys and Girls! You can help your Uncle Sam Win the War: Save your Quarters, Buy War Savings Stamps," poster by James Montgomery Flagg.

FIG. 29. "Save your Child from Autocracy and Poverty," poster by Herbert Paus.

Paus poster "Save your Child from Autocracy and Poverty" (fig. 29). The rosy-cheeked blonde child who is grasping an image of Liberty's torch is nude except for shoes and socks, an image that today might raise eyebrows. We might almost see this drawing as an inappropriate exploitation of children. Images of perfect boys and girls are positioned both to exhibit patriotism and to raise the specter, at least in the imagination, of the child ravished by the shameless Hun, a ploy that cannot help but loosen the purses of patriotic Americans.

Hoover and the U.S. Food Administration and the American Red Cross targeted school children with textbooks and activities manuals. *Food Saving and Sharing* was sponsored by the National Education Association in cooperation with the Food Administration and intended to be used in "the instruction of American children."[20] Among its contributors were the editor of the *Journal of Home Economics* and a professor of food chemistry at Columbia University. *Food Saving and Sharing* asks children to contribute to national security and world health by saving food, specifically to "prove your Americanism by eating less."[21] According to the then most recent knowledge on nutrition, the five food groups—fruits and vegetables; meat, eggs, milk and cheese; cereals and grain; sugar and sweets; and fats—are represented by imaginary booths at a food market, which intelligent children visit with shopping baskets. In this way children are instructed in domestic science and politics at the same time, and little girls are prepared to become culinary soldiers like their mothers. On the small-town level, a 1917 photograph of an unidentified local store front displays Food Administration signs and a mannequin dressed in a Food Administration uniform. The photo also places live children at a table having tea. A sign at the foot of the table tells window-shoppers that this is "A War Time Tea Party." Other signs in the

FIG. 30. Storefront tea party display.

window convey Food Administration directives such as "Give the Kiddies the New War Time Dishes and Watch Them Thrive" and "Make Baking Day Hoover Day." The children around the tea table range in ages from seven or eight to around four and, as children would, they are all looking at something outside the window and show little interest in the contents of their cups (fig. 30). Children walking by the window display will undoubtedly get the message that eating the correct foods is patriotic and that their tea parties, play ones or otherwise, must conform to Food Administration standards. Domestic science thus becomes another method of engaging children directly in the war. Like the Food Administration poster "Little Americans Do your Bit," by Cushman Parker, the textbook and store front suggest that children are not exempt from war service (fig. 31). The poster shows a bibbed, rosy-cheeked male toddler saluting a bowl of oatmeal. The remaining copy tells children they

FIG. 31. "Little Americans Do Your Bit," poster by Cushman Parker.

must "Eat Oatmeal—Corn meal mush—Hominy—other corn cereals—and Rice with milk. Save the wheat for our soldiers. Leave nothing on your plate." The message on the poster, that children should revise their eating habits for the duration of the war, is not as problematic as the saluting child. Like Davy and Dorfy and the children who follow the Pied Piper to the school garden, this child is also enlisted, but when he can barely walk. "A Children's Promise" reprinted from *John Martin's Book: The Child's Magazine*, includes a rhyming form of the same message and a place for children to sign their names, as their mothers have on the Food Administration Pledge Card. The family, in this case the mother-child unit, works together to save soldiers—their fathers and brothers—and the global but sociologically identical community of starving refugees.

The Junior Red Cross

The American Red Cross also made use of the school room to swell the ranks of the membership of the Junior Red Cross. A Teachers Manual issued in October of 1918 instructs teachers in methods of raising money for local school chapters and gives detailed instructions for making garments for European refugees. In the foreword to the manual, teachers are told that while local modifications to the classroom instruction may be necessary, they should "recogniz[e] the urgency of making it possible for our young citizens to become real and active participants in the great struggle for freedom."[22] To maintain a viable chapter, each member was expected to donate a quarter, a sum that might have been difficult for some families to raise. Schools could also devise entertainments for fund-raising, and the manual offers suggestions such as a "Nature Pageant" in which young girls perform dances to Mendelssohn's "Spring Song" and a number called "The First

Daffodil." Each entertainment was to be advertised to bring in parents and the general public. According to the instructions, "attention need only be called to the patriotic purpose of the entertainment to insure support."[23] As an example, the manual cites a circus held by students in Huerfano County, Colorado, a mining community. The children, "none of whom were above the fourth grade," turned each room in the school into a side show, including pets doing tricks and others on display in cages. Each child contributed one lemon to make the "circus lemonade."[24] In another school, the kindergarten class put on an afternoon matinee, charging a nickel for other students and a dime for adults. For their efforts, the kindergarten was allowed to hang a 100 Percent Red Cross poster in its window.[25] And overlapping with the Food Administration, some rural schools earned money for their chapters by growing vegetables and raising livestock. Several Oklahoma schools raised pigs in their schoolyards. The girls bought the young animals and the boys constructed pig pens and took care of the growing pigs.[26] In the back of the manual are instructions for cutting and sewing garments for refugee children. A photograph in this section shows children, including both boys and girls, proudly wearing the clothing they have made to be sent abroad. We are reminded here of Margaret Higonnet's assertion that "through propaganda in school and at home, children were mobilized as patriotic citizens."[27] We might also wonder when, during the course of the patriotic day, students devoted their energies to traditional classroom endeavors. While the National Security League Poster and "The Junior Four Minute Men War Savings Contest" have students writing essays, albeit patriotic ones, the rest seem to abandon intellectual activities altogether. The war and wartime duties take every waking minute of the child's life.

While some of the above materials, Captain Tick-Mouse in particular, do not gender war participation, most do. Home is represented by the traditional nuclear family in which males go off to fight and young females nurse them when they are wounded. Mother, of course, remains at home when she is not doing the work of the U.S. Food Administration or out recruiting more soldiers. *Soldier Bob*, a large picture book written and illustrated by Florence Notter, genders the children's war play along those traditional lines. Soldier Bob is another round-cheeked youngster who plays general to a regiment of tin soldiers. Soldier Bob's orders are to guard the family unit, "dear Mother's land," to see that his men remain close by "to stand and fight for her alone." When Soldier Bob's men come under fire, they are graphically wounded. Tin soldiers minus arms, legs, and even heads surround Soldier Bob as he aims and fires his rifle. Once the battle is over, Bob's sister Betty arrives in a nurse's cap, ready to take the soldiers to Mother, who will glue them back together. The two succeeding pages depict Soldier Bob on one page drilling his remaining troops (fig. 32), while on the opposite page, Mother and Nurse Betty tend to the wounded.

Bob and Betty are dead ringers for Davy and Dorfy, except that Dorfy shoulders a rifle and Bob's sister wears the Red Cross. Still, the story demands war play of both genders, and in that play instills in the children the idea that they are responsible for the safety of adults. In the opening lines of the rhyming text, Bob declares, "How glad I am that I'm a boy! / So I can fight for right." We are not told if Bob's father is actually fighting in the war or has perhaps been killed, but Mother is definitely alone during the action of the story, making the little toddler her protector.[28] The home is the focus of Bob's war play, and even

FIG. 32. Soldier Bob "Guarding Mother's Home," by Florence Notter.

though Bob is only a boy, like Marieken de Bruin he becomes the head of household. While Marieken dealt with live German soldiers and Bob deals with toy ones, the idea is similar, except that the protectors of home and hearth have become much younger. The primary relationship between mother and child informs Bob's actions, yet his war play serves the state. Once again Gemeinschaft and Gesellschaft overlap.

Sheet music also reflects the notion of the child protector of home and family (fig. 33). In the song "There's Nobody Home but Me," some young recruits spy a boy of eight wearing a khaki

FIG. 33. Cover illustration from the sheet music for "There's Nobody Home but Me."

uniform. In response to the question, "Who's home with you, my boy?" the child replies:

> My brother's over in the trenches,
> And sister's gone to nurse out there
> While Daddy's making ammunition,

My Mama also does her share.
I've got my uniform all ready,
A soldier boy, I'd like to be
So if you're over here
For a brave volunteer,
There's nobody home but me."[29]

The young soldier boy in the song is guarding the home front, as does Bob, but at the same time he is ready to enlist, albeit ten years too soon. Like Bob's sister, this boy's sister is a nurse, adhering to the expected gender roles that seem to be ignored only in the Captain Tick-Mouse series and to an extent in the adolescent novels we examined in chapter 3. Young girls are taught to nurture and comfort the soldiers who fight for glory. Once again the primary unit, the family, is served in the children's service to the state. These girls will marry and become the mothers of tomorrow who will hold the family unit together while father goes off to work or to war, and later when the state demands more aid, she will send her sons, the boy soldiers off to war and her daughters to nurse them.

Bob's sister and the sister of the soldier boy comfort their soldier protectors by tending their wounds and tucking them into their cots. Wartime paper dolls feature similar play images. A collection of war-inspired paper dolls published in 1918 by the Reilly and Britton Company as a supplement to the *North American* offers young girls examples of French, British, American, and Belgian nurses as well as a Sister of Mercy. Entitled "Fold-A-Way War Nurses," the paper dolls, drawn front and back, can be cut out and folded to stand up (fig. 34). The nurses' faces are young and rosy-cheeked, and two of the five are either bandaging or tucking in wounded soldiers. The Belgian nurse cradles an infant, no doubt an orphan, an image

FIG. 34. "Fold-A-Way War Nurses" paper dolls.

consistent with propaganda stories of Belgian women and children being raped and murdered.[30] *American Heroes: Paper Posters to Make* also involves cut-outs, meant to be pasted into a book. The "General Directions" at the beginning of the book explain that it "contains the outlines for ten posters representing our heroes in war."[31] Children are directed to cut out the colored parts, also included, and paste them onto the outline. Among the heroes included are a marine, an aviator, and an "aeroplane" gun. The only female "hero" is a Red Cross nurse, which in my copy of the poster book is the only figure pasted in, suggesting that a patriotic little girl was the owner. Already tuned in to her gender role, she has picked the single image applicable to her experience and used it as part of her child's play.

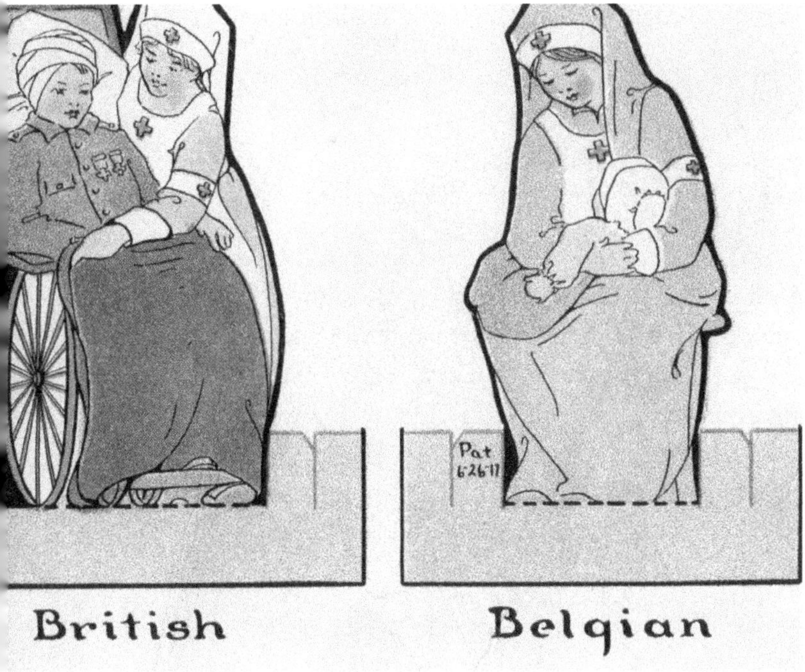

A further playful, highly unrealistic look at nursing appears in *Our Hospital* ABC, which offers a satirical but ultimately upbeat look at nursing and chastises young girls who have not answered the call. In spite of the warning on the inside cover that the book is "Not to Be Taken Seriously," the nurses who are depicted are capable and, to an extent, attractive. The ABC is both literal—that is, each page offers a verse beginning with the appropriate letter of the alphabet—and an anagram for Anzac British Canadian. Along with the British, the Anzacs (Australian and New Zealand forces) and Canadians represent British colonial troops, at least of the Anglo variety. All are served by clean and sturdy young girls who work night and day for the Empire. Under the letter *C*, a Canadian soldier with his arm in a sling smiles down on two small children, a boy and girl, accompanied by the lines:

C is for Canada
Gallant and true
whose sons make the Huns
Decidedly blue.

Satirical or not, the message is clear: children must worship the wounded—although only slightly wounded—soldier who has been bandaged up by a nurse, and of course, they must remember that the shameless Hun is the source of the wounds. VADs, as we have noted, also did scullery work, which is reflected under *F*:

F is the food
I am sure it will please
When prepared by the hands
of fair damsels like these.

Although the verse under *N* refers to the girls as wenches to get a rhyme with trenches, the nurse in the illustration is still decidedly young and middle class. *Our Hospital* ABC also addresses the slacker or complainer under the letter G, which proclaims:

G are the grouses
One has to suppress
At being cut off
from more picturesque dress.

The young woman pictured wears a large hat and rather foolish dress while a nurse frowns from a window in the background. Satire functions here as a means of admonishing those young girls who are not willing to sacrifice for the war effort and rewarding those who are willing. In the final illustration, a nurse polishes a doorknob with Bluebell Metal Polish, and the verse declares:

> Z is the Zeal
> Which inspires ev'ry one
> To make their own hospital
> Second to none.

Young girls cannot help but be inspired by the hard work of the nurses, in spite of the humor, because no one wants to be considered a grouse. But *Our Hospital* ABC goes even further in its recruitment of youngsters. The letter *J*

> is for John
> The ubiquitous scout
> Whose manner is recal
> When showing you out.

John is dressed in khaki and red, and he wears a supercilious smile of the stiff-upper-lip variety. John is clearly pleased with himself and his willingness to wear a uniform and participate in war activities; no doubt as soon as he can, he will join one of the British armies represented so as to protect his home and all those pretty nurses.[32]

Les Soldats de la Grande Guerre

The French text *Les Soldats de la Grande Guerre* also takes a playful and unrealistic, if subtly jingoistic and anti-German, view of the war. Published in Paris in 1914, *Les Soldats* depicts first mobilization, then various French, British, and colonial troops as they march off to the trenches. The text, in both French and English, is brief. A French shepherd gets his marching orders from the postman as the shepherd tends his sheep. Both figures are dressed in colorful, almost clownish, garments and what appear to be wooden shoes, not normally associated with French shepherds. In the second panel, the shepherd has given his staff to the sheep dog, which holds it between his teeth. The caption instructs him, "Doggie, take care of our Sheep, I must go to kill the wolves."[33] Subtle but dehumanizing nonetheless, wolves refers to Germans. The same postman delivers orders to a cattle farmer and an urban toy maker, and all march off to receive their uniforms.

In every frame, children—some little boys also dressed in uniform—and dogs watch and wave at the soldiers as they are deployed. In one frame a little boy dressed in the uniform of a dragoon rides a wooden horse. Other children and dogs also stand by watching and waving. In the panel depicting Marines, the uniformed little boy and his dog both salute as the troops march past (fig. 35). Dogs also pull toy cannons in scenes showing artillery. Along with the colorful, happy drawings of war preparations, all observed by eager children, *Les Soldats* includes drawings of colonial troops, both French and British, that employ racial stereotypes, although all the colonials are armed to fight the wolves. Many colonials in fact were not armed and performed hard labor, which still proved deadly in some cases. The final panel shows a trench, manned by all the troops, looking out over a pristine landscape. All the little children, including colonial children, cheer as Germans and Turks flee. The text declares, "Take one more good look, for you will never see them again."[34]

The belief that the war would be over quickly obviously proved erroneous. But beyond that error, the drawings suggest that war is clean and soldiers are cute and always smiling, including Russian Cossacks. While *Les Soldats* does not threaten children the way much British and American propaganda does,

FIG. 35. Saluting dog from *Les Soldats de la Grande Guerre,* by Niké.

it calls them to arms, as does *Soldier Bob,* and the text cannot refrain from referring to the German prisoners of war as "Square-Heads." Equally unrealistic is the final drawing on the back cover, in which all the little children, colonial, French, and British, sit atop a cannon. In many ways, colonialism was as ugly as the war, and this little book sanitizes both. Unlike the French texts Margaret Higonnet examines, *Les Soldats* does not "question the inevitability of war" or, for that matter, of colonialism.[35] And while the text does not dwell on the idea of separation, the shepherd, cattle farmer, and toy maker must temporarily break up home and family to serve the state. The children and their dogs remain involved in the war by following its progress, however sterilized, into the trenches.

Indeed, every aspect of the child's life becomes fodder for propaganda. A coloring book called *The Soldier Painting Book,* published in New York in 1917 but most likely before the United States entered the war, includes the German uniform as well as others and does not depict the soldier in a negative light. Ironically, the inscription in my copy is in German: "[To] Würgel from Grandma." Still, the book is intended as U.S. propaganda. The cover, partly colored in, shows a marine and an infantry officer. The marine bears a U.S. flag and the words *E Pluribus Unum* emerge from beneath the flag. Other books for young readers, *In the Ranks* and *Our Army*, define and depict tanks, anti-aircraft guns, and other weapons new to the First World War, all with the idea of preparing young boys to defend the home front, to serve the state in the service of family.[36]

Postcards and Potty Humor

Both sides made use of children in propaganda postcards. In several instances the postcards employ sweet-faced little children to depict risqué images meant to demean the Hun and celebrate the Allies. The postcards also endorse behavior that during peace would be considered inappropriate for children. A French postcard depicts a pink-cheeked little girl wearing the cap of a French soldier and using an inverted pickelhaube as a chamber pot (fig. 36). Her toilet paper is labeled "Kultur" and "Deutschland Über Alles." The little verse, which rhymes in French, translates "To all pointed helmets, I offer this pot of jam; it is excellent for the health of people of Kultur! Take it, Wilhelm, my Emperor, it is said to bring good luck." The innocence and beauty of the child's face in juxtaposition with the potty humor seems benign, but once again this is a child who has been taught to hate the German beast, to defile and demean, if not to kill. So much the better if the defecating child provides a laugh for German-hating adults. Less risqué but nevertheless dismaying in their promotion of childhood militarism, two American postcards depict a young boy dressed in an army uniform. The caption on one card asks, "Wonder when they'll

FIG. 36. French postcard of defecating child.

FIG. 37. Postcard of a child soldier.

let me go?" The other card depicts the same child, legs spread defiantly, declaring "Conscription for me? Not likely!" (fig. 37). Both postcards picture the same grown-up male face in a circle at the top, undoubtedly this little boy when he can really enlist. The idea here is obviously to suggest to male children, in the same way Soldier Bob suggests, that his job is to fight and the sooner the better. The home, the abode of the Gemeinschaft, is in danger, and in the father's absence the male child, the boy must become the protector of both home and mother.

A third postcard genders war behavior in the same way Soldier Bob does. A young boy in a uniform lounges next to a dog with a bandaged paw. A little girl in a Red Cross uniform fusses over the dog with a roll of gauze, beneath the caption "Fit Again." Here the dog is the patient, not the soldier, but both children are playing at war games by dressing like their adult role models. Soon the children in the postcards will be grown up as well and will be ready for war.

German propaganda postcards also depicted uniformed children in adult settings. One such postcard shows a small boy and girl embracing. The boy is uniformed and wearing a pickelhaube (fig. 38). The caption, "Du, Du liegst mir im Herzen!" translates roughly as "You will remain in my heart!" The image of the children serves two purposes. First, it prepares children for the eventual and inevitable parting of war that according to the state will be part of their adulthood; the family must protect itself by serving the state. Second, the postcard sentimentalizes, if possible, the notion of parting for adults, the breaking up of the family in service to the state.

Like the French, the British and Australians used war postcards for humor. One example, actually mailed to an address in Blackpool, shows a little boy staring at a plain slice of white bread and lamenting:

FIG. 38. Postcard of a German child soldier and his girlfriend.

We've hardly any butter,
And we can't get any jam;
Really it's enough to make
A saint say . . .

The poem is printed above the boy's head on what appears to be a scroll, and the part of the scroll that would contain the word "damn" is torn away. While this child's potential hunger is not at all funny, the omission of the expletive expresses adult frustration with food shortages and rationing, although the Ministry of Food did issue Rationing Books for children providing additional meat and fats for their growing bodies.[37] Reminiscent of Dorfy posing with a rifle, an Australian postcard pictures a small girl, her blonde curls, with one exception, tucked under the wide-brimmed hat of the Australian Army. She waves an Australian flag with one hand and holds the rifle in the other. The caption reads, "My word, when the Kaiser sees Me coming, he'll stop it." Unlike Captain Tick-Mouse's portrayal of Dorfy, which is serious, this postcard, in one stroke, endorses patriotism and makes fun of the little girl who ignores gender roles and sports the masculine trappings of war.

Hot Dogs and Bayonets

One of the most violent and dehumanizing of the British publications is *Ten Little Sausages*, written and illustrated by Stanley L. Wood and based on the racist *Ten Little Indians*. Illustrator of numerous books both British and American, Wood is well known for painting scenes of the American West, where he lived periodically—that is, his sensibilities are both British and American.[38] The little sausages, German soldiers, have stick arms and legs, and they are wearing spiked helmets and Kaiser-like mustaches. The rhyming text describes how each of the ten sausages meets his demise, but the illustrations convey the book's real message. The first little sausage is shot, but the second is bayoneted. The illustration shows the little sausage impaled on the end of a Frenchman's rifle and lifted wriggling into the air (fig. 39). The soldier smiles broadly at the skewered German. If depicting Germans as glorified hot dogs were not enough, the bayoneting and the soldier's glee at hoisting the sausage overhead further illustrate for children the "enemy's" total lack of humanity. Sausages three and four are similarly bayoneted by grinning soldiers, but sausage number seven is sliced in half by a Gurkha (fig. 40). The soldier's Nepalese origins are obvious in his hat, which is pinned up on one side; his shorts; and more important, in the shape of the blade he wields, a kind of scimitar distinctive to Gurkhas. Like the colonials in *Les Soldats*, the Gurkha here is as grotesquely stereotyped as are the German sausages. The final sausage, retreating to Germany, is set upon by three soldiers, one Russian, one French, and one British, according to the text. The unarmed sausage kneels with arms raised in a gesture of surrender, yet the soldiers charge as if they mean to bayonet him, a violation of the rules of war. The final text declares:

> No little sausage left
> And no one to deplore it;
> Everything will be OK
> And the world much better for it.

The lack of an American soldier in this last scene suggests that the undated publication must have been printed before April of 1917. Still, in its complete dehumanization of German soldiers, it closely parallels the "Liberty Loan Primer." Possibly the most stunning aspect of my copy of the book is that the child who owned it has drawn little sausages on the front and

FIG. 39. Impaled sausage from *Ten Little Sausages*, by Stanley L. Wood.

back covers, and one of the sausages has a bayonet through it (fig. 41). Clearly, the author has achieved his purpose.

The problem with propaganda, especially that involving children, is the obvious fact that in its use of stereotypes, it dehumanizes. If the enemy is less than human, it is easier to kill. While this concept may serve the soldier on the front lines, it also enables ordinary citizens to stone German dogs to death or,

FIG. 40. Sliced sausage from *Ten Little Sausages*.

as in the United States near St. Louis in 1918, to lynch German-born Robert Prager, whose assailants were tried but acquitted. On a lesser note, this hatred enabled the governor of Iowa to forbid public use of the German language, including the words hamburger and sauerkraut, which became Victory sandwich and Victory cabbage.[39] Functioning to protect the family unit that would act in the service of the state, propagandists justified the ethnic and racial stereotyping and the scatological humor used to amuse and instruct children. Stereotypes of course underscored the us/them dichotomy that solidified family unity and

FIG. 41. Back cover of *Ten Little Sausages* with child's drawing.

loyalty to the state. But in teaching children to hate and defile those of a different nationality, in teaching them to follow the Pied Piper, propaganda creates potential killers, children who will disappear like the children of Hamelin, or at the very least become strangers to themselves and their parents.

Keeping a Stiff Upper Lip

Propaganda or no, children will inevitably be touched by war. In a little booklet called *Records of the Raids*, published by the Society for Promoting Christian Knowledge, the Right Reverend Henry Luke Paget discusses the effects of Zeppelin raids on citizens of London and surrounding areas. In a chapter called "The Children," Paget explains, "The children are at once our main anxiety and our greatest comfort."[40] He goes on to say that the clergy had arranged for eighty shell-shocked children to be sent to the country. In his words, these are "children whose nerves have suffered," some from having their homes destroyed (17). "But as a rule," he continues, "the children are splendid, and it required something more than threats and warnings to prevent the small boys from darting out after souvenirs in the beginning of the raids" (17). The remark implies that the shell-shocked children are not splendid, that they have not lived up to the expectations of their propaganda role models. On the other hand, the boys who risk their lives for fun are noteworthy, and Paget relates several anecdotes that suggest such bravado is appropriate. He quotes a little boy who observes "how slow [the bombs] drop" (17). Another child declares, "I ain't afraid of vem 'air pins'" (17). Other children accordingly play at air raids. In Paget's words, "one boy was trying to imitate the sound of falling bombs, and the others were tumbling over, heels in air" (18); that is, the children are pretending to have been impacted by a bomb. We might see this behavior in two ways. Children certainly try to act out things of which they are afraid in order to diminish the effects of fear. But on the other hand, children who are taught to hate the enemy become desensitized to the real effects of war and see it as a delightful game without any real consequences. If a soldier is wounded, a beautiful nurse will patch him up, and he and his family will be whole again.

Virtually oblivious to the psychological damage children experience in these bombing raids, Paget does express concern for the possibility of illness, "of pneumonia and bronchitis and of infectious complaints" (18) among the children. Nevertheless, his concerns are short-lived. Within the next paragraph, he is describing babies, "nestle[d] down upon the tables like birds in a nest, or a litter of puppies" (19). This stroke of sentimentality obliterates the reality that children are hauled down to bomb shelters on a nightly basis and expected to sleep through the mayhem. The alternative, as he has suggested earlier, is to remove children as far away as possible from war, a feat admittedly not always possible. One of the most obvious tragedies of war, and one that should perhaps ask us to rethink our militaristic methods of settling disputes, is that children die, to paraphrase Robert Graves, if "only" from shelling.[41] Perhaps the worse tragedy is that children become pawns in the struggle. As members of the family group and as citizens of the state, they are taught to stereotype and dehumanize others, to be prepared if necessary to kill others in the name of the state. Made aware through propaganda of their membership in the local community, and by extension in the larger community as well, children are easily directed to make enemies of groups other than their own. If children have learned sufficiently to hate the German beast, to embrace killing as an alternative to fear, then as Ponsonby suggests, governments have "sufficiently secure[d] recruits for the continuance of the struggle."[42] Of course, the operative word here is "continuance." If children are taught to hate sufficiently, then the likelihood of hostilities continuing is strong.

FIVE

The Hun Is at the Gate

Protecting the Innocents

In his 1914 poem "For All We Have and Are," Rudyard Kipling writes:

For all we have and are,
For all our children's fate,
Stand up and meet the war,
The Hun is at the gate![1]

Kipling's lines aptly summarize the application of First World War propaganda with the use of two images: that of the child and, by extension, the mother in danger, and that of the marauding Hun not only ready but eager to destroy everything in his path. In preceding chapters, we have examined propaganda directed at women and children, propaganda that enlists both in a variety of war services from nursing, gardening, and conserving food to financing the war through Thrift Stamps, War Savings Stamps, and Liberty Bonds. As part of their war service, propaganda also demands that women and children pressure the men in their lives—fathers, husbands, sons, and brothers—to fight the Hun who will offer no mercy to women and children when he invades England or the United States. The family group and its status in the local community, as we have seen, is the focus of posters, magazine stories, textbooks, and novels, inviting the participation of women and children in war activities. The war undoubtedly could not have been conducted to the extent it was without the Red Cross, VADs, canteen workers, and food service volunteers. And the pennies collected by the Junior Red Cross did swell the coffers of that organization.

But women and children had that second role to play in the war as well. The images of these "innocents," or noncombatants, were also part of the propaganda campaign designed to shame men into war service. As Kipling's poem insists, the fate of Allied women and children depends on men standing to meet the war and the "shameless Hun."[2] The specters of the *Lusitania* and Edith Cavell, and atrocity stories, many of which were apocryphal, all manipulated the images of the dead and mutilated to serve the voice of war fervor. Novels and stories, some popular and some "literary," as well as films, raised these specters in order to incite violence against Germany and ultimately to justify the severe war reparations assessed against Germany, reparations that many historians agree opened the political door to Adolph Hitler. Patrick Quinn in *The Conning of America: The Great War and American Popular Literature* writes of the fear of imminent threat from Germany as it was expressed in popular literature before America joined the Allies. Quinn links the "German invasion of American novels," as he calls them, to propaganda that evolved in the United States because of financial arrangements between American banks and both sides of the conflict. Based on Teddy Roosevelt's advocacy of preparedness, these novels, according to Quinn, portray the apocalyptic destruction of major U.S. cities and German demands for astonishingly large sums of money.[3]

Quinn maintains that "the logistical and military realities of a large-scale invasion by Germany on the United States in 1915 do not play much of a part in these novels."[4] That is, the Hun was indeed not at the gate, nor was he likely to be, but reality generally bears little relation to atrocity stories and the fear mongering that they induce. Yet because of these early propaganda novels, the preparedness movement gained a foothold, according to Quinn, "foster[ing] the establishment of a training camp for young men in Plattsburg, New York, where in July of 1915 nearly two thousand business and professional men received instruction in the art of warfare."[5] Roughly the same as the number of women who applied to serve in the marines in New York City, the figure suggests that whatever the aim of propaganda, if it garners enough fear, it will work.

Propaganda and Atrocity Stories

The number of atrocity stories involving women and children abounded, and the number of books expressing outrage over the atrocities multiplied exponentially in the early days of the war. Among the atrocity stories Robert Ponsonby reports in *Falsehood in War-Time* is that of the handless Belgian baby: "Not only did the Belgian baby whose hands had been cut off by the Germans travel through the towns and villages of Great Britain, . . . it went through Western Europe and America, even into the Far West."[6] Stories of otherwise mutilated, impaled, or crucified babies also survived scrutiny. *Our War for Human Rights,* a hyperbolic collection of atrocity stories, descriptions of weapons, and explanations of war tactics, is full of reports of raped girls and mutilated babies. Under the header "Shocking Barbarities" is an account by a Belgian farmer similar to those included in the Bryce Report.[7] The farmer tells of "young girls and little children outraged at Orsmael, where several inhabitants suffered mutilations too horrible to describe."[8] The book contains photographs of Belgian refugees who have been rendered homeless by the impact of bombs and shells. Nevertheless, the two infants in the picture are very much alive and whole, if frightened.

FIG. 42. "Hun or Home?" poster by Henry Patrick Raleigh.

FIG. 43. "Hunger," poster by Henry Patrick Raleigh.

Beyond the butchered, Belgian babies and their mothers became a staple of propaganda that vilified Germany and promoted the U.S. Food Administration and Liberty Bonds. Two American posters by Henry Patrick Raleigh, "Hun or Home" and "Hunger" (figs. 42 and 43), wring the consciences of secure

FIG. 44. "Don't waste food while others starve!" poster by L. C. Clinker and M. J. Dwyer.

Americans by depicting starving or orphaned children—in the case of "Hunger," a baby at its emaciated mother's breast. Likewise, a third Food Administration poster by L. C. Clinker and M. J. Dwyer shows a weeping baby in its mother's arms and numerous emaciated children over the caption "Don't waste food while others starve!" (fig. 44). While hunger existed in Belgium during the war, it existed in Germany as well. The problem with propaganda posters based on hunger is that they sentimentalize the plight of Belgian refugees in ways that disingenuously exploit their misery to manipulate those on the home front.

Hunger was a fact of life in war-torn Europe, but the question of mutilated babies is more problematic. Alluding to several more or less official investigations of these stories after the war, Ponsonby concludes that most, if not all, were apocryphal. Given our current knowledge of mass Nazi atrocities during the Second World War, we might find denials like those of Ponsonby dubious. Nevertheless the physical evidence of legitimate photographs and exhumed bodies from the First World War does not exist. Personal memoirs, Robert Graves's *Good-Bye to All That*, for instance, also allude to atrocity stories. While Graves did see children who had been wounded, he believed the wounds were the result of "shell-fire, British or French shell-fire as likely as not."[9] One of the tragedies of war is that civilians are wounded and die; they get caught in the cross-fire at the behest of neither combatant force but within the realm of culpability of both. Historians seem to be willing only to estimate the numbers of civilian casualties. G. J. Meyer refers to "the numberless millions of civilians who . . . died in every imaginable way."[10] According to Martin Gilbert, more Serbian civilians were killed than Serbian soldiers, more than a million Armenians were murdered in an example of pre-holocaust genocide, and at least 750,000 Germans died because of Allied blockades.[11] These figures do not include British, French, and Belgian civilians. That children are among those wounded and dead is particularly troubling, and if anything ought to provoke caution in those considering armed military action, the involvement of children should. Instead, dead children, like hungry children, are too often used to prove how bestial is the enemy and how righteous the local community and the attendant state.

The threat of rape is one of the persistent fears in the wake of advancing troops and, like the fear for children in harm's way, is often one of war's despicable realities. Reality notwithstanding, the fear of rape, like the fear of hunger, was exploited in propaganda images and proliferated there. Among posters capitalizing on the fear of rape, "Destroy This Mad Brute," "Beat Back the Hun," and "Keep the Hun Out" (fig. 2) all depict the German soldier as an apelike brutish beast. Rape also appears in both popular and "literary" fiction from the war. We saw in Porter Emerson Browne's sentimental "Mary and Marie" the Belgian girl brutalized to death by the invading Huns. At the other end of the literary spectrum, Ernest Hemingway deals with rape and its representation in propaganda images in the Nick Adams story "A Way You'll Never Be." As a badly shell-shocked Nick bicycles past the dead from a just-ended "attack" in Italy, he sees littered around the bodies of the dead a mass of paper ephemera. Among the litter Nick describes are "propaganda postcards showing a soldier in Austrian uniform bending a woman backward over a bed; the figures were impressionistically drawn; very attractively depicted and had nothing in common with actual rape in which the woman's skirts are pulled over her head to smother her, one comrade sometimes sitting upon the head."[12]

The text, in typical Hemingway iceberg fashion, does not explain how Nick knows about "actual rape." Readers may assume Nick has seen such rapes, which suggests the possibility that the Allies are committing them, or that Nick has come across the corpses of women who have been suffocated during the course of such rapes and whose bodies remain in the position described. A third possibility is that the "actual rape" described in the paragraph is itself propaganda, an apocryphal story like all the other apocryphal stories, including the postcards. This conflict appears in other Hemingway stories as well: in "Soldier's Home," it fosters the psychic dissociation of Harold Krebs, who is unable finally to sort out the "truth" of his war experiences from the mass of apocryphal stories that have followed him home after the war, and the same may be true of Nick's experience.[13]

As in the case of hunger, the individual tragedy of rape is exploited in the service of the state. In this case women are doubly violated, first as victims of rape and then as propaganda icons. Certainly the exploitation of the fear of rape is not new to World War I. In colonial India and Africa, and in the post–Civil War South, the subject was ubiquitous and was the source of much racial enmity. But coupled with the prospect of hunger, mutilation, and cannibalism, rape became part of a much larger depiction of the brutish German, of autocracy, and of Kultur, and as such exhorted husbands, fathers, and brothers to "Stand up and meet the war," as in Kipling's verse, or risk being called cowards.

The Question of the *Lusitania*

Not all propaganda stories from the Great War were entirely false. Two in particular had a basis in reality but were mined for all they were worth in the press and in the books mentioned. The sinking of the *Lusitania* and the execution of Edith

Cavell formed persistent focal points for the suggestion that the Germans were barbarians and, given the chance, would impose their brutal autocracy, their valueless *Kultur*, on the rest of the world.

On May 7, 1915, the passenger ship *Lusitania* was sunk just off the coast of Ireland. Germany had issued warnings that ships crossing the Atlantic would be torpedoed by the new U-boats, or submarines. No one seemed to believe Germany would sink a ship carrying nearly two thousand noncombatant passengers, but Germany did, and of those two thousand, twelve hundred drowned, more or less within sight of land. The blatant use of these civilians as propaganda images victimizes them twice, as befalls the victims of rape; sentimentalizes their deaths in a way that ignores, even dehumanizes, their individual tragedies; and by promoting war as a form of vengeance for the act, brings about further civilian and combatant casualties.

If the sinking itself were not bad enough in the Allied world, a short time later, a memorial coin appeared in Germany advertising the event as a German naval victory. Accounts vary as to who actually minted the coin, but its presence in the hands of the British became a powerful propaganda tool. A British version of the coin followed quickly on the heels of the original. Issued in a commemorative box, the medal, like the German original, depicts passengers lining up at the Cunard ticket window behind which Death stands as the ticket agent. The other side of the coin shows the liner sinking under the waves. The date on the coin is May 5, which suggests that the German navy had been planning to sink the ship sooner than it did, and that the coin had already been minted before the ship went down. The copy on the inside of the box explains that the coin is "an exact replica of the medal which was designed in Germany and distributed to commemorate the sinking of the

'Lusitania.'" The explanation of Germany's motives continues in larger copy: "This indicates the true feeling the War Lords endeavor to stimulate, and is proof positive that such crimes are not merely regarded favorably, but are given every encouragement in the land of Kultur." German autocracy, synonymous with the word Kultur, cares nothing for the lives of women and children, and is so cruel in the accomplishment of its own ends that it will let nothing stand in the way, especially not women and children. That Germany appeared to celebrate the event provided the perfect propaganda tool.

Among the books decrying the sinking of the *Lusitania*, Logan Marshall's *Horrors and Atrocities of the Great War: The Tragic Destruction of the Lusitania* calls the action "THE SUPREME CRIME AGAINST CIVILIZATION." According to Marshall, the submarine, "a venomous instrument of destruction . . . has sent headlong to the bottom of the everlasting sea more than a thousand unarmed, unresisting, peace-bent men, women, and children—even babes in arms."[14] Before the opening chapter of the book, Marshall includes photographs of many of the *Lusitania*'s dead, among them the wife and six children of American Paul Crompton, and "prominent" American Alfred G. Vanderbilt. Another photo shows a mass grave containing "sixty-six coffins." James M. Beck in *The War and Humanity* calls the sinking "a foul crime . . . [that] will never be fully redressed unless the watery grave of the *Lusitania* shall prove to be the lasting grave of the Hohenzollern dynasty."[15] Referring to the children aboard the ship, Beck quotes scripture: "And whoso shall offend one of these little ones, which believe in me, it were better for him that a millstone were hanged about his neck and he were drowned in the depth of the sea."[16] Both books employ the event to its maximum potential as powerful anti-German propaganda bound to stir the hearts and minds of

God-fearing citizens everywhere, except of course in the land of the evil Hun.

In spite of general condemnation of the sinking of the *Lusitania* and the large number of Americans among the dead, the United States remained neutral for almost two years after the event. Already in its second printing, clearly Beck's book was widely read before the date the United States entered the war. To the issue of diplomacy rather than action, Beck expresses dismay. In Europe in the summer of 1916, Beck reports "surprise and disappointment in the failure of America to enact full and swift atonement for this murder of American women and children."[17] His own assessment of the lack of retribution is that "the honour of a nation, once compromised, is not so easily regained."[18] The American author Henry James was so incensed over the failure of the United States to enter the war immediately that he became a British citizen.

Possibly the most stunning use of *Lusitania* victims as propaganda is the Fred Spear recruiting poster "Enlist." One of the most highly sought-after posters from the Great War, "Enlist" shows a drowning mother cradling an infant. Two years after the event, no explanation of the image is needed; only the word "Enlist" is necessary. Less well executed but equally effective, a Navy recruiting poster by W. A. Rogers shows sailors underwater reaching for the drowned children who wait on the bottom of the ocean in or near a sunken life boat (fig. 45). The portholes of the submerged ship loom in the background. The caption on the poster announces, "When You Fire Remember This." Across the bottom, the plea "Enlist in the Navy" completes the message. The back of the poster, however, continues with a lengthy argument that declares: "American bluejackets are now fighting to avenge the little children of the *Lusitania*." Once the memory of the children has been invoked, the copy

FIG. 45. "When You Fire Remember This," poster by W. A. Rogers.

moves on to the image of living mothers and sweethearts by reminding potential sailors that "you are going to be a man . . . so that your mother shall be proud of you, and your sweetheart look up to you. For Boy, no woman likes a 'slacker.'" Men who don't enlist, in fact, are worse than slackers; the poster implies that men who are not moved by the sight of drowned children are cowards or traitors sympathetic to the power of German autocracy.

While the poster suggests to all eligible men that "the corsair of today is the dastardly U-boat, the murderer of American women and children," the sinking of the *Lusitania* was not without controversy of another kind. Part of that controversy was whether the ship was actually transporting munitions to the Allies, of which at the time, as noted, the United States was not one. Reports of secondary explosions after the ship was torpedoed leave the question open. Quinn, who also devotes a lengthy chapter to Cavell and the *Lusitania*, wonders if the secondary explosion resulted from the "cargo of 2400 cases of rifle cartridges, 1250 cases of shrapnel, [and] ten tons of gun powder" on board the ship.[19] As a propaganda issue, however, it seems unlikely that the presence of weapons on board would have cooled public outrage. A "civilized" nation would have allowed women and children to flee the ship before sinking it, and therein lay its continuing propaganda value. If the Kaiser would be willing to eat little British and American babies, if he would cut off their hands in Belgium, he would surely fail to refrain from drowning them. When the Hun is at the gate, home and family are in danger of being destroyed. The local tragedy once more becomes emblematic of the nation in danger. As we have seen repeatedly, the Gemeinschaft serves the Gesellschaft in ways that ostensibly keep both intact.

The Martyrdom of Edith Cavell

We have seen how the figure of Edith Cavell became a model for young women considering becoming nurses. But Cavell's martyrdom went far beyond an image of bravery meant to inspire young girls. Her death served an even greater purpose as an international reminder that Germany would stop at nothing in its perceived quest for world dominance. Beck, in *The War and Humanity,* devotes an entire chapter, "Belgium and the Cavell Tragedy," to Cavell's execution. No one, not even Beck, denies that Cavell, in one way or another, helped French, Belgian, and British soldiers escape to Holland, after which many resumed their posts as combatants in their respective units. But Beck argues that Cavell should not have been executed because she was not guilty of "High Treason"—that is, "murdering or attempting to murder a sovereign or prince of Germany or an attempt by violence to overthrow the Imperial Government or any State thereof."[20] Of her execution on October 12, 1915, Beck remarks, "Miss Cavell's fate only differs from that of hundreds of Belgian women and children in that she had the pretense of a trial and presumably had trespassed against military law, while other victims of the rape of Belgium were ruthlessly killed in order to effect a speedy subjugation of the territory."[21] Later, after describing Cavell's trial and execution, Beck somewhat modifies his assertions by saying, "She at least had committed some violation of German military law. She at least had the form of a trial."[22] An article in the December 1915 issue of the *American Review of Reviews* reports the execution with slightly more restraint than does Beck. According to the article, "there was no question raised by [Brand Whitlock, American Minister to Brussels] as to the fairness of the trial or the technical legality of the sentence under military rules."[23] Nevertheless, the article concludes by suggesting that "it would have been quite sufficient to make Miss Cavell's sentence that of mere expulsion from the country."[24] Drinker's *Our War for Human Rights* also addresses the case of Edith Cavell in a close paraphrase of the *American Review of Review*'s article, which appeared two years before Drinker's book. According to both accounts, in nearly

FIG. 46. Photo of Edith Cavell in the garden with her dogs.

identical language, "no one thing so stimulated the enlistments for service as the execution of Miss Edith Cavell, the English nurse who was shot as a spy by Germany."[25] Drinker, like Beck, sees the execution as a further example of the rape of Belgium; opposite a photo of Belgian refugees he includes a photograph of Cavell in the garden with her dogs (fig. 46).

According to the introduction to the 1928 novelization of the silent film *Dawn*, Cavell was undoubtedly guilty as charged. Reginald Berkeley, author of the novelization, details Cavell's actions leading up to her arrest in August of 1915. She went to Belgium in 1907 at the request of a Belgian physician by the name of Depage, who wanted Cavell to run a nursing school in Brussels. There she founded the Ecole Belge d'Infirmières Diplômées, often referred to as the Berkendael Institute. Technically, Cavell was in charge of a private institute, not associated with the Red Cross. Among the "conspirators" who worked with Cavell to get wounded or escaped soldiers out of the country were an Irishwoman, Ada Bogart; Louise Thuliez, a French citizen; Philippe Baucq, a Belgian; and Louis Severin. Also among the conspirators were Prince Reginald of Croy and Princess Croy, whom Cavell tried to protect during the course of her testimony. In addition to hiding the escaped soldiers, the group provided fake identities, money, and civilian clothing. When the prosecution pointed out to Cavell that she had returned soldiers fit for duty to "enemy" territory, Cavell replied, "My aim has never been to benefit the enemy, but to help the men to reach the frontier. Once at the frontier, they were free."[26] Most accounts agree on the details provided here, but most accounts also suggest that the trial was a showcase for "German militarism" and that Cavell never tried to conceal the details of her actions. Of the above conspirators, only Baucq was executed along with Cavell.

Accounts differ widely in the description of her actual execution, a function of its propaganda value. Ernest Protheroe, in *A Noble Woman: The Life Story of Edith Cavell*, relates two versions of her death. One taken from the Amsterdam *Telegraaf* reports that the entire firing squad was so "impressed by the courage and fortitude of the nurse" that they all fired over her head. When Cavell collapsed, the commanding officer shot her in the head "as she lay mercifully unconscious of her surroundings."[27] The second account claims that Cavell chose to go to her death without a blindfold, and that "the Germans, with one of their acute refinements of cruelty, allowed her to witness the execution of M. Bancq [sic]," at which point Cavell collapsed.[28] Berkeley reports the undocumented execution of a German soldier, Private Rammler, who refused the order to shoot a woman. Two clergymen, including Horace Gahan, deny the event, but Berkeley believes it, along with the fact that the body of the soldier was interred next to Cavell's body.[29] Both Berkeley and Beck report that Cavell was conscious and standing when she was shot and was killed immediately.

However Edith Cavell went to her death, she became an immediate martyr and her name continued to invoke cries of outrage against Germany and to symbolize the bravery and dedication of British, and ultimately Allied, womanhood. Like the sinking of the *Lusitania*, the execution of Edith Cavell became a rallying cry for "civilization" against the forces of Kultur. The power of her martyrdom survived well beyond the war and to an extent survives today, a testament to the unassailable power of propaganda. Two films, the 1929 silent film *Dawn* and the 1939 version, *Nurse Edith Cavell*, extol the virtues of her actions well after the end of the war. As noted earlier, Cavell continued as a propaganda tool into World War II, and she continues to be the subject of books, including the 1956 novel *Edith Cavell: Heroic Nurse*. Written for young girls, the novel includes the account of Private Rammler; although the text does not name him, it declares that the commanding officer "shot the soldier on the spot."[30] Cavell's "last words" parallel those of the 1944 propaganda ad using the still from *Nurse Edith Cavell*: "Patriotism is not enough."[31] Even historian Arthur Marwick, in his 1965 book, *The Deluge: British Society and the First World War*, refers to the execution as "one of the most senseless of all the senseless acts of German militarism."[32]

By 1965 when the Cuban Missile Crisis, the Kennedy assassination, and the beginning of the Vietnam War threatened world stability in ways not possible in 1915, we might imagine that indignation over Cavell's death would have cooled, especially in the minds of serious historians such as Marwick, but the power of propaganda is not easily challenged. Ethnic hatreds worldwide are fed by martyrdoms such as that of Cavell, and often the legends surrounding such deaths grow in proportion to those hatreds, one feeding the other, until the truth becomes entirely moot; but as we have also noted, propaganda bears only scant relation to the truth to begin with. Fortunately, mythologizations of the kind surrounding the death of Edith Cavell are rare. Along with the sinking of the *Lusitania*, her death suggested that a nation committing such "atrocities" deserved to be obliterated because its citizens were less than human, a belief that made killing Germans an act of morality.

"Both cows . . . and my own three ducks": Kipling's "Swept and Garnished"

Whether Rudyard Kipling's fiction is "literary" or "popular" is a highly debatable question. The jingoism of much of his work is distasteful to contemporary readers, and today Kipling is not widely read. Nevertheless, in his time, Kipling published in American magazines such as *McClure's* and his work was widely read in Great Britain and the United States, lending propaganda value to his war fiction and poetry. Kipling was virulently anti-German well before he wrote "For All We Have and Are." The phrase "the Goth and the shameless Hun" concludes his 1902 poem "The Rowers," written on the occasion "when Germany proposed that England should help her in a naval demonstration to collect debts from Venezuela." Linking Germany with the enemy in the Boer War, Kipling declares:

> Our dead they mocked are scarcely cold,
> Our wounds are bleeding yet—
> And you tell us now that our strength is sold
> To help them press for a debt![33]

But Kipling's hatred grew with the onset of war, even before the disappearance of his son Jack at the Battle of Loos in September of 1915. First published in January of that year and later in the 1917 collection *A Diversity of Creatures*, the story "Swept and Garnished" builds on anti-German stereotypes and uses images of dead Belgian children to sentimentalize war casualties and villainize German civilians as well as the German military.

Middle-aged and substantially middle-class, Frau Ebermann, at the beginning of the story, suffers from influenza and waits in her bedroom for her servant Anna to return from the pharmacist with medicine for her fever. While Frau Ebermann's fever is a potentially important element in the story, two other details may be of greater importance. First, the name Ebermann itself is significant because *Eber* in German means wild boar. From the very beginning then, we have the association of Germans and swine. Second, Frau Ebermann's obsessive-compulsive behavior dominates the story. Completely inflexible about the arrangement of her household goods, Frau Ebermann has taught Anna "with her knuckle" to "measure the equal margins" of the lace cover on the "imitation" marble that tops her radiator.[34] Both details articulate the conflicting stereotype of Germans as swine-like sticklers for order. When Anna tells Frau Ebermann that the Germans have achieved a victory, "Frau Ebermann purred, one might almost say *grunted*, contentedly" (412, italics mine).

The word *grunted* furthers the image of Germans as swine and prepares readers for the events to follow.

Even before Anna returns with her medicine, Frau Ebermann begins to see ragged children in her bedroom. They appear dirty and threaten to upset the order in which Frau Ebermann keeps all her possessions. Associating order with Godliness, Frau Ebermann believes that "if it pleased our dear God to take her to Himself, . . . He should find all her belongings fit to meet his eye. 'Swept and garnished' were the words that shaped themselves in her intent brain" (413). Frau Ebermann's priorities, according to Kipling, are confused, and the appearance of the Belgian children is intended as an object lesson to the old woman. "Never . . . a child-lover in any sense," although she has a son, Frau Ebermann is disgusted to find not God but "a parcel of dirty children" at the foot of her bed (413). To her horror, the children sit on the velvet sofa, ignoring Frau Ebermann's insistence that they go away. At the beginning of their conversation with Frau Ebermann, Kipling parallels their entry into the bedroom uninvited to the German invasion of Belgium. One of the three little girls repeats Frau Ebermann's words and the words of one of their dead elders, for whom the children wait. No one should go into "houses nor bedrooms, nor dining-rooms nor churches, nor all those places. Shouldn't come in. It's rude" (415). The little girl continues in the words of her dead elder, "only pigs would do that" (415). Linking the ill old woman with the marauding troops through her name Ebermann and the word pig, Kipling begins to lay at the door of ordinary German citizens the actions of their soldiers.

Sentimentality kicks in when the children reply to Frau Ebermann's repeated request that they "go, home to your father and mother!" (416). In echoes of descending age, the children reply, beginning with the oldest, "There isn't anything left" (416). A younger child mimics the sound of an explosion and adds "like that, uncle told me. Both cows too" (416). The youngest child adds his "own three ducks" to the inventory of destruction, and the picture of German brutality is complete.

Frau Ebermann counters with two propaganda explanations of her own. The inhabitants of the villages the children came from fired on the advancing German troops and "were punished" (417). Her second justification, like the first, claims that the civilian deaths were their own fault. Frau Ebermann's son has written to her that "accidents to the children happen" (419). She tells the children, "You should have been more careful. You should not have run out to see the horses and guns passing" (419). Frau Ebermann will not admit to herself or to the phantom children the possibility of German atrocities, and she also refuses to believe the numbers of dead the children report. Nevertheless, the story the children narrate begins to affect Frau Ebermann, and several times she tells them to go to the kitchen where Anna will give them sweets.

Kipling, who in some ways believed in the concept of mass hallucination, either situates the children in Frau Ebermann's unconscious and retrieves them through her fever, or he actually envisions the ghosts of dead Belgians taking vengeance on ordinary Germans who would prefer not to know the truth about their countrymen.[35] Hallucination or no, the children, at least temporarily, drive Frau Ebermann mad. When Anna enters her room, she finds the elderly woman cleaning "blood" from the floor with the lace doily off the radiator, so that her "dear Lord when He came might find everything as it should be" (420). The doily, which earlier has been symbolic of the necessity for order, now becomes a tool for clearing up disorder, for erasing death by erasing the blood from her floor. In Kipling's economy, Germany's crimes would never be atoned for; that is, the "dear Lord" would never find anything in order as long as children and ducks died in the name of Kultur. Never one to avoid the jingoistic or for that matter racist attitude, Kipling delivers a potent propaganda message with these small Belgian specters—German swine do not care whom they kill, and kill they will unless Allied men "stand up and meet the war."

Brutality and Debauchery in *Hearts of the World* and *The Little American*

Among the films produced during the Great War, D. W. Griffith's *Hearts of the World* and Cecil B. De Mille's *The Little American* employ many of the stereotypes—brutality, drunkenness, and lechery—associated with Kultur. While the Kipling story "Swept and Garnished" relies on the stereotypes of neatness and orderliness to the point of obsessive-compulsive disorder, the two films, with equal strokes of sentimentality, present a vicious conqueror. Both Gish sisters, Lilian and Dorothy, star in *Hearts of the World,* Lilian as Marie Stephenson, the innocent fiancée of Douglas Gordon Hamilton, and Dorothy as "The Little Disturber," Marie's potential rival until The Little Disturber falls in love with Monsieur Cuckoo, who provides comic relief in the film when he is not bravely performing his duty as a soldier. Like George Campton of Edith Wharton's *A Son at the Front,* Douglas, referred to as "the boy" in the captions, is the son of an American artist and a hopeless romantic. He woos Marie by the garden wall of "the double house in which live the two American families on the Rue de la Paix" and gallantly fights off the advances of The Little Disturber.[36]

When war interrupts the lives of the two couples, both men go off to fight. The village, of course, is shelled and eventually occupied by the evil Huns. On the day that was to have been her wedding day, Marie loses her grandfather and her mother to German shells. Wearing her wedding veil and dragging the tattered dress behind her, Marie wanders onto the battlefield in a daze, where she finds Douglas wounded. Believing him to be dead, she lies down beside him, head on his shoulder, and spends what would have been their wedding night. The next morning, she leaves Douglas for dead and wanders back to the inn in the village where The Little Disturber nurses her back to health.

As part of the German occupation, villagers are forced to work in the fields. In one scene Marie is digging potatoes, and when she cannot lift a bushel basket onto a cart, she is brutally beaten with a whip. Gish, whose facial expressions were made for the silent screen, attempts to lift the heavy basket several times as the stout German taskmaster looks on. After she is beaten, she once again wanders to the inn, where she collapses. But Marie is not the only victim of the occupation. Douglas's old mother and his three younger brothers are hidden in the basement of their shelled home when the mother collapses and dies of exhaustion. As she lies on her deathbed, the three children kiss her one by one, including the smallest, who weeps tragically before all three kneel by her corpse. To prevent her corpse from being violated by the Huns, the three small boys dig a six-foot-deep hole in the basement, where they bury her. Marie, recovered from the lashing, encounters the children and takes food to their basement hideout. Most of the scenes in the film depict the German invaders as evil swine, capable of the most vile actions. In an almost comically anti-German scene, the evil von Strohm, a member of the German secret service, entertains the other officers at the inn. Complete with dancers who are visibly uncorseted and twirl to show panties, the scene is one of total revelry; the Germans are drunk and very nearly sleeping with the dancers in public.

Back in the trenches, Douglas is not dead. He has healed from his wounds and becomes a spy. Dressed in a German uniform, Douglas briefly infiltrates the German lines, taking viewers into the trenches with him. Oddly enough, many of the battle scenes in the film are authentic. The movie opens with D. W. Griffith obtaining the permission of the British War Office to film at the front lines, and much of that footage is included. A determined Douglas, under fire, crawls to a German trench and, for a time, deceives the Germans in it until the officers find him out. Still he escapes and makes his way back to the village as the French troops advance and retreat repeatedly in an attempt to retake it. At the inn, the evil von Strohm threatens to rape Marie, but she escapes, only to run into another German whom she refuses to look at. Of course, this second soldier is Douglas, and viewers are treated to a gradual moment of recognition, which once again profits from the expressive face of Lilian Gish. A second moment of recognition follows in which The Little Disturber, who happens along, believes Marie is consorting with the enemy until she, in a contrastingly humorous moment, also recognizes Douglas.

The film's climax employs numerous propaganda images, including those of female bravery reflected in a willingness to kill without fear of losing the stereotypical feminine qualities of kindness and acquiescence. As the retreating Germans shell the town, the camera cuts to the villagers who are sheltered in a basement, where the scenes parallel some of the scenes from the Raleigh and other posters. A woman nurses an infant and another woman cradles the head of a dead friend or sister on her lap. When the stout German finds Douglas hidden in Marie's room and tries to kill him, Marie stabs the German several times in the back with a carving knife. The two retreat to the bombed-out upper floor of the inn, where the evil von Strohm, along with several other officers, tries to break down the door. Having seen one of the Germans playing with a grenade earlier, The Little Disturber employs one and kills the Germans as they are about to capture Douglas and Marie. The Little Disturber, who turns out to have a heart of gold after all, is rewarded with the hand of Monsieur Cuckoo and Marie with the hand of Douglas. Ironically, one of the final captions—undoubtedly added after the war, describing American troop ships returning home—declares: "America—Returning home after freeing the world from Autocracy and the horrors of war—we hope forever and ever."[37] The central claim of World War I propaganda, that this was the war to end wars, speaks in this last moment of the film. But the war is over only because women such as Marie and The Little Disturber fight for their men and their children, even as their men fight for them. Home and village may be threatened, but through the efforts of local women, the community will survive, and with it the state.

The Little American, directed by Cecil B. De Mille, stars Mary Pickford and was produced by her film company, Artcraft Pictures. The film was released in August of 1917 but begins prior to the war in 1914, perhaps as a way of revealing Germany's descent into a completely immoral and tyrannical state. Not quite as sentimental as *Hearts of the World, The Little American* still employs the same anti-German stereotypes of brutality, drunkenness, and lechery, although with a surprising twist.[38] At the beginning of the film Angela More, Pickford, is being courted by two aristocratic suitors, one French and one German. Initially viewers might see the suitors as representatives of the two combatant nations courting America, but the conclusion of the film does not bear out this assumption. Angela clearly prefers Karl Von Austreim, whose mother is American and whose father is German, over the Frenchman, Count Jules De

Destin. In a comic scene at the beginning of the film, Karl has Angela and her little brother Bobby, played by Ben Alexander, who also plays the youngest brother of Douglas Hamilton in *Hearts of the World*, goose-stepping around the parlor. Angela jokes that Karl will make a Prussian of Bobby before he learns his ABCs. But the film's humor is short-lived. Both men, of course, end up fighting for their respective countries, although Karl does not go willingly.

Angela is also summoned to France to tend to her dying aunt, who lives in a large chateau and has made Angela her heir. In an obvious allusion to the sinking of the *Lusitania*, Angela's ship, the *Veritania*, is torpedoed by a German submarine. The link between the name of the ship and the word *veritas*, Latin for "truth," is obvious, as is the word's resemblance to *Lusitania*. Germans have torpedoed the truth and in the process killed hundreds of civilians. Three important scenes are involved in the sinking of the ship. First, ignoring German warnings that the ship may be sunk, the passengers are partying, complete with champagne, streamers, and confetti, when the torpedo hits, underscoring the belief that the United States was not prepared for German brutality. Cinematically, the film employs artful cutting as it switches from the ballroom of the ship to the U-boat where the gunners are setting the liner in the torpedo's sights. Right before the explosion Angela has just declared that "ocean travel has no thrills," that they might as well be dancing at a local club.

In the second crucial scene after the ship sinks, Angela, the Little American, stands on the makeshift raft she and her companions cling to in order to taunt the German U-boat captain, who has come to the ship's lookout to observe his handiwork. Waving an American flag she has tucked into her bodice, Angela screams, "You've fired on American women and children."

Ironically, the flag was part of her birthday gift from Karl on the evening he taught Bobby to goose-step. The third scene occurs when the camera cuts to a German camp where Karl, who knows Angela has sailed for France, learns that the *Veritania* has been destroyed. At first Karl refuses to toast the German "victory," but his fellow officers insist, and he reluctantly complies. But Karl is not completely innocent. By the time Angela arrives at the chateau, her aunt is dead and the chateau is serving as a field hospital where, she runs into Jules briefly before the advancing Germans take over the house.

Before they arrive, Jules, who has lost an arm but is still acting as an officer, installs a telephone in the fireplace, similar to the Marconi hidden in the fireplace in *The White Feather*. A French soldier pretending to be the butler is supposed to telephone the position of the German guns to Jules. Angela and her maids stay with the wounded because Angela still believes the Germans will honor her neutrality. In a scene similar to the drunken party in *Hearts of the World,* the Germans break into the chateau, pillage the wine cellar, step on the wounded soldiers, and rape the maids. When Angela reminds the German officers that she is an American, they laugh. One of the central scenes in the film occurs when Angela is herself attacked by a German officer. She fights him off and is about to stab him when she discovers her attacker is Karl. Why she releases the letter opener when she discovers Karl's identity is unclear. His behavior is as ruthless as that of the enlisted men who are raping the servants in the next room, but Angela demands of him, "If there's a spark of manhood left in you—go and save those women!" Karl cannot, but he does his best to protect Angela, who is forced at one point to remove the boots from the feet of his commanding officer.

The Germans also shoot most of the male civilians in the

area, including an old man and a boy. Angela must operate the telephone herself because the French "butler" has been killed when the Germans take over the chateau. Knowing she will be shot if she is caught, she telephones Jules with the location of the guns because she is sick of German brutality. Angela does not seem at all conflicted by her actions—she is trying to kill every German except Karl, whose attempted rape is all but forgotten. When Angela is caught, she tells the commanding officer that "I was neutral—'till I saw your soldiers destroying women and shooting old men! Then I stopped being 'neutral' and became a human being!" Karl also denounces Germany, and they are about to be shot together when Jules fires on the chateau again and the French retake it. Totally unrealistic in its conclusion, *The Little American* closes with Angela and Karl free to return to America and the armless Jules heartbroken. Except when he offers to die with Angela, Karl seldom appears sympathetic in the film, and his fellow countrymen are the usual beasts. One possible explanation for Karl's redemption is the fact, alluded to only once, that his mother is American. That civilizing force, both feminine and non-German, must ultimately remind Karl of his humanity and his real community in America, to which he returns. Still, the truth that his father is German and that Karl has fought on behalf of the Kaiser will make living in the United States virtually impossible, no matter how aristocratic he is. Angela's bravery in the face of German brutality, even though she ignores Karl's complicity in it, establishes the film's propaganda value. When Angela telephones Jules with the locations of the guns, he hesitates until she tells him, "Don't worry about me! You have no choice when it's *one* woman—or the battle line of France!" The Little American follows through, as does her country, albeit a bit later. Very nearly drowned when the *Veritania* is sunk, almost raped by her "fiancé," and placed before a firing squad, Angela demonstrates bravery equal to that of other heroines. She graciously forgives Karl, as Edith Cavell forgave her executioners, saves Karl from his Prussian dark side, and returns him to his American mother, thus preserving some remnant of home and family. The Frenchman, who does not need to be reminded of honor, continues to fight even though he is maimed and does not get the girl.

"Are You Half the Man Your Mother Thought You'd Be?"

Sheet music was another form of propaganda that, in addition to recruiting women, shamelessly used images of women and children to goad men into service. Music from the First World War remains legendary. Songs such as "Keep the Home Fires Burning" and "Over There" are indeed familiar to most of us born shortly after the Second World War because they remained in use as inspirational songs through that war as well. While phonographs were in use during the first war, singing along as someone played the piano was a widespread form of entertainment. Many of the pieces in my collection have names written on the front, which leads me to believe young women took the music to get-togethers and put their names on the music so they could retrieve it at the event's conclusion.

While "Are You Half the Man Your Mother Thought You'd Be" does not directly refer to war service—the publication date is 1916—it does depict a number of men in service uniforms on the cover, as well as roughly drawn images of George Washington, Abraham Lincoln, and Teddy Roosevelt, arranged around an image of a mother reading to her young son (fig. 47). That circle of family unity, the mother and son, exhibits the kernel of the Gemeinschaft, not just the mother and child but mother and male child, the essence of the future, the source of future families and future armies. In this particular illustration, the mother is young and pretty, in contrast to other images; she is

FIG. 47. Cover illustration from the sheet music for "Are You Half the Man Your Mother Thought You'd Be?"

the mother who will later demand her son become a soldier. In preparation for that eventuality, the refrain asks, "Are you all she planned and prayed for, / all she raked, and scrap'd, and slaved for?"[39] Only the son who answers the call to war can claim to be the man the song exalts.

FIG. 48. Cover illustration from the sheet music for "I'd Be Proud to Be the Mother of a Soldier."

Even before 1916, however, Americans were being prepared to send their sons off to war. "I'd Be Proud to Be the Mother of a Soldier," published in 1915, uses what became the classic image of the mother volunteering her son for military service. Unlike the mother on the previous sheet music, this mother is far too old to have a son like the young man depicted in the drawing (fig. 48). White-haired and lace-collared, she appears grandmotherly, undoubtedly a calculated stroke of sentimentality to further the popular propaganda appeal of the songs. In this song the family sits at the dinner table talking of the European war. While the son initially declares that "it's not right that men should fight," his mother reminds him that his father has fought, and "Just like your Dad before, you'd march away to war, / And the same as any other, leave your sweet-heart and your mother."[40] American patriotism steps in at this point as the Mother continues:

> Now that others are fighting, I pray for peace, it's true,
> But it would be a different story,
> If they trampled on *Old Glory*,
> I'd be proud to be the mother of a soldier.[41]

This mother demands service of her sons, as we imagine the mother demanding in the previous song. In this cycle of birth, death, and violence, mothers bear the sons who fight for the families who will bear more sons to be sacrificed in future wars.

Cover art on a number of other war songs employs the same image of the older woman wearing a lace collar and white hair pulled back into a bun. The 1917 "That's a Mother's Liberty Loan," which declares "when the battle's won, I'll then take back my Son," actually uses a photograph of actors Edward Earle and Mary Maurice on the cover.[42] The mother does not anticipate her son returning limbless or in a coffin; she merely offers him up. "America Here's My Boy" declares "America I raised a boy for you, America you'll find him staunch and true, / Place a gun upon his shoulder, He is ready to die or do." The mother continues that this is her only son, but if she had more, she would send them as well, a sentiment echoed in "If I Had a Son for Each Star in Old Glory (Uncle Sam, I'd Give Them All To You)."[43] The mothers in these songs express little concern for the lives of their sons, only the desire that they should conform to the role of protector, that they should be the man the mother expects.

British sheet music conveyed similar messages. "Your King and Country Want You (A Woman's Recruiting Song)" actually mirrors the Siegfried Sassoon poem "Glory of Women." The mother in the song declares:

> No matter what befalls you,
> We shall love you all the more,
> So come and join the forces
> As your fathers did before.

The sheet music, "Dedicated by special permission to Her Majesty the Queen," promises that "The entire profits from the sale of this song will be devoted to Queen Mary's 'Work for Women' Fund."[44] Unlike the American songs, this British song does admit that horrors may befall the soldier. Still, those mutilations will only be endearing, and they will become decorations in which the mothers express pride.

Two war songs, one British, one American, literally convert the local image of family to the image of the state; Gemeinschaft, in the service of the state, becomes one big family, a gigantic national one. Britannia becomes a mother image in the colonial war song "Britannia Needs You Like a Mother (Would You Turn Your Mother Down)?" published in Sydney (fig. 49). The song begins by speaking of a mother adoring her children, some "adopted," but "the mother is in trouble / And she needs her children's aid." Britannia and the colonies are one big happy family; thus, colonial men must respond to the call. Indeed,

FIG. 49. Cover illustration from the sheet music for "Britannia Needs You Like a Mother (Would You Turn Your Mother Down?)."

earlier, we have seen Australian Edward Smout declare that signing up was the "thing to do." Issues of colonialism aside for the moment, state and family converge here, become undifferentiated by the demands of war.[45] Similarly, "That Family

Called the U.S.A." looks to the individual states as the previous song looks at British colonies. Declaring initially that "Our land of liberty is one big family," the song continues:

> When good old Uncle Sam
> Got mixed up in a jam, He just spoke to all
> His relatives by dozens,
> Nephews, brothers, cousins,
> And forty-nine [sic] states answered to his call.

Copyrighted in 1919, the song concludes that the United States "stuck and licked the Hun."[46] States are depicted in various roles on the cover—Missouri, for instance, is a nurse's cap on a pretty young nurse (fig. 50). These direct links between family and state underscore the role of the family unit, especially women and children, in war propaganda. To survive in its local form, the family must serve the state, must in fact become the state. War dissolves local boundaries, and in the process Gemeinschaft and Gesellschaft merge. The state takes on the qualities of the smaller unit, and all relationships become primary relationships. War erases the idea of the secondary relationship because, as the song declares, we are all "nephews, brothers, cousins."

War as Product: The Message of Advertising

As we saw in chapter 1, advertisements promoting domestic science and wartime food economy abounded, especially after the formation of the U.S. Food Administration late in 1917. But the war infiltrated ads for everything from corsets to soap. The October 1918 issue of the *Ladies' Home Journal*, after promoting women's war service, features an advertisement for NuBone Corsets, which are supposedly designed for the heightened activity of war work. Speaking directly to the woman who is engaged in war work, the ad maintains, "You need freedom

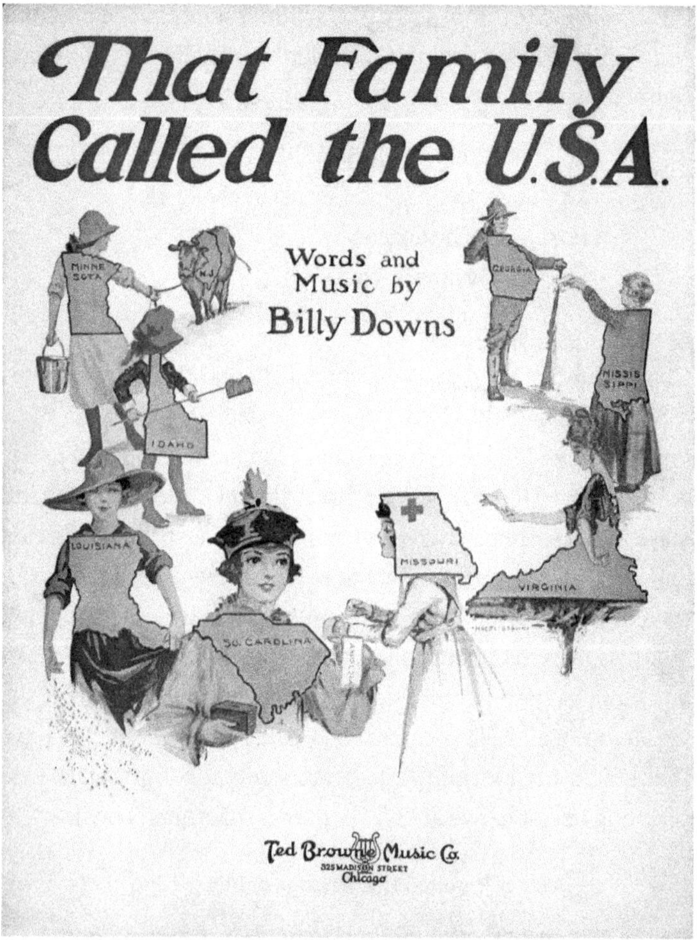

FIG. 50. Cover illustration from the sheet music for "That Family Called the U.S.A."

to assume any position easily and comfortably, yet in every position you should be perfectly supported. Modesty, no less than comfort and safety, requires this. And your native pride demands that there be no abatement of style!"[47] The reference to style parallels the importance of shirt collars in "One

Hundred Percent," and the articles on wartime patterns and remaking last year's clothes in the *Delineator*. Illustrated by both drawings of women engaged in "wartime activities" and discreet photographs of women wearing the corsets, the corset ad guarantees the made-to-measure garments.

The ad is followed by two food ads, one for Swans Down Cake Flour—cake flour, not oat or barley flour—which will produce "War Cake You Will Be Proud to Serve," and another for the ubiquitous Crisco, which includes a recipe for "Barley Doughnuts."[48] A color ad for Woodbury's Facial Soap does not mention the war, but the drawing of an upper middle-class woman playing a piano includes a young man in military uniform pressing his cheek to hers. While the drawing is anonymous, it depicts the softness and female charm of a Haskell Coffin magazine cover. In the Butterick pattern magazine the *Delineator*, the ad for Woodbury's Soap features a drawing by illustrator Paul Starr. Featuring "A Skin You Love to Touch," the illustration is available, along with samples of soap, for the small price of fifteen cents.

McClure's Win-the-War Magazine also features advertisements that appeal to female readers. The March 1918 issue, the first of the issues devoted entirely to war, concludes with two ads, one for Borden's Eagle Brand Milk, the other for toothpaste. Slightly more subtle than the Crisco ads, the Eagle Brand Milk ad claims the milk is "economical" when used in "Baby's Fifth Birthday" cake because it is "the milk that saves the sugar," a scarce commodity during the war. Perhaps the most curiously nationalistic ad, one for the "Pro-phy-lac-tic Tooth Brush," graces the back cover of the magazine. According to the ad's headline, the toothbrush is "Made in America by Americans under American Sanitary Conditions." Without directly maligning German products, as much war propaganda did, the ad blatantly promotes the "American" value of cleanliness and connects patriotism with the use of the product. "As a good citizen of the U.S.A.," the ad continues, "you should use the Pro-phy-lac-tic Tooth Brush because it is made under factory conditions which Americans demand." The drawing in the ad depicts a cheerful red-brick factory covered with ivy and surrounded by trees, in contrast to a propaganda ad featured in the July 10, 1917, issue of the *Augusta Herald*, which depicts a German factory guarded by soldiers who force workers inside with bayonets.[49] Contrasting "The American Way" with "The Prussian Way," the newspaper ad also depicts German soldiers dragging women by the hair and threatening to bayonet them. Using these images to promote male war service, the ad declares the Prussians are "fiends that are Itching to Kill You Off—so they may possess your House, your Lands, your Chattels, your Women—all?" The solution, of course is that "Every Man in Augusta Who Is a Man Must Do His Part to Win the War. GET IN THE GAME! DO YOURS?"[50] While the question mark at the end of the command seems curious, the message is clear: men must rise to the occasion to protect their women, who are listed immediately after chattels.

Personal care products for men were also targeted toward women in war advertisements. The September 1918 issue of *McClures's Win-the-War Magazine* opens with an ad for Durham-Duplex razor blades. Central to the ad is a drawing of a smiling mother holding a box of the blades. A smaller drawing of her uniformed son, pictured to look like a photograph atop a service flag, stares directly at readers. The ad copy claims, "One Durham-Duplex Razor will shave a man—or a regiment—for a lifetime."[51] Since men are at the front and cannot purchase their own personal care products, the choice falls to mothers and wives. The woman in this ad is coifed and dressed as "mother," but wives must understand the ad is meant for them as well.

Ivory soap also appeals to those at home purchasing products to send "Over There" by appealing to a preference for the American way of life, which the Huns threaten on a daily basis. The drawing depicts happy soldiers in various stages of undress, some discreetly nude, bathing or about to bathe in a stream that is neither foul nor bloody. Touting Ivory and the American way, the ad proclaims: "IVORY SOAP follows the flag. Wherever America goes, it is 'among those present.' Ivory's use is as unchangeable a part of American life as the practice of cleanliness. Ivory Soap is, in fact, the very joy of living to Our Boys when they are relieved from the front lines for rest, recreation, clean clothes and a bath."[52] Like the toothbrush ad and the Georgia recruiting ad, the Ivory soap ad suggests in hyperbolic language that cleanliness is an American commodity, the "joy of living" to soldiers. The ad neglects to allude to the question of lice, which the soap cannot kill—which in fact industrial steam vats used to disinfect uniforms did not kill. Indeed, these men appear never to have set foot in a trench.

An ad for Cream of Wheat, unremarkable in itself, appears on the inside front cover of the November 1918 issue of *Today's Housewife* (fig. 51). The ad depicts a French waitress serving a bowl of Cream of Wheat to a soldier over the caption, "NONE BUT THE BRAVE DESERVE THE FARE." We know the waitress is French because a sign in the background declares "Nous Servons Cream of Wheat" (We Serve Cream of Wheat).[53] Even in France, this homespun fare will comfort the soldier. The cover of the magazine, drawn by Edna F. Hart, is, however, remarkable (fig. 52). Over the caption "WASTE NOT—WANT NOT," two toddlers, one a girl dressed in a U.S.

FIG. 51. "Nous Servons Cream of Wheat," Cream of Wheat advertisement from *Today's Housewife*, 1918.

Food Administration uniform, prepare "Best War-Time Recipes." The girl holds a knife with which she has just trimmed the crust from a pie that she holds proudly in her other hand, and the younger child, a boy, licks a mixing spoon over a bowl

FIG. 52. Cover illustration from *Today's Housewife*, November 1918.

of batter. Like the children in war posters, these toddlers are blonde and rosy-cheeked. Itself an advertisement for the Food Administration, the cover once more exploits the ideal American family, the quintessential American child, the American way.

The family group, the Gemeinschaft, conveys the message of nationalism, of patriotism, to a nation at war.

Propaganda clearly finds a way into all of these forms of popular culture, compelling men, women, and children to serve in whatever ways they can. Propaganda creates popular culture as it mythologizes war martyrs such as Edith Cavell and the victims of the sinking of the *Lusitania*. Starving children, ghost children, and violated women all become emblematic of the cruelty and insensitivity of autocracy, examples of what will happen if the Hun is not stopped. The primary relationships of the local community—mother and child, wife and husband, and brother and sister—all fall into place as both subjects and objects of propaganda as a way to promote service to the larger community, or the state. As we observed, Ferdinand Tönnies argues that propaganda in some ways creates itself by making alternative opinions impossible—not just expressing dissenting opinions but even having them. As Tönnies explains, "Real Public Opinion . . . [vilifies] a deviant opinion as a sin. Even though they are not interested in having a deviant opinion expressed or disseminated ("propagandized"), its assessment (i.e., its rejection) is based on *having* the opinion."[54]

For loyal citizens, the opinions expressed in popular literature, film, and magazines, and direct propaganda such as posters, were the only opinions possible without risking the epithets *slacker* or *coward*. Various implementations of the Panopticon serve as a kind of "Thought Police" preventing, for the most part, the formation of dissenting opinions, even if not quite as severely as in the witch hunts of the McCarthy era. Public opinion maligned everything German, everything in any way connected with Germany. While German Americans were not interned as were Japanese Americans in World War II, they were placed in the precarious position of being suspected traitors at the same time they grieved over loved ones fighting on both sides. But propaganda does not acknowledge a middle ground, details that might foster moral conflicts. For the propagandist, the concepts "we" are good and "they" are evil are fixed and incontrovertible.

Conclusion

Learning to Love Big Brother—or Not

Committee on Public Information Chairman George Creel became, when the war was over, a spokesperson for the success of the U.S. propaganda campaign. Congress, fearing a voter backlash to the manipulation of public information, quickly dissolved the committee. In the "Dedicatory" to his 1920 book *How We Advertised America,* Creel insists that Congress, in its "annihilation" of the committee and its final report on propaganda, attempted to "keep the committee from making a statement of achievement for the information of the public."[1] It did not occur to Creel that the public might take exception to being propagandized, nor did Creel have to fear an angry constituency, as did Congress. Creel published his book, as he puts it, not as "a compilation of incident and opinion, but [as] a *record* and a *chronicle.*"[2] Creel's battle with Congress over the revelation of potentially controversial material suggests Congress might have had some qualms about the propaganda campaign it had supported during the war and did not want to agitate those same people who during the war bought bonds and curbed their consumption of scarce food items at the government's behest. Too much information might scare off potential voters, a risk few public servants are willing to take. Creel, as well as Newton D. Baker, then secretary of war and author of the book's foreword, both believed that a unified nation was essential in the victory over Germany, that in Baker's words, "it was of the greatest importance that America in this war should be represented not merely as a strong man fully armed, but as a strong man fully armed and believing in the cause for which he was fighting."[3] In his defense of the most massive propaganda campaign in U.S. or British history, Baker goes on to say that the Allies "were fighting for ideas and ideals, and somebody who realized that, and knew it, had to say it and keep on saying it until it was believed."[4] In other words, the governments that had declared war and were asking their citizens to go out and fight had to articulate in the most basic terms what the war was ostensibly about and had to convince those citizens that great consequences would result if they refused to fight. As we have seen repeatedly, those basic terms suggest that the enemy is evil and dangerous and that the very core of civilization, the nuclear family, is in danger of being destroyed if the enemy is allowed to prevail. While war may temporarily break up the family unit, when the war is won, the family will be reunited and all will be well. Men can resume their positions as heads of households, and women and children can go back to doing whatever it was they were doing before war broke out. Young girls can marry their war heroes and produce more soldiers for the next war. The nature of war propaganda, in the event we have not yet learned it, becomes clear, as does Creel's and Baker's naiveté that no one would mind.

As chairman of the Committee on Public Information, naive or not, George Creel must go down as one of history's villains, albeit a lesser known one. While Creel was no Stalin, no Hitler, his contribution to the demise of honesty in the flow of public information was substantial, and by way of that contribution, a thinly veiled Creel appears in at least one major work of cynical postwar fiction, John Dos Passos's *U.S.A.* trilogy. Portrayed in *The 42nd Parallel* as an opportunistic public relations magnate who sees publicity as the solution to any problem, J. Ward Moorehouse reappears in *Nineteen Nineteen* as "one of the best known publicity experts in New York before the war."[5] When readers see Moorehouse in *Nineteen Nineteen,* he has just arrived in Paris to run the war-stressed publicity department of the Red Cross. Dos Passos's summary of Moorehouse's motivational speech to the Red Cross volunteers could very nearly have been lifted from *How We Advertised America.* Through the voice of Eveline Hutchins, who briefly becomes Moorehouse's lover, we learn that

> he made a little speech about the importance of the work the Red Cross was doing to keep up the morale of civilians and combatants, and that their publicity ought to have two aims, to stimulate giving among the folks back home and to keep people informed of the progress of their work . . . ; and that the American people and the warwracked populations of the Allied countries *must be made* to know the splendid sacrifice the Red Cross workers were making, as splendid in its way as the sacrifice of the dear boys in the trenches.[6]

Toward the end of this rousing speech, Moorehouse declares that their publicity must produce in their mass audience "the catch in the throat, the wrench to steady the nerves, the determination to carry on."[7] Moorehouse's goal here is to produce an emotional response in the public, a response parallel to the visceral fear that images of an apelike Hun produced in civilians and soldiers alike. As does Creel, Moorehouse believes that public opinion must not deviate from the popular mythology of the war, and that it is his job to create that popular mythology. A powerful public spokesperson, Moorehouse is one of the "bigmouthed officials with too many bank accounts" Dos Passos refers to in the brief introduction to *U.S.A.*[8] Even though Moorehouse, in his feigned sincerity, may initially remind Eveline of her father, he is never a positive character and in fact serves as a model of the carelessness and cynicism of the presumptuous and power-hungry.

Propaganda, it is true, has many purposes. In my introduction, I examined Vance Packard's important work on advertising, *The Hidden Persuaders*. Indeed, the use of propaganda in advertising during the First World War has been one of the subjects under consideration here. We might also note the connection between war propaganda and advertising in the figure of Edward Bernays, who worked with Creel on the Committee on Public Information. According to Creel, Bernays coordinated the export of goods to a war-torn Europe and disseminated the propaganda accompanying those exports. As part of his duties on the committee, Bernays wrote articles and published photographs "telling of war aims and activities."[9] Bernays is perhaps better known for his book *Propaganda*, in which he defends the art and applies its methods to advertising. We might incidentally note here that Bernays made a career in advertising, not in government. Although Bernays believes propaganda is a science and therefore neutral, he opens his book with the statement: "The conscious and intelligent manipulation of the organized habits and opinions of the masses is an important element in democratic society. Those who manipulate this unseen mechanism of society constitute an invisible government which is the true ruling power of our country."[10] In this oxymoronic declaration, Bernays in a way expresses the fears embedded in studies such as Packard's and expressed in the present study. Chilling in his disregard for personal choice, or for that matter personal freedom, Bernays condones the use of whatever means necessary to sway public opinion and in a way foreshadows the invisible power of the military-industrial complex that later became the brunt of protest during the Vietnam war.

In his introduction to Bernays's *Propaganda,* Mark Crispin Miller also focuses on the neutral nature of the "science," at one point comparing to propaganda the efforts to improve public health through vaccination. Promoting public health through statistics, in Miller's words, is "no less a propaganda drive than any anti-clerical or socialist or nativist crusade. Evidently this fact was apparent to those few who used the word—which did not become a synonym for big black lies until the Allies made the word familiar to the masses of Great Britain and America."[11] Like Bernays, Miller refuses to acknowledge that the manipulation of political information, or any information, is negative. The key word here is *manipulation*. First, the word propaganda became a synonym for "big black lies" because through the manipulation of information, most war propaganda contained them; and second, Miller's analogy is faulty. Campaigns promoting public health are not, by any stretch of the imagination, propaganda. Vaccination, except in rare cases, prevents disease—an objective quantifiable scientific fact. A case in point is the disease smallpox, which has all but been eradicated worldwide because of efforts to vaccinate potential victims of the disease, and the same can be said of polio. Even today, public health officials are struggling to control the spread of AIDS with campaigns that debunk myths about the disease; that is, by disseminating scientific truth about the nature of the disease and how to prevent it. Scientists are in fact fighting some local propaganda campaigns that suggest homeopathic remedies will cure AIDS or that the AIDS epidemic was incurred through the wrath of God.

In its inception, propaganda was not neutral; it was designed to "propagate" the Catholic faith, to convert the nonbeliever.

Through its promotion of consumer products, propaganda as advertising is not neutral; its bottom line after all is to increase profits by increasing sales. During World War I, propaganda was not neutral; as Baker and Creel have declared, citizens needed to back the war. According to Ponsonby, "every country uses [falsehood] quite deliberately to deceive its own people, to attract neutrals, and to mislead the enemy. The ignorant and innocent masses in each country are unaware at the time that they are being misled, and when it is all over only here and there are the falsehoods discovered and exposed."[12]

As noted, Ponsonby's goal in writing his book is that "the common people may be more on their guard when the war cloud next appears on the horizon."[13] Still proponents of propaganda argue for its continued use. In an attempt to justify his role in advertising, Bernays asserts that although "the instruments by which public opinion is organized and focused may be misused . . . such organization and focusing are necessary to orderly life."[14] To allude once again to *Brave New World*'s Mustapha Mond, "No civilization without social stability. No social stability without individual stability."[15] While society has not yet resorted to genetic manipulation of individuals to achieve the stability Mond refers to, it does manipulate individual thought, and the dissemination of lies or half-truths to achieve that goal is not neutral. Propaganda advocating flag waving or the purchase of Pro-phy-lac-tic toothbrushes is not neutral. Propaganda violates one of the foremost tenets of democracy, albeit an idealistic one: that of the educated population making decisions based on the acquisition of facts. Even Bob Dylan, in his despair that "[all is] propaganda / All is phoney," ultimately hopes to awaken his listeners, as did Harold Lasswell and Arthur Ponsonby. Cynicism of the sort promulgated by Edward Bernays can only allow those "big black lies" to flourish.

In the debate that surrounded the framing of the U.S. Constitution, Alexander Hamilton argues for a government strong enough to resist the powers of demagoguery. While Hamilton fails to see the potential for government itself as demagogue, he describes the effects of propaganda on an unsuspecting public, although he does not use the word. Speaking of those who opposed a strong constitution and the force of that opposition, Hamilton declares: "A torrent of angry and malignant passions will be let loose. To judge from the conduct of the opposite parties, we shall be led to conclude, that they will mutually hope to evince the justness of their opinions, and to increase the number of their converts by the loudness of their declamations, and by the bitterness of their invectives."[16] Hamilton concludes this part of his argument by warning that such zealots open the door to "despotism," that "of those men who have overturned the liberties of republics the greatest number have begun their career, by paying an obsequious court to the people, commencing Demagogues and ending Tyrants."[17]

Perhaps the most significant part of Hamilton's argument, however, is the statement that his intention is to put his fellow citizens upon their guard "against all attempts . . . to influence [their] decision in a matter of the utmost moment to [their] welfare by any impressions other than those which may result from the evidence of truth."[18] While we must admit that truth in the twenty-first century is an elusive construct at best, we must appreciate Hamilton's warning as well as the implication of his words: we must look for truth wherever we can find it, and we should know those big black lies when we see them. To paraphrase Ponsonby, if after serious reflection we can conclude that "such obvious bias [of propaganda] cannot possibly represent the truth," if through serious reflection we can detect what he refers to as "sham ideals" and "collective hysteria," we may begin to know it when we see it. It is, after all, the power of propaganda that to an extent makes truth so elusive, that makes detecting propaganda such an arduous task.

Whatever we may have learned from World War I propaganda, it remains one of the most remarkable phenomena of the twentieth century in its shameless use, among other things, of noncombatants as recruits and as propaganda images. Reflected and repeated in popular fiction, advertising, and films, the message of World War I propaganda became a pervasive fact of life in the Allied nations. Effective to the extent that dissent was virtually nonexistent, and those who dared dissent faced ostracism or in some cases jail, propaganda created a pre-Orwellian state or states.[19] By enlisting women and children in the absence of their fighting men, the family unit, the essential structure of the Gemeinschaft, participated, coerced, and informed in ways that promoted and achieved the goals of the state. In Orwell's *1984*, Winston Smith scribbles on a scrap of paper, "Freedom is the freedom to say that two plus two make four. If that is granted, all else follows."[20] But propaganda has the power, as does O'Brien in the novel, to make two plus two equal five. Propaganda has the power to make children inform on their parents. Parsons, who lives in Winston Smith's building, is proud of his daughter for stalking a "strange man" and turning him in as a spy.[21] The same daughter later turns Parsons in for ostensibly saying "Down with Big Brother!" in his sleep.[22] This is an accusation we might doubt, given the effects of propaganda on the child, effects we see in the Tick-Mouse series from World War I.

Orwell wrote *1984* perhaps with Stalinist Russia in mind, but the setting of the novel in London and the ideas Orwell expresses in the ubiquitous essay "Politics and the English Language" suggest that the power of the state is also ubiquitous, and that language, deceitfully or manipulatively used in the service of the state, is at the root of that power.[23] While Orwell's focus is language rather than images, the combination of the two, as we have seen, is even more powerful. Still the state continues to rely on the linguistic obfuscations Orwell deplores. The phrase "Mistakes were made" has become a political cliché. In its use of passive voice, the phrase automatically obliterates the truth, the crucial details—who made the mistake and why—and thereby becomes a form of propaganda. If we ask the questions who and why, if we endeavor, as I declared in my introduction, to know propaganda when we see it, be it words or images, if we learn from the lessons of World War I that propaganda can become pervasive, we may retain the right to say two plus two make four, an alternative far superior to learning to love Big Brother.

NOTES

Introduction

1. Dylan, "It's Alright, Ma (I'm Only Bleeding)."

2. Armstrong, "American Idiot."

3. Ponsonby, *Falsehood in War-Time*, 128. Most contemporary examinations of the Bryce report concur with Ponsonby. Peter Buitenhaus in *The Great War of Words* argues that the Bryce report was "largely a tissue of invention, unsubstantiated observations by unnamed witnesses, and second-hand eyewitness reports, depending far more on imagination than any other factor. The witnesses were not put on oath, nor were they cross-examined" (27). More recent than Buitenhaus's study, Horne and Kramer's *German Atrocities, 1914* examines atrocity stories from all perspectives, both Allied and German, "adopt[ing] the approach of a transnational cultural history" (5). In other words, Horne and Kramer actually attempt to sort out the truth, to determine what really happened during those early days of the war, an undertaking both difficult and admirable.

4. For an important essay on Smith's novel, see Jane Marcus's "Corpus/Corps/Corpse," 124–67. Marcus's essay also serves as the afterword to Feminist Press's 1988 reprint of Price's novel. My own essay "Propaganda, Militarism, and the Home Front" examines the cultural contexts of the home front as the novel sees them.

5. Goldman, *Women Writers and the Great War*, 77; and Cardinal et al., eds., *Women's Writing on the First World War*.

6. Haytock, *At Home, at War*, 8.

7. Haytock, *At Home, at War*, 118.

8. Haytock, *At Home, at War*, 119.

9. Banta, *Imaging American Women*, 590.

10. For a thorough historical examination of World War I propaganda in the United States, including a lengthy discussion of George Creel and the Committee on Public Information, see Stewart Halsey Ross's *Propaganda for War*.

11. Fraser, *Propaganda*, 1.

12. Fraser, *Propaganda*, 2 (my emphasis).

13. Fraser, *Propaganda*, 8.

14. Foucault, *Discipline and Punish*, 195–200.

15. Foucault, *Discipline and Punish*, 200.

16. Foucault, *Discipline and Punish*, 205.

17. Foucault, *Discipline and Punish*, 205.

18. Taylor, *Munitions of the Mind*, 8.

19. Taylor, *Munitions of the Mind*, 8.

20. Pratkanis and Aronson, *Age of Propaganda*, 24–26.

21. Pratkanis and Aronson, *Age of Propaganda*, 25.

22. Fraser, *Propaganda*, 2.

23. Huxley, *Brave New World*, 13.

24. Huxley, *Brave New World*, 28.

25. Huxley, *Brave New World*, 27.

26. Huxley, *Brave New World*, 47.

27. Huxley, *Brave New World*, 22.

28. Huxley, *Brave New World*, 42.

29. Pratkanis and Aronson, *Age of Propaganda*, 25.

30. Packard, *The Hidden Persuaders*, 1.

31. Packard, *The Hidden Persuaders*, 4.

32. Packard, *The Hidden Persuaders*, 2.

33. Louis Rose, in a 2003 essay, examines the work of art historian Ernst Kris, who applied the studies of Aby Warburg involving classic drama as well as the works of Freud to examine caricature art and ultimately to apply his theories to Nazi propaganda. According to Rose, Kris believed "caricature portraits possessed regressive traits—fusions, distortions, exaggerations, and schematized expressions—similar to those found in psychotic creations." In a convoluted process of ego adaptation to the perceived aggression of the caricature, according to Kris's theories, "caricature drawings demonstrated the psychological essence of art in the ability of the ego to confront visual images at different mental and emotional levels, and to respond to them from

shifting distances" (Rose, "Interpreting Propaganda," 124). Certainly Kris's views of Nazi propaganda, at least those involving caricature, can in Freudian terms be extended to World War I propaganda, much of which involves the use of caricature or of stereotype.

34. Gay, *Freud*, 368. Although Freud was Austrian and supported the German war effort in the beginning, he eventually tired of the war, and according to Gay, "by 1917, he mainly longed for the slaughter to end" (370).

35. Gay, *Freud*, 355.

36. Fraser, *Propaganda*, 32 (parentheses in original).

37. Keen, *Faces of the Enemy*, 1.

38. Keen, *Faces of the Enemy*, 19.

39. Keen, *Faces of the Enemy*, 8.

40. Keen, *Faces of the Enemy*, 12.

41. Jung is very clear in his definition of archetypes that their source is not social. In the opening essay of *Man and His Symbols*, Jung declares: "What we properly call instincts are physiological urges, and are perceived by the senses. But at the same time, they also manifest themselves in fantasies and often reveal their presence only by symbolic images. These manifestations are what I call archetypes. They are without known origin; and they reproduce themselves in any time or in any part of the world." Joseph Campbell in his work on world mythology also uses a Jungian approach. Campbell sees variations of basic archetypes in major religious figures and mythological heroes. His work encompasses the mythology of ancient cultures and more recent ones including Native American and African American folklore. It is Campbell's belief that all myth springs from the human psyche, thus confirming Keen's theory that our visions of the enemy also come from the same source. See Jung, "Approaching the Unconscious," 58; and J. Campbell, *The Masks of God*.

42. LeShan, *Psychology of War*, 36.

43. LeShan, *Psychology of War*, 36 (emphasis in original).

44. LeShan, *Psychology of War*, 36.

45. LeShan, *Psychology of War*, 34.

46. LeShan, *Psychology of War*, 24.

47. Lasswell, *Propaganda Technique*, 9 (my emphasis).

48. Lasswell, *Propaganda Technique*, 11.

49. Ponsonby, *Falsehood in War-Time*, 14–15.
50. Ponsonby, *Falsehood in War-Time*, 14.
51. Ponsonby, *Falsehood in War-Time*, 15.
52. Mills, *Power Elite*, 300.
53. Mills, *Power Elite*, 303.
54. Mills, *Power Elite*, 303.
55. Mills, *Power Elite*, 304.
56. Bailey, *Captain Tick-Mouse . . . Secret Service*.
57. Tönnies, *Ferdinand Tönnies*, 118.
58. Tönnies, *Ferdinand Tönnies*, 118.
59. Tönnies, *Ferdinand Tönnies*, 168 (my emphasis).
60. Tönnies, *Community and Society*, 37.
61. Tönnies, *Community and Society*, 37.
62. Tönnies, *Community and Society*, 65.
63. Elshtain, *Women and War*, 107 (emphasis in original).

1. Food Will Win the War

1. Mullendore, *History of the United States Food Administration*, 12.
2. Mullendore, *History of the United States Food Administration*, 12.
3. Merritt, *War Time Control of Distribution of Foods*, 148.
4. Merritt, *War Time Control of Distribution of Foods*, 148.
5. Mullendore, *History of the United States Food Administration*, 87.
6. Pollock, *The Food Administration in Iowa*, 122–23.
7. Shapiro, *Perfection Salad*, 4. For further discussions of domestic science and World War I see James, "The 'Enid Problem,'" 92–128.
8. Shapiro, *Perfection Salad*, 4.
9. Hoover depended upon "the spirit of self-sacrifice of the American people . . . to accomplish the necessary results upon a voluntary basis" (Mullendore, *History of the United States Food Administration*, 12).
10. Franks, *The Margin of Happiness*, 3–4.
11. Franks, *The Margin of Happiness*, 22.
12. Franks, *The Margin of Happiness*, 27.
13. Franks, *The Margin of Happiness*, 118.
14. Franks, *The Margin of Happiness*, 134.
15. Franks, *The Margin of Happiness*, 118.
16. Franks, *The Margin of Happiness*, 114.
17. Franks, *The Margin of Happiness*, 149.

18. Franks, *The Margin of Happiness*, 148.

19. *Selected Recipes for Wartimes*.

20. Franks, *The Margin of Happiness*, 152.

21. Franks, *The Margin of Happiness*, 212.

22. Hoover, "What I Would Like Women to Do," 25.

23. *Selected Recipes for Wartimes*, 1.

24. Hoover, "What I Would Like Women to Do," 25.

25. Hoover, "What I Would Like Women to Do," 25–26.

26. Kennedy, *Over Here*, 118.

27. Mullendore, *History of the United States Food Administration*, 12.

28. U.S. Food Administration, *War Cook Book for American Women*, 5.

29. The U.S. Food Administration Home Card for 1918 asks "every loyal American to help win the war by maintaining rigidly, as a minimum of saving, the following program." The plan outlined by the Home Card includes two wheatless days a week, every Monday and Wednesday; a meatless day on Tuesday; and porkless days on Tuesday and Saturday. Sugar and fats are to be saved every day, and vegetables used "abundantly." In case the purpose of the effort is not clear, the card states in all capital letters: "DISLOYALTY IN LITTLE THINGS GIVES AID TO THE ENEMY."

30. U.S. Food Administration, *War Cook Book for American Women*, 5.

31. U.S. Food Administration, *Food and the War*, introductory pages.

32. U.S. Food Administration, *Food and the War*, 372–74.

33. My own copy of *Food and the War*, obtained from an antique dealer, is inscribed by a Wellesley student in October of 1918. On the back flyleaf, she has penciled in the proportions of flour, fat, liquid, and salt for cream soup, gravy, and soufflé.

34. New Hampshire College Extension Service, "Extension Circular No. 21," 2.

35. New Hampshire College Extension Service, "Extension Circular No. 21," 4.

36. Mullendore, *History of the United States Food Administration*, 83.

37. Mullendore, *History of the United States Food Administration*, 84.

38. Mullendore, *History of the United States Food Administration*, 85.

39. Northend, "Harmony in the Breakfast Room," 91–94.

40. Pamphlet issued by Federal Food Administration for Nebraska.

41. Hill, "Food Suggestions for August–September," 124.

42. "Queries and Answers," 135.

43. Hill, "Seasonable and Tested Recipes," 500–502.

44. Plumley, "The Basis of Victory," 484.

45. "To Teach Cooking to College Girls," 575–76.

46. "The Wiser Person," "On Having a Case," 590.

47. "The Wiser Person," "On Having a Case," 590. Popular music of the day also reflected Hoover's call to conserve food. "Hoover Hooverize" by Mrs. Melrose Scales declares,

> We'll Hoover Hooverize
> We'll cut out cakes and pies
> Have bread puddin's
> O they're good uns
> We must all economize.

The song is, of course, dedicated to Herbert Hoover and approved by the U.S. Food Administration (Scales, "Hoover Hooverize").

48. Neal, "Helping Hoover on Thanksgiving Day," 26.

49. Neal, "Helping Hoover on Thanksgiving Day," 27.

50. Leffingwell and Lucas, "Don't Forget the Salvation Army (My Doughnut Girl)." My copy of this sheet music, according to a stamp on the cover, belonged to the Thelma Leah Rose School of Dancing, which we might speculate used it as the score for a dance number.

51. "The Weaker Sex?" 3.

52. "The Weaker Sex?" 3.

53. "The Weaker Sex?" 3.

54. "The Weaker Sex?" 12.

55. Goewey, "Women to the Farmer's Rescue," 444.

56. Scott, "How to Save Half the Wheat."

57. National War Garden Commission, *Home Drying and Canning*, 1.

58. Fussell, *The Great War and Modern Memory*, 116.

59. Fussell, *The Great War and Modern Memory*, 116.

60. Quoted in Ponsonby, *Falsehood in War-Time*, 103.

61. Ponsonby, *Falsehood in War-Time*, 108–10.

62. *Selected Recipes for Wartimes*, 1.

63. *Best War Time Recipes*.

64. U.S. Food Administration, *War Economy in Food*, 8.

65. U.S. Food Administration, *War Economy in Food*, 11.

66. U.S. Food Administration, *War Economy in Food*, 9. Much of this exhortation is repeated in U.S. Food Administration, *War Cook Book for American Women*, 11–12, this time attributed to Herbert Hoover.

67. Hill, *War Time Recipes*, 4.

68. *Recipes for War Breads*, 6–7. The C. I. Hood Company, makers of Hood's Sarsaparilla, Peptiron, and Hood's Pills, also put out a war cookbook, *Hood's Leftovers: War Edition*. In the introduction, this booklet repeats the admonition, "If we are selfish or even careless, we are disloyal, we are the enemy at home" (4). This warning shares the same page with a testimonial for Hood's Sarsaparilla.

69. *Hood's Leftovers: War Edition*, flyleaf.

70. Hoover, "What I Would Like Women to Do," 25.

71. Banta, *Imaging American Women*, xxviii.

72. Banta, *Imaging American Women*, xxviii.

73. Banta, *Imaging American Women*, xxviii.

74. Hull, "Food for Thought?" 265.

75. Hull, "Food for Thought?" 266.

76. Hull, "Food for Thought?" 270.

77. For a study of food rationing in World War II, see Bently's *Eating for Victory*. Bently focuses on World War II propaganda and what she refers to as the "Wartime Homemaker," devoting limited space to the precedent of Hoover's World War I propaganda campaign, the U.S. Food Administration, and the National War Garden Commission, which in posters asks women "Are YOU a Victory Canner?"

78. Marwick, *The Deluge*, 193.

79. Both American and British posters appealed to women to conserve food. Often posters are class specific, not only in the food items depicted but in the clothing and hairstyles of the women.

80. Peel, *The Eat-Less-Meat Book*, 19.

81. Peel, *The Eat-Less-Meat Book*, 32.

82. Marwick, *The Deluge*, 196.

83. Peel, *The Eat-Less-Meat Book*, 42.

84. "Ham Croquettes That Are Different," 2.

85. *War-Time Cook and Health Book*. The date printed on the Hoover conservation request is July 23, 1917, roughly three weeks before Congress formally appointed Hoover head of its newly created Food Administration.

86. In his strongest antiwar poem, "Dulce et Decorum Est," Owen indirectly addresses poet Jessie Pope, author of numerous children's books as well as *War Poems* and *More War Poems*, verse of the newspaper variety, by suggesting that if she had seen the death from phosgene gas described in the poem,

> My friend, you would not tell with such high zest
> To children ardent for some desperate glory,
> the old Lie: Dulce et decorum est
> Pro patria mori.

Owen had in early drafts dedicated the poem to Pope but removed the dedication in the final draft. See Owen, *The Collected Poems of Wilfred Owen*, 55.

87. Wells, *Mr. Britling Sees It Through*, 188.

88. Wells, *Mr. Britling Sees It Through*, 188.

89. Wells, *Mr. Britling Sees It Through*, 253.

90. Peel, *The Eat-Less-Meat Book*, 32.

91. Smith, *Not So Quiet*. References to the novel are cited parenthetically in the text.

2. "One Hundred Percent"

1. Keen, *Faces of the Enemy*, 12.

2. For a discussion of popular literature that encouraged American participation in the war see Quinn, *The Conning of America*. Quinn argues that among other issues, American "financial houses" had an economic interest in seeing that the Allied nations were not defeated because the Allies owed American banks for loans issued prior to the war. American popular literature, according to Quinn, used prevalent stereotypical images of German militarism to sway public opinion to favor a declaration of war against Germany, and "once war was declared, the German military and their people could be easily demonized into

being seen as a threat to American democracy and traditions" (vi). While Quinn touches on some of the same areas as this study, his focus is on work intended for a more general audience.

3. Ponsonby, *Falsehood in War-Time*, 78.

4. Ponsonby, *Falsehood in War-Time*, 78.

5. Ponsonby, *Falsehood in War-Time*, 79.

6. Graves, *Good-Bye to All That* (1930), 223. The 1957 reprint omits the phrase "British or French shell-fire as likely as not" (183). Both versions call the shelling or bombing "accidental-on-purpose."

7. Ponsonby, *Falsehood in War-Time*, 78.

8. Kipling, "The Vampire," 220 (the edition does not use line numbers).

9. Browne, "The Mellow-drammer," 348–49.

10. Browne, "Mary and Marie," 13.

11. Browne, "Mary and Marie," 79.

12. *McClure's Magazine* 5, no. 47 (September 1916): 25.

13. Gatlin, "New York Stuff," 13. Further references are cited parenthetically in the text.

14. "With Such a Spirit—," 5.

15. "With Such a Spirit—," 5.

16. Witwer, "It's the Huns!" 46–48.

17. According to a review in the April 4, 1918, issue of the *New York Times*, the play "acquired an American background to its action [and] in the total effect [the two plays] are quite different" (11).

18. Worrall and Terry, *The White Feather*, 1915), 21. The book was published in England by Howard J. Clode. Further references are cited parenthetically in the text.

19. Gullace, "White Feathers and Wounded Men," 182. Further references are cited parenthetically in the text.

20. As we saw earlier, Jennifer Haytock raises a similar issue in terms of American culture when she suggests "women were resented by veterans" for their participation in the war and because they could not "comprehend [the soldier's] experiences and resulting psychological trauma" (*At Home, at War*, 119).

21. "Killing Fields: The First World War," videocassette.

22. Ferber, "One Hundred Percent," 11. Further references are cited parenthetically in the text.

23. Roosevelt, "The Great Adventure," 9.

24. Gilbert, *The First World War*, 441.

25. Gilbert, *The First World War*, 441.

26. Gatlin, "A Star in the Window," 36. Further references are cited parenthetically in the text.

27. Graves, *Good-Bye to All That* (1930), 273.

28. Graves, *Good-Bye to All That* (1930), 271.

29. Owen, *The Collected Poems of Wilfred Owen*, 67–68.

30. Sassoon, *The War Poems of Siegfried Sassoon*, 30. In one of the private listening booths at the Liberty Memorial, the official U.S. World War I Museum in Kansas City, Missouri, visitors can hear a British actor reading Sassoon's poem.

31. "Letters of a Japanese Schoolboy" first appeared as a column in *Collier's* weekly magazine. In 1909 a collection of the early columns appeared in book form. In the letters, Irwin created the fictional character Hashimura Togo, a stereotypical and racist caricature that was nevertheless popular in the United States until the beginning of World War II. Yoshiko Uzawa writes extensively about the character's reception, including Mark Twain's endorsement of him as the "dearest & sweetest & frankest & wisest & funniest & delightfulest & loveablest creation that has been added to our literature for some time." (Uzawa, "'Will White Man and Yellow Man Ever Mix?'" 202–3).

32. Irwin, "One of Ten Million," 15. Further references are cited parenthetically in the text.

33. *The Delineator* 91, no. 3 (September 1917): 21.

34. "*The Delineator*'s Women's Preparedness Bureau," 34.

35. "*The Delineator*'s Women's Preparedness Bureau," 34.

36. "Women, War and the New Fashions," 53.

37. Chalmers, "Remade Dresses that Gratify the Craving," 62–63.

38. Shepherd, "The Soul That Stirs," 56.

39. Shepherd, "The Soul That Stirs," 5.

40. "Service Uniforms of Red Cross Workers," 45–51.

3. VADs and Khaki Girls

1. Cather, *One of Ours*, 194.

2. Gilbert, *The First World War*, 514.

3. *Life Magazine*, April 17, 1944, 87.

4. Gilbert, *The First World War*, 202–3.

5. Caddigan and Brenan, "The Rose of No Man's Land."

6. Rogers and Monaco, "I'm Going to Follow the Boys."

7. Since love is the outcome of "Twenty-Two," calling it a love story on the cover is not misleading. In fact, the only reference to war on the cover of this issue of *Metropolitan* is the Teddy Roosevelt article that deals with "Volunteering and Conscription." The Haskell Coffin cover illustration is of a young woman in a filmy white dress cradling a dozen roses and holding what appears to be a diploma in her hand. Although the United States entered the war in April of 1917, war fervor had not yet come to dominate popular magazines.

8. Rinehart, "Twenty-Two," 10. Further references are cited parenthetically in the text.

9. R. W. Campbell, *Dorothy, VAD and the Doctor*, 12. Further references are cited parenthetically in the text.

10. Gurlitz, "The Dog of War," 18. Further references are cited parenthetically in the text. Although most of the features in this issue of *Metropolitan* focus on the war, the cover is another Haskell Coffin illustration of a young woman, this one in a red raincoat posing with her umbrella.

11. Emerson, *Ruth Fielding in the Red Cross*, 42. Further references are cited parenthetically in the text.

12. U.S. Committee on Public Information, "Spies and Lies," 38.

13. Emerson, *Ruth Fielding at the War Front*, 61. Further references are cited parenthetically in the text.

14. Emerson, *Ruth Fielding Homeward Bound*, 145. Further references are cited parenthetically in the text.

15. Trent, *Alice Blythe Somewhere in England*, n.p.

16. Trent, *Alice Blythe Somewhere in England*, n.p.

17. Trent, *Helen Carey Somewhere in America*, 11. Further references are cited parenthetically in the text. Continuing in the tradition of the spunky heroine, the 2007 novel *The Hearts of Horses* by Molly Gloss is similar at least in tone to *Helen Carey Somewhere in America*. Set in 1917, the Gloss novel follows nineteen-year-old Martha Lessen, a horse whisperer, as she negotiates the difficulties of doing a man's job in the rough terrain of eastern Oregon. While the war plays a smaller

role in Martha's life than it does in Helen Carey's, Martha is a tough girl who is at times more comfortable with a horse than she is with humans.

18. Trent, *Marieken De Bruin Somewhere in Belgium*, 13–14. Further references are cited parenthetically in the text.

19. Trent, *Valerie Duval Somewhere in France*, 12. Further references are cited parenthetically in the text.

20. Trent, *Alice Blythe Somewhere in England*, 211.

21. While Hemingway and other war writers who were in Italy denigrate the Italian Army to the extent that the Italian front is more or less a joke, that sentiment is lacking in the Martha Trent series, not surprising since the idea here is to garner support for all of the Allies, not just some of them.

22. Trent, *Lucia Rudini Somewhere in Italy*, 156.

23. Trent, *Phoebe Marshall Somewhere in Canada*, 129.

24. Van Dyne, *Aunt Jane's Nieces in the Red Cross*. Similar novels include *Mary Louise and the Liberty Girls*, also by Edith Van Dyne, and the 1918–20 Khaki Girls series by Edna Brooks: *The Khaki Girls of the Motor Corps*, *The Khaki Girls behind the Lines*, *The Khaki Girls at Windsor Barracks*, and *The Khaki Girls in Victory*. While the postwar publication dates of the last two Khaki Girls novels renders them moot in terms of propaganda, they still serve as exemplars for young girls who want to perform public service within the realm of acceptable boundaries.

25. Brett, Cover illustration, *Ladies' Home Journal*, October 1918.

26. Warwick, "To You: The American Girl War Worker," 1.

27. Wyckoff, "The Girls behind the Men," 3.

28. Deland, "The American Girl 'Over There,'" 20.

29. Deland, "The American Girl 'Over There,'" 20.

30. Meyer, *A World Undone*, 576–77.

31. Meyer, *A World Undone*, 577.

32. Meyer, *A World Undone*, 577.

33. Marcus, "Corpus/Corps/Corpse," 124–67.

34. Haytock, *At Home, at War*, 119.

4. "Learning to Hate the German Beast"

1. Ponsonby, *Falsehood in War-Time*, 14.

2. Higonnet, "War Games," 4.

3. Higonnet, "War Games," 12.

4. Browne, "A Liberty Loan Primer," n.p.

5. Browne, "A Primer for Pacifists," 17.

6. Browne, "A Primer for Pacifists," 17.

7. Wilcox, "One Night in May," 30 (emphasis in original).

8. Lupton, "ABC for Little Willie and Others."

9. Bailey, *Captain Tick-Mouse . . . Secret Service*, 6.

10. Bailey, *Captain Tick-Mouse . . . Secret Service*, 7.

11. Bailey, *Captain Tick-Mouse . . . Torch Bearers*.

12. Burgess, *Happy Jack's Thrift Club*, n.p.

13. Burgess, *Happy Jack's Thrift Club*.

14. Burgess, *Happy Jack's Thrift Club*.

15. "Attention, American School Children!"

16. "The Junior Four Minute Men War Savings Contest," 2.

17. "The Junior Four Minute Men War Savings Contest," 6.

18. Owen, *The Collected Poems of Wilfred Owen*, 26.

19. Owen, *The Collected Poems of Wilfred Owen*, 29–30.

20. U.S. Food Administration, *Food Saving and Sharing*, v.

21. U.S. Food Administration, *Food Saving and Sharing*, v.

22. American Red Cross, *Junior Activities Teachers Manual*, flyleaf.

23. American Red Cross, *Junior Activities Teachers Manual*, 242–43.

24. American Red Cross, *Junior Activities Teachers Manual*, 243–44.

25. American Red Cross, *Junior Activities Teachers Manual*, 245.

26. American Red Cross, *Junior Activities Teachers Manual*, 248–49.

27. Higonnet, "War Games," 4.

28. Notter, *Soldier Bob*, n.p.

29. Conrad and Ehrlich, "There's Nobody Home but Me."

30. "Fold-A-Way War Nurses," supplement to the *North American* (Philadelphia) January 27, 1918.

31. Orville, *American Heroes*, n.p.

32. Cordon and Tindall, *Our Hospital* ABC.

33. Niké, *Les Soldats de la Grande Guerre*, n.p.

34. Niké, *Les Soldats de la Grande Guerre*.

35. Higonnet, "War Games," 4.

36. *The Soldier Painting Book*, no. 43. *In the Ranks*, no. 244, depicts

the story of Bobby and Eleanor, whose Uncle Jack enlists in the U.S. Army. Jack tells Eleanor that he is not afraid of being wounded because "if I do, I will be well taken care of by the Red Cross Doctors and nurses. There is always an ambulance nearby to take the wounded to the hospital"—unless Jack is wounded in No Man's Land and no one can reach him. *Our Army*, no. 65 in Our Allies Series, is a collection of color drawings of anti-aircraft guns, a parachute, and a dirigible (9). The format of the postwar *My Book of Sailors* is similar to that of the *Soldier Painting Book* except that it is illustrated with color drawings.

37. The booklet in my collection was issued in Newcastle-upon-Tyne on October 28, 1918, only a few days before the end of the war. Many of the meat and lard coupons have been used.

38. Wood, *Ten Little Sausages*, n.p.

39. Kennedy, *Over Here*, 68.

40. Paget, *Records of the Raids*, 17. Further references are cited parenthetically in the text.

41. "True Stories" by John Lea in his *Brave Boys and Girls in Wartime* tells the stories of Allied children who contributed to the war effort, including the stories of children who died bravely. "The Story of Doris Walton" chronicles the death of a young girl who was wounded on a playground during a bombing raid in London in 1917. Two Canadian soldiers wearing wound stripes carry her to the ambulance and she kisses them both because they have also suffered. "They were the last [kisses] that the little heroine would give," we are told, because she dies before midnight. The undated publication refers to dates as late as February 1918 but may well have been published after the war as an example to children should the opportunity arise again.

42. Ponsonby, *Falsehood in War-Time*, 14.

5. The Hun Is at the Gate

1. Kipling, "For All We Have and Are," 328–29. The poem first appeared in the *Times* of London.

2. Kipling, "The Rowers," 281–82.

3. Quinn, *The Conning of America*, 72–73.

4. Quinn, *The Conning of America*, 97.

5. Quinn, *The Conning of America*, 99.

6. Ponsonby, *Falsehood in War-Time*, 78.

7. Bryce, comp. *Evidence and Documents Laid Before the Committee on Alleged German Outrages*.

8. Drinker, *Our War for Human Rights*, 48.

9. Graves, *Good-Bye to All That* (1930), 223.

10. Meyer, *A World Undone*, 609.

11. Gilbert, *The First World War*, 540–41.

12. Hemingway, "A Way You'll Never Be," 306.

13. Hemingway, "Soldier's Home," 111–16.

14. Marshall, *Horrors and Atrocities of the Great War*, n.p.

15. Beck, *The War and Humanity*, 152.

16. Beck, *The War and Humanity*, 152.

17. Beck, *The War and Humanity*, 153.

18. Beck, *The War and Humanity*, 154.

19. Quinn, *The Conning of America*, 50.

20. Beck, *The War and Humanity*, 246–47.

21. Beck, *The War and Humanity*, 214.

22. Beck, *The War and Humanity*, 268.

23. "Miss Cavell's Execution," 660.

24. "Miss Cavell's Execution," 661.

25. Drinker, *Our War for Human Rights*, 242.

26. Berkeley, *Dawn*, xxvii.

27. Protheroe, *A Noble Woman*, 66. Protheroe repeats verbatim the chapter "Blood of the Martyr," describing her execution in the later volume *Edith Cavell: Nurse and Martyr*, 63–74. In a chapter called "The World's Press" Protheroe transcribes a number of press releases about Cavell's death. One newspaper account from the French *L'Homme Enchainé* declares that Cavell collapsed "in a moment of weakness and distress by which the splendour of His sacrifice was increased." In this version, the officer who shoots Cavell "with his hand red with blood, signed to his 'men,' if such I may call them, that the work of Germania was done" (153).

28. Protheroe, *Edith Cavell: Nurse and Martyr*, 69.

29. Berkeley, *Dawn*, xxxiv–xxxv.

30. Elkon, *Edith Cavell: Heroic Nurse*, 185–86.

31. Elkon, *Edith Cavell: Heroic Nurse*, 186.

32. Marwick, *The Deluge*, 98.

33. Kipling, "The Rowers," 281–82.

34. Kipling, "Swept and Garnished," 411. Further references are cited parenthetically in the text.

35. Bella Armine in Kipling's "A Madonna of the Trenches" appears as a ghost or mass hallucination after her death from an apparent abortion. Both her nephew Clem Strangwick and her lover John Godsoe see her as they walk though the trenches. The apparition finally lures Godsoe to commit suicide so he can spend eternity with Bella.

36. *Hearts of the World: The Story of a Village*, scenario by M. Gaston de Tolignac.

37. *Hearts of the World.*

38. *The Little American*, screenplay by Jeanie Macpherson. The version referred to here was issued on DVD in 2007 by Televista, Incorporated.

39. De Costa and Wood, "Are You Half the Man Your Mother Thought You'd Be?"

40. Bayha, "I'd Be Proud to Be the Mother of a Soldier."

41. Bayha, "I'd Be Proud to Be the Mother of a Soldier" (emphasis in original).

42. Gaskill et al., "That's a Mother's Liberty Loan."

43. Lang and Sterling, "America, Here's My Boy."

44. Rubens, "Your King and Country Want You."

45. Clark and Schwartz, "Britannia Needs You Like a Mother."

46. Downs, "That Family Called the U.S.A."

47. *Ladies' Home Journal*, October 1918, 55.

48. *Ladies' Home Journal*, October 1918, 59–60.

49. *Augusta (Georgia) Herald*, July 10, 1917, 9.

50. *Augusta (Georgia) Herald*, July 10, 1917, 9 (emphasis in original).

51. *McClure's Win-the-War Magazine*, front cover.

52. *McClure's Win-the-War Magazine*, 6.

53. *Today's Housewife* 7, no. 14 (November 1918).

54. Tönnies, *Ferdinand Tönnies*, 168 (my emphasis).

Conclusion

1. Creel, *How We Advertised America*, ix.

2. Creel, *How We Advertised America*, ix (emphasis in original).

3. Newton D. Baker, foreword to Creel, *How We Advertised America,* xv.

4. Baker foreword to Creel, *How We Advertised America,* xv.

5. Dos Passos, *Nineteen Nineteen,* 221.

6. Dos Passos, *Nineteen Nineteen,* 221 (my emphasis).

7. Dos Passos, *Nineteen Nineteen,* 222.

8. Dos Passos, U.S.A., vii.

9. Creel, *How We Advertised America,* 266.

10. Bernays, *Propaganda,* 37.

11. Bernays, *Propaganda,* 11.

12. Ponsonby, *Falsehood in War-Time,* 13.

13. Ponsonby, *Falsehood in War-Time,* 14–15.

14. Bernays, *Propaganda,* 39.

15. Huxley, *Brave New World,* 42.

16. Hamilton, "Vigour of Government Is Essential," 221.

17. Hamilton, "Vigour of Government Is Essential," 221.

18. Hamilton, "Vigour of Government Is Essential," 221–22.

19. The socialist poet Ralph Chaplin was sentenced to twenty years in prison for his antiwar opinions.

20. Orwell, *1984,* 69.

21. Orwell, *1984,* 50.

22. Orwell, *1984,* 193.

23. Orwell, "Politics and the English Language," 77–92.

BIBLIOGRAPHY

American Red Cross, Department of Development, Junior Membership. *Junior Red Cross Activities Teachers Manual*. New York: Douglas C. MacMurtrie, 1918.

Armstrong, Billie Joe. "American Idiot." *American Idiot*, Green Day, Reprise Records, 2004.

"Attention, American School Children!" Washington: National Committee of Patriotic Societies, Division on Women's War Work, n.d.

Augusta Herald. Augusta GA. Advertising Section. July 10, 1917, 9.

Bailey, Roy Rutherford. *Captain Tick-Mouse and his Adventures in Secret Service*. Chicago: Elgin National Watch Company, 1917.

———. *Captain Tick-Mouse and His Adventures with the Torch Bearers* Chicago: Elgin National Watch Company, 1918.

Baker, Newton D. Foreword to *How We Advertised in America* by George Creel. New York: Harper and Brothers, 1920. xi–xviii.

Banta, Martha. *Imaging American Women: Ideas and Ideals in Cultural History*. New York: Columbia University Press, 1987.

Bayha, Charles. "I'd Be Proud to Be the Mother of a Soldier." New York: Shapiro, Bernstein and Company, 1915.

Beck, James M. *The War and Humanity*. 2nd ed. New York: G. P. Putnam's Sons, 1917.

Bently, Amy. *Eating for Victory: Food Rationing and the Politics of Domesticity*. Urbana: University of Illinois Press, 1998.

Berkeley, Captain Reginald, M.P. *Dawn*. New York: J. H. Sears and Company, 1928.

Bernays, Edward *Propaganda*. Introduction by Mark Crispin Miller. 1928; reprint, Brooklyn: Ig Publishing, 2005.

Best War Time Recipes. New York: Royal Baking Powder Company, 1918.

Brett, Harold. Cover illustration. *Ladies' Home Journal*, October, 1918.

Brooks, Edna. *The Khaki Girls behind the Lines*. New York: Cupples and Leon Company, 1918.

———. *The Khaki Girls in Victory*. New York: Cupples and Leon, 1920.

———. *The Khaki Girls of the Motor Corps*. New York: Cupples and Leon Company, 1918.

———. *The Khaki Girls at Windsor Barracks*. New York: Cupples and Leon Company, 1919.

Browne, Porter Emerson. "A Liberty Loan Primer." Illustrated by James Montgomery Flagg. Washington: Liberty Loan Committee, 1918.

———. "Mary and Marie." *McClure's Magazine* 5, no. 47 (September 1916): 13+.

———. "The Mellow-drammer." *Everybody's Magazine*, September 1909, 348–349, qtd. in Lewin Goff, "The Owen Davis–Al Woods Melodrama Factory," *Educational Theater Journal* 11, no. 3 (1959): 201.

———. "A Primer for Pacifists." *McClure's Magazine*, May 1917, 17.

Bryce, Viscount O. M., comp. *Evidence and Documents Laid before the Committee on Alleged German Outrages: Being an Appendix to the Report of the Committee Appointed by His Britannic Majesty's Government*. Ottawa: Government Printing Bureau, 1916.

Buitenhaus, Peter. *The Great War of Words: British, American, and Canadian Propaganda and Fiction, 1914–1933*. Vancouver: University of British Columbia Press, 1987.

Burgess, Anthony. *A Clockwork Orange*. New York: W. W. Norton, 1995.

Burgess, Thornton W. *Happy Jack's Thrift Club*. Illustrated by Harrison Cody. Boston: Savings Division of the First Federal Reserve District, 1918.

Caddigan, Jack, and James A. Brenan. "The Rose of No Man's Land." New York: Leo Feist, 1918.

Campbell, Joseph. *The Masks of God*. 4 vols. New York: Viking, 1959–68.

Campbell, R. W. *Dorothy, VAD and the Doctor*. London: W. and R. Chambers, 1918.

Cardinal, Agnès, Dorothy Goldman, and Judith Hattaway, eds. *Women's*

Writing on the First World War. Oxford: Oxford University Press, 1999.
Cather, Willa. *One of Ours*. 1922; reprint, New York: Vintage, 1991.
Chalmers, Eleanor. "Remade Dresses that Gratify the Craving for New Clothes and Satisfy Your War-Time Conscious." *Delineator* 92, no. 3 (March 1918): 62–63.
Clark, Grant, and Jean Schwartz. "Britannia Needs You Like a Mother (Would You Turn Your Mother Down?)." Sydney: D. Davis and Company, n.d.
Conrad, Con, and Sam Ehrlich. "There's Nobody Home but Me." New York: Broadway Music Corporation, 1918.
Cordon, Hampden, and M. C. Tindall. *Our Hospital ABC*. Illustrated by Joyce Dennys. 3rd ed. London: John Lane, n.d.
Creel, George. *How We Advertised America: The First Telling of the Amazing Story of the Committee on Public Information That Carried the Gospel Of Americanism to Every Corner of the Globe*. New York: Harper and Brothers, 1920.
De Costa, Harry, and Leo Wood. "Are You Half the Man Your Mother Thought You'd Be?" New York: Leo Feist, 1916.
Deland, Margaret. "The American Girl 'Over There.'" *Ladies' Home Journal*, October 1918, 20.
"*The Delineator*'s Women's Preparedness Bureau: How a Typical American Village Solved the Problem." *Delineator* 91, no. 3 (September 1917): 34.
Dos Passos, John. *Nineteen Nineteen*. In the *U.S.A.* trilogy. New York: Modern Library, 1937.
Downs, Billy. "That Family Called the U.S.A." Chicago: Ted Browne Music Company, 1919.
Drinker, Frederick E. *Our War for Human Rights: Being an Intensely Human and Brilliant Account of the World War and Why and for What Purpose America and the Allies Are Fighting*. Washington: National Publishing Company, 1917.
Dylan, Bob. "It's Alright, Ma (I'm Only Bleeding)." *Bringing It All Back Home*, Columbia Records, 1965.
Elkon, Juliette. *Edith Cavell: Heroic Nurse*. New York: Julian Messner, 1956.
Elshtain, Jean Bethke. *Women and War*. New York: Basic Books, 1987.

Emerson, Alice B. *Ruth Fielding Homeward Bound*. New York: Cupples and Leon Company, 1919.

———. *Ruth Fielding in the Red Cross*. New York: Cupples and Leon Company, 1918.

———. *Ruth Fielding at the War Front*. New York: Cupples and Leon Company, 1918.

Ferber, Edna. "One Hundred Percent." *Metropolitan*, October 1918, 5+.

"Fold-A-Way War Nurses." Supplement to *The North American* (Philadelphia), 27 January, 1918.

Ford, Ford Madox. *Parade's End*. 1950; reprint, New York: Vintage, 1979.

Foucault, Michel. *Discipline and Punish: The Birth of the Prison*. Translated by Alan Sheridan. 1975; reprint, New York: Vintage, 1995.

Franks, Thetta Quay. *The Margin of Happiness: The Reward of Thrift*. New York: G. P. Putnam's Sons, 1917.

Fraser, Lindley. *Propaganda*. London: Oxford University Press, 1957.

Fussell, Paul *The Great War and Modern Memory*. New York: Oxford University Press, 1975.

Gaskill, Clarence, lyricist, and Mayo and Tally, composers. "That's a Mother's Liberty Loan." New York: M. Whitmark and Sons, 1917.

Gatlin, Dana. "New York Stuff." *McClure's Magazine*, March 1918, 13+.

———. "A Star in the Window." *McClure's Magazine*, August, 1918, 24+.

Gay, Peter. *Freud: A Life for Our Time*. New York: W. W. Norton, 1988.

Gilbert, Martin. *The First World War: A Complete History*. New York: Henry Holt, 1994.

Gloss, Molly. *The Hearts of Horses*. (Boston: Houghton Mifflin, 2007).

Goewey, Edwin A. "Women to the Farmer's Rescue: The Hand That Rocks the Cradle Must Be the Hand to Feed the World." *Leslie's Weekly Illustrated Newspaper* 3264 (1918): 440+.

Goldman, Dorothy, with Jane Gledhill and Judith Hattaway. *Women Writers and the Great War*. New York: Twayne Publishers, 1995.

Graves, Robert, *Good-Bye to All That*. New York: Vail-Ballou Press, 1930; reprint, New York: Anchor-Doubleday, 1957.

Gullace, Nicoletta F. "White Feathers and Wounded Men: Female Patriotism and the Memory of the Great War." *Journal of British Studies* 36 (April 1997): 178–206.

Gurlitz, Amy Landon. "The Dog of War." *Metropolitan*, April 1918, 16+.

"Ham Croquettes That Are Different." *Saturday Evening Post*, September 21, 1918, 2.

Hamilton, Alexander. "Vigour of Government Is Essential to the Security of Liberty," *The Federalist I*, in *The Debate on the Constitution: Federalist and Antifederalist Speeches, Articles, and Letters during the Struggle over Ratification*, Part One. New York: Library Classics of the United States, 1993. 219–23.

Haytock, Jennifer. *At Home, at War: Domesticity and World War I in American Literature*. Columbus: Ohio State University Press, 2003.

Hearts of the World: The Story of a Village. Scenario by M. Gaston de Tolignac. Trans. Captain Victor Marler. Directed by D. W. Griffith. D. W. Griffith Production Company, 12 March, 1918.

Hemingway, Ernest. "A Way You'll Never Be." *The Complete Short Stories of Ernest Hemingway*, Finca Vigia Edition. New York: Charles Scribner's Sons, 1987. 306–15.

———. "Soldier's Home." *The Complete Short Stories of Ernest Hemingway*, Finca Vigia Edition. New York: Charles Scribner's Sons, 1987. 111–16.

Higonnet, Margaret R. "War Games." *The Lion and the Unicorn* 22 (1998): 1–17.

Hill, Janet McKenzie. "Food Suggestions for August–September." *American Cookery* 23, no. 2 (August–September 1918): 124.

———. "Seasonable and Tested Recipes." *American Cookery* 22, no.7 (February 1918): 500–502.

———. *War Time Recipes*. Cincinnati: Procter and Gamble Company, 1918.

Hood's Leftovers: War Edition. Lowell MA: C. I. Hood Company, 1918.

Hoover, Herbert. "What I Would Like Women to Do." *Ladies' Home Journal*. August, 1917, 25.

Horne, John, and Alan Kramer. *German Atrocities, 1914: A History of Denial*. New Haven: Yale University Press, 2001.

Hull, Andrew J. "Food for Thought? The Relations between the Royal

Society Food Committees and Government, 1915–19." *Annals of Science* 59 (2002): 263–98.

Huxley, Aldous. *Brave New World*. 1932; reprint, New York: Perennial Classics, 1998.

In the Ranks. No. 244. New York: Sam Cabrill Sons and Company, 1918.

Irwin, Wallace. "One of Ten Million." *McClure's Magazine*, December 1917.

James, Pearl. "The 'Enid Problem': Dangerous Modernity in *One of Ours*." In *Cather Studies, Volume 6: History, Memory, and War*, ed. Steven Trout, 92–128. Lincoln: University of Nebraska Press, 2006.

"The Junior Four Minute Men War Savings Contest: For the United States of America." Washington: Government Printing Office, 1918.

Jung, Carl. "Approaching the Unconscious." In *Man and His Symbols*, ed. M.-L. Von Franz. New York: Dell, 1964.

Keen, Sam. *Faces of the Enemy: Reflections of the Hostile Imagination*. 1986; reprint, San Francisco: Harper Collins, 1991.

Kennedy, David M. *Over Here: The First World War and American Society*. Oxford: Oxford University Press, 1980.

"Killing Fields: The First World War." *People's Century*. Produced and directed by Bill Treharne Jones. Videocassette, 60 in. WGBH Boston, 1997.

Kingsbury, Celia M. *The Peculiar Sanity of War: Hysteria in the Literature of World War One*. Lubbock: Texas Tech University Press, 2002.

———. "Propaganda, Militarism, and the Home Front in Helen Zenna Smith's *Not So Quiet . . . Stepdaughters of War*." In *War and Words: Horror and Heroism in the Literature of Warfare*, ed. Sara Deats, Lagretta Tallent Lenker, and Merry G. Perry. New York: Rowman and Littlefield, 2004. 235–51.

———. "Squeezed into an Unnatural Shape: Bayliss Wheeler and the Element of Control in One of Ours." *Cather Studies, Volume 6: History, Memory, and War*, ed. Steven Trout, 129–44. Lincoln: University of Nebraska Press, 2006.

Kipling, Rudyard. "For All We Have and Are." In *Rudyard Kipling's Verse*. New York: Doubleday, 1940.

———. "A Madonna of the Trenches." In *Debits and Credits*. London: Macmillan, 1926.

———. "The Rowers." In *Rudyard Kipling's Verse*. New York: Doubleday, 1940.

———. *Rudyard Kipling's Verse: The Definitive Edition*. New York: Doubleday, 1940.

———. "Swept and Garnished." In *A Diversity of Creatures*. New York: Doubleday, 1917.

———. "The Vampire." In *Rudyard Kipling's Verse*. New York: Doubleday, 1940.

Ladies' Home Journal, October 1918.

Lang, Arthur, and Andrew B. Sterling. "America, Here's My Boy." New York: Joe Morris Music Company, 1917.

Lasswell, Harold D. *Propaganda Technique in World War I*. MIT Studies in Comparative Politics. 1927; reprint, Cambridge: MIT Press, 1971.

Lea, Fannie Heaslip. "Half-Past the Eleventh Hour." *Good Housekeeping*, July 1918, 29+.

Lea, John. *Brave Boys and Girls in War-Time*. London: Blackie and Son, n.d.

Leffingwell, Elmore, and James Lucas. "Don't Forget the Salvation Army (My Doughnut Girl)." New York: Broadway Music Corporation, 1918.

LeShan, Lawrence. *The Psychology of War: Comprehending Its Mystique and Its Madness*. Chicago: Noble Press, 1992.

Life Magazine. April 17, 1944, 87.

The Little American. Screenplay and story by Jeanie Macpherson. Directed by Cecil B. DeMille. Artcraft Pictures Corporation, 27 August, 1917.

Lupton, S. "ABC for Little Willie and Others." London: Daily News, n.d.

Marcus, Jane. "Corpus/Corps/Corpse." In *Arms and the Woman: War, Gender, and Literary Representation*, ed. Helen M. Cooper, Adrienne Auslander Munich, and Susan Merrill Squier, 124–67. Chapel Hill: University of North Carolina Press, 1989.

Marshall, Logan. *Horrors and Atrocities of the Great War: The Tragic Destruction of the Lusitania*. Philadelphia: P. W. Ziegler Company, 1915.

Marwick, Arthur. *The Deluge: British Society and the First World War*. New York: Norton, 1970.

McClure's Win-the-War Magazine 11, no. 50 (September 1918).

Merritt, Albert N. *War Time Control of Distribution of Foods*. New York: MacMillan, 1920.

Meyer, G. J. *A World Undone: The Story of the Great War 1914–1918*. New York: Delacorte Press, 2006.

Miller, Mark Crispin. Introduction to *Propaganda* by Edward Bernays. 1928; reprint, Brooklyn: Ig Publishing, 2005. 9–33.

Mills, C. Wright. *The Power Elite*. Afterword by Alan Wolfe. 1956; reprint, New York: Oxford University Press, 2000.

"Miss Cavell's Execution." *American Review of Reviews* 52, no. 6 (December 1915): 659–61.

Mullendore, William Clinton. *History of the United States Food Administration: 1917–1919*. Introduction by Herbert Hoover. Stanford: Stanford University Press, 1941.

My Book of Sailors. United States: Salfield Publishing Company, 1919.

National War Garden Commission. *Home Drying and Canning of Vegetables and Fruits*. Washington DC: National War Garden Commission, 1919.

———. *War Vegetable Gardening and the Home Storage of Vegetables*. Washington DC: National War Garden Commission, 1918.

Neal, Marion Harris. "Helping Hoover on Thanksgiving Day." *People's Home Journal* 33, no. 11 (1918): 26.

New Hampshire College Extension Service, "Extension Circular No. 21," *Food Emergency Demonstrations*, September 1917.

Niké. *Les Soldats de la Grande Guerre*. Paris: Pierre Lafitte, 1914.

Northend, Mary Harrod. "Harmony in the Breakfast Room," *American Cookery* 23, no. 2 (August–September 1918): 91–94.

Notter, Florence. *Soldier Bob*. No. 4. New York: M. A. Donohue and Company, 1918.

Orville, Florence. *American Heroes: Paper Posters to Make*. New York: Platt and Nourse Company, 1918.

Orwell, George. *1984*. 1949; reprint, New York: Signet, 1992.

———. "Politics and the English Language." In *Shooting an Elephant and Other Essays*, 77–92. New York: Harcourt, Brace, 1950.

Our Army. No. 65, Our Allies Series. Newark: Charles E. Graham, n.d.

Owen, Wilfred. *The Collected Poems of Wilfred Owen*. New York: New Directions Books, 1965.

Packard, Vance. *The Hidden Persuaders*. 1957; reprint, New York: Cardinal Editions, 1960.

Paget, Henry Luke. *Records of the Raids*. London: Society for Promoting Christian Knowledge, 1918.

Peel, Dorothy C. *The Eat-Less-Meat Book*. 1917; reprint, New York: Gordon Press, 1975.

Plumley, Ladd. "The Basis of Victory." *American Cookery* 22, no. 7 (February 1918): 484.

Pollock, Ivan L. *The Food Administration in Iowa*. Vol. 1. Iowa City: State Historical Society of Iowa, 1923.

Ponsonby, Arthur. *Falsehood in War-Time*. New York: Dutton, 1928.

Post, Edwin M., Jr. *Henri War Dog*. Reprint from *New York Times*, April 1915 Sunday Supplement for Allies Special Aid, New York, n.d.

Pratkanis, Anthony, and Elliot Aronson. *The Age of Propaganda: The Everyday Use and Abuse of Persuasion*. 1992; reprint, New York: W. H. Freeman, 2001.

Protheroe, Ernest. *Edith Cavell: Nurse and Martyr*. London: Epworth Press, 1928.

———. *A Noble Woman: The Life Story of Edith Cavell*. 4th ed. London: Epworth Press, 1916.

Purdy, Mabel Dulon. "Into the Kitchen with Hoover! What the Food Administration Has Accomplished in Just One Year." *McClure's Magazine*, September 1918, 28.

"Queries and Answers." *American Cookery* 23, no. 2 (August–September 1918): 135.

Quinn, Patrick. *The Conning of America: The Great War and American Popular Literature*. Amsterdam: Editions Rodopi, 2001.

Recipes for War Breads. Philadelphia: Dr. D. Jayne and Son's Family Medicines, 1918.

Rinehart, Mary Roberts. "Twenty-Two." *Metropolitan*, June 1917, 10+.

Rogers, Howard, and James V. Monaco. "I'm Going to Follow the Boys." New York: M. Witmark and Sons, 1917.

Roosevelt, Theodore. "The Great Adventure." *Metropolitan* 5, no. 48 (October 1918): 9.

Rose, Louis. "Interpreting Propaganda: Successors to Warburg and Freud in Wartime." *American Imago* 60, no. 1 (2003): 122–30.

Ross, Stewart Halsey. *Propaganda for War: How the United States Was Conditioned to Fight the Great War of 1914–1918*. Jefferson NC: McFarland, 1996.

Rubens, Paul A. "Your King and Country Want You (A Woman's Recruiting Song)." London: Chappell and Company, 1914.

Sassoon, Siegfried. *The War Poems of Siegfried Sassoon*. 1919; reprint, Teddington, Middlesex: Echo Library, 2006.

Scales, Mrs. Melrose. "Hoover Hooverize." Dallas: Scales Music Publishing Company, 1918.

Scott, Mrs. Anna B. "How to Save Half the Wheat." *North American* (Philadelphia), April 14, 1918. Supplement.

Selected Recipes for Wartimes. N.p.: Calumet Baking Powder Company, 1918.

"Service Uniforms of Red Cross Workers." *Red Cross Magazine*, August 1918, 45–51.

Shapiro, Laura. *Perfection Salad: Women and Cooking at the Turn of the Century*. New York: Henry Holt, 1986.

Shepherd, William G. "The Soul That Stirs in Battalions of Death." *Delineator* 92, no. 3 (March 1918): 56.

Smith, Helen Zenna. *Not So Quiet . . . Stepdaughters of War*. Foreword by Jane Marcus. 1930; reprint, New York: Feminist Press at the City University of New York, 1989.

The Soldier Painting Book. No. 43. Rochester NY: Stecher Lith, 1917.

Taylor, Philip M. *Munitions of the Mind: A History of Propaganda from the Ancient World to the Present Era*. 3rd ed. Manchester: Manchester University Press, 2003.

Today's Housewife 7, no. 14 (November 1918): back cover.

Tönnies, Ferdinand. *Community and Society*. Trans. and ed. by Charles P. Loomis. 1887; reprint, Mineola NY: Dover, 2002.

———. *Ferdinand Tönnies on Public Opinion: Selections and Analyses*. Ed. and trans. Hanno Hardt and Slavko Splichal. Foreword by Gary T. Marx. Oxford: Rowman and Littlefield, 2000.

"To Teach Cooking to College Girls," editorial. *American Cookery* 23, no. 8 (March 1918): 575–76.
Trent, Martha. *Alice Blyth Somewhere in England*. New York: Barse and Hopkins, 1918.
———. *Helen Carey Somewhere in America*. Cleveland: Goldsmith Publishing, 1918.
———. *Lucia Rudini Somewhere in Italy*. New York: Barse and Hopkins, 1918.
———. *Marieken De Bruin Somewhere in Belgium*. Cleveland: Goldsmith Publishing, 1918.
———. *Phoebe Marshall Somewhere in Canada*. Cleveland: Goldsmith Publishing, 1919.
———. *Valerie Duval Somewhere in France*. New York: Barse and Hopkins, 1918.
U.S. Committee on Public Information. "Spies and Lies." *Pictorial Review*, July 1918, 38.
U.S. Food Administration. *Food and the War: A Textbook for College Classes*. Boston: Houghton, Mifflin, 1918.
———. *Food Saving and Sharing*. New York: Doubleday, Page, 1918.
———. *War Cook Book for American Women: Suggestions for Patriotic Service in the Home*. Comp. Frederic J. Haskin. Washington DC: National Capital Press, 1918.
———. *War Economy in Food*. Hammond IN: W. B. Conkey, 1918.
Uzawa, Yoshiko. "'Will White Man and Yellow Man Ever Mix?' Wallace Irwin, Hashimura Togo, and the Japanese Immigrant in America." *Japanese Journal of American Studies* 17 (2006): 201–22.
Van Dyne, Edith. *Aunt Jane's Nieces in the Red Cross*. Chicago: Reilly and Britton, 1915.
———. *Mary Louis and the Liberty Girls*. Chicago: Reilly and Lee, 1918.
"A War Play Comes Home to Roost: 'The Man Who Stayed at Home' Is *The White Feather* Americanized." *New York Times*, April 4, 1918.
War-Time Cook and Health Book. Lynn MA: Lydia E. Pinkham Medicine Company, 1917.
Warwick, Ann. "To You: The American Girl War Worker." *Ladies' Home Journal*, October 1918, 1.
"The Weaker Sex? No, Not Woman, but Man!" *St. Louis Post-Dispatch Sunday Magazine*, October 21, 1917, 3.

Wells, H. G. *Mr. Britling Sees It Through*. 1916; reprint, London: Hogarth Press, 1985.
What to Eat: How to Cook It. "Official Recipe Book, State Council of Defense of Illinois." 1918; reprint, Waco TX: B. J. Enterprises, 1979.
Wilcox, Ella Wheeler. "One Night in May." *McClure's Magazine*, May 1917, 30.
"The Wiser Person," "On Having a Case." *American Cookery* 23, no. 8 (March 1918): 588–90.
"With Such a Spirit—." *McClure's Magazine* 5, no. 50 (March 1918): 5.
Witwer, H. C. "It's the Huns." *McClure's Magazine* 5, no. 50 (March 1918). 46–48.
"Women, War and the New Fashions." *Delineator* 91, no. 3 (September 1917): 52–53.
Wood, Stanley L. *Ten Little Sausages*. N.p.
Worrall, Lechmere, and J. E. Harold Terry. *The White Feather*. New York: Grosset and Dunlap, 1918.
Wyckoff, Elizabeth Porter. "The Girls behind the Men behind the Guns." *Ladies' Home Journal*, October 1918, 3.

INDEX

Page numbers in italic refer to illustrations.

"ABC for Little Willie and Others" (pamphlet), 176

advertising, 100, 265; Black Cat Cigarettes, 154–55, *156–61*, 162, *163*; and the food industry, 51, 53, 58–59, 255; in magazines, 70–71, 76–77, 253–59; and psychology, 16–17. *See also* propaganda

The Age of Propaganda (Pratkanis and Aronson), 14

"America Here's My Boy" (song), 250–51

American Cookery (magazine), 40–43, 53

"Are YOU a Victory Canner?" (poster), *48*, 49

"Are You Half the Man Your Mother Thought You'd Be" (song), 247–48

Aronson, Elliot: *The Age of Propaganda*, 14

At Home, at War (Haytock), 5–6, 167, 279n20

atrocity stories, 6, 224–25, 271n3; corpse factory, 49, 51; mutilated children and refugees, 67–68, 220; and rape, 225–26; and rumor, 2–3. *See also* propaganda

Aunt Jane's Nieces series, 153–54. *See also* fiction

Bailey, Roy Rutherford, 22, 177. *See also* Captain Tick-Mouse series

Baker, Newton D., 262–63

Banta, Martha: *Imaging American Women*, 9

Baucq, Philippe, 234

Baum, L. Frank ("Edith Van Dyne"), 153–54, 282n24

"Beat Back the Hun" (poster), 225

Beck, James M.: *The War and Humanity*, 228, 229, 232

Belgium, 4, 52, 234; atrocity stories from, 2–3, 67–68, 220, 224; fiction set in, 69–70

Benson, Mildred Wirt, 125

Bentham, Jeremy, 12

Berkeley, Reginald, 234

Bernays, Edward: *Propaganda*, 265–66, 267

Black Cat Cigarettes, 154–55, *156–61*, 162, *163*. *See also* advertising

Bogart, Ada, 234

Booth, Charles: *Life and Labour of the People in London*, 57–58

"Boys and Girls! You can help your Uncle Sam Win the War" (poster), 185, *189*

Brave Boys and Girls in Wartime (Lea), 284n41

Brave New World (Huxley), 14–16, 267

"Britannia Needs You Like a Mother (Would You Turn Your Mother Down)?" (song), 251–52

Brittain, Vera, 4, 116
Brooks, Edna, 282n24
Browne, Porter Emerson, 76, 225; *A Fool There Was*, 68–69; "A Liberty Loan Primer," 172–75; "Mary and Marie," 68–71, 83, 225
Bryce Report, 2, 220, 271n3
Burgess, Anthony: *A Clockwork Orange*, 14, 16

Campbell, James B., 54–55
Campbell, Joseph, 273n41
Campbell, R. W.: *Dorothy, VAD, and the Doctor*, 117–21
Captain Tick-Mouse and His Adventures in Secret Service (Bailey), 177–79
Captain Tick-Mouse and His Adventures with the Torch Bearers (Bailey), *180*
Captain Tick-Mouse series, 177–81
Cather, Willa, 5, 101; *One of Ours*, 106
Cavell, Edith, 77, *108*, 167–68, 233, 234; burial site of, 106, *107*; execution of, 106, 110, 113, 226–27, 231–33, 234–36, 285n27; postcards of, 106, *107*, *108*, *109*; as recruiting tool, 106, 110–12. *See also* nurses
children, 171–72; and gender roles, 196–200, 209; images of, in propaganda, 169–71, 185–94, 206–11, 219, 220, 224, 229–31, 237, 238–39, 247, 257–59; and the Junior Red Cross, 194–95; and "A Liberty Loan Primer," 172–75; and patriotism, 171, 177, 183–85; and propaganda in children's books, 4, 9, 176–81, 196–97, 201–6, 211–13, 283n36, 284n41; and school, 182–85, 191; and war play, 9, 169, 196–97, 199–200, 209, 216; and War Savings Stamps, 175, 177, 179, 181–82, 183, *190*. *See also* family relationships
Christy, Howard Chandler, 8, *89*, 90
civilian deaths, 224–25, 227
Clinker, L. C., 223, 224
A Clockwork Orange (Burgess), 14, 16
Committee on Public Information, 126–27, 182, 183, 262–63, 265
Community and Society (Tönnies), 22–24, 27, 68, 104, 260
The Conning of America (Quinn), 219–20, 231, 278n2
Conrey, Lee, 45
Costello, Maude Marie, 51
Creel, George, 126–27, 182, 262–65; *How We Advertised America*, 262–63
cummings, e. e., 167

Dawn (film), 234, 235
De Mille, Cecil B., 240, 243
"Destroy This Mad Brute" (poster), 225
Dewey, 185, *188*
"Disabled" (Owen), 95–96
Discipline and Punish (Foucault), 12–13
A Diversity of Creatures (Kipling), 237
"The Dog of War" (Gurlitz), 121–24
domestic science movement, 30–34, 37, 42, 53–54, 191, 192; journals of the, 40–43. *See also* food conservation
"Don't Forget the Salvation Army (My Doughnut Girl)" (song), 43–44
"Don't waste food while others starve!" (poster), 223, 224
Dorothy, VAD, and the Doctor (Campbell), 117–21
Dos Passos, John, 167, 263–65
"Dulce et Decorum Est" (Owen), 278n86
Dwyer, M. J., 223, 224
Dylan, Bob, 1–2, 267

Eat-Less-Meat Book (Peel), 57–58, 61
Edith Cavell: Heroic Nurse (Elkon), 235
Elkon, Juliette: *Edith Cavell: Heroic Nurse*, 235

Emerson, Alice B., 125. *See also* Ruth Fielding series
"Enlist" (poster), 68, 229
Enright, Macinel Wright, *170*
Evidence and Documents Laid Before the Committee on Alleged German Outrages. *See* Bryce Report

Faces of the Enemy (Keen), 17–18
Falsehood in War-Time (Ponsonby), 20–21, 51, 67–68, 169, 220, 267
family relationships: and the *Gemeinschaft* (community), 23–24, 68, 71–72, 91, 104, 113, 169, 247, 251–53, 260, 269; and propaganda, 7–8, 23–24, 176–77, 218–19. *See also* children; women
Ferber, Edna: "One Hundred Percent," 87–88, 90–91, 92
fiction, 8–9, 14–16; children's books, 4, 9, 177–81, 196–97, 201–5, 211–13; and food, 59–65; and literary modernism, 3, 4–6; magazine, 66–67, 68, 69–76, 97–101, 113–16, 121–24, 281n7; novels, 3–4, 77–79, 82, 83–87, 117–21, 124–44, 146–54, 171–72, 235; postwar novels, 59, 263–65, 269–70; and rape, 225–26; Ruth Fielding series, 125–34; short stories, 67, 68, 69–76, 83, 87–88, 90–91, 92–95, 96–100, 113–16, 121–24, 237–40; "Somewhere" series, 3, 132, 135–53, 282n21. *See also* propaganda
films, 106, 110, 234, 235, 240–47. *See also* propaganda
Fitzgerald, Charles Penrose, 80
Flagg, James Montgomery, *7*, 8, 172–73, 175, 185, *189*
"Follow the Pied Piper" (poster), 169–71
Food and the War, 37–38, 42
food conservation, 40–42, 45, 274n9, 277n79; and children, 191–94; and the food industry, 51–53, 58–59; in Great Britain, 55–59, 60–65; and rationing, 27–28, 57, 277n77; and the United States Food Administration, 27–29, 31, 35–37, 38–40, 42–43, 46–47, 49, 51–54, 61, 65, 275n5. *See also* domestic science movement
Food Saving and Sharing (textbook), 191
A Fool There Was (Browne), 68–69
"For All We Have and Are" (Kipling), 218, 236
"For Home and Country" (poster), 25, 26
The 42nd Parallel (Dos Passos), 263–64
Foucault, Michel: *Discipline and Punish*, 12–13
Franks, Thetta Quay, 37, 42; *Household Organization for War Service*, 38–39; *The Margin of Happiness*, 30–33, 38–39
Freud, Sigmund, 17, 273n34
Fuhr, Ernest, *47*

Gahan, Horace, 110
Gatlin, Dana: "The Mating," 101; "New York Stuff," 71, 72–76; "A Star in the Window," 92–95, 96–97
Gemeinschaft (community), 5, 136, 165; and community standards, 120–21; definition of, 23–24; and family relationships, 23–24, 27, 68, 71–72, 91, 104, 113, 169, 247, 251–53, 260, 269; and gender roles, 30, 129, 139; and *Gesellschaft* (society), 33, 100, 177, 231. See also *Gesellschaft* (society)
gender roles, 54; and children, 196–200, 209; in fiction, 134, 137, 139, 143–44, 146, 148–49, 152, 165–66; and the *Gemeinschaft*, 30, 129,

gender roles (*cont.*)
139; and male duty, 78–80, 82, 91–97, 230–31, 247–53, 256. *See also* stereotypes; women
Gesellschaft (society): and community standards, 120–21; definition of, 23–24; and family relationships, 65; and *Gemeinschaft* (community), 33, 100, 177, 231; and social acceptance, 64. See also *Gemeinschaft* (community)
Gibson, Hugh: *The Rape of Belgium*, 77, 83
Gish, Lilian, 240–41, 242
"The Glory of Women" (Sassoon), 96, 251
Gloss, Molly, 281n17
Goldman, Dorothy, 5
Goldman, William: *Lord of the Flies*, 171
Good-Bye to All That (Graves), 67, 95, 217, 224
Graves, Robert: *Good-Bye to All That*, 67, 95, 217, 224
Great Britain: and food conservation, 55–58, 60–65; and propaganda, *56*, 57, 209, 211–13, 216–17, 227–28, 251–52; and rationing, 57, 211; and Voluntary Aid Detachment (VAD) workers, 4–5, 61–64, 116–20
Green Day, 2
Griffith, D. W., 240, 242
Gurlitz, Amy Landon: "The Dog of War," 121–24

Hamilton, Alexander, 268
Hardy, William Bate, 55, 57, 62
Hart, Edna F., 257
Haytock, Jennifer: *At Home, at War*, 5–6, 167, 279n20
The Hearts of Horses (Gloss), 281n17
Hearts of the World (film), 240–43
Helen Carey Somewhere in America (Trent), 135, 136–39. *See also* "Somewhere" series
Hemingway, Ernest, 3, 5, 167, 282n21; "Soldier's Home," 226; "A Way You'll Never Be," 225–26
The Hidden Persuaders (Packard), 14, 16–17, 265
Hill, Janet M., 40–41, 53, 58–59
History of the United States Food Administration (Mullendore), 27–28, 29, 39
Hoover, Herbert, 35–36, 42–43, 54, 59, 65, 191, 276n47, 278n85; and "Hooverization," 31; and the press, 39; and rationing, 27–28, 274n9. *See also* United States Food Administration
Horrors and Atrocities of the Great War (Marshall), 228
Household Organization for War Service (Franks), 38–39
How We Advertised America (Creel), 262–63
"Hunger" (poster), 52, 222, 224
"Hun or Home?" (poster), *221*, 222
Huxley, Aldous: *Brave New World*, 14–16, 267

"I'd Be Proud to Be the Mother of a Soldier" (song), 249–50
imagery: Belgium, 4, 52, 220, 224; cannibalism, 99; children, 169–71, 185–94, 206–11, 219, 220, 224, 229–31, 237, 238–39, 247, 257–59; German Huns, 6, 10–12, 24, 26, 218, 225, 256; Kaiser Wilhelm, 49, *50*, 51, 67, 98–99, 172, *173*; nurses, 106–13, 184, 200–201; and the *Pickelhaube*, 6, 209; Uncle Sam, 53, 169–71, 173, 185, *189*; women, 9, 46–47, *48*, 49, 53, 54–55, 80–95, 96–99, 106, 110, 219, 220, 224, 226,

235, 247, 279n20. *See also* posters; propaganda
Imaging American Women (Banta), 9
"I'm Going to Follow the Boys" (song), 112
Ireland, Billy, 10, *11*
Irwin, Wallace, 67, 97–99, 280n31
"I Want YOU for the Navy" (poster), *89*

Jacobs, Leonebel, *48*
James, Henry, 3, 171, 229
Jung, Carl, 17–18, 273n41
Junior Red Cross. *See* Red Cross

Kealey, E. V., *81*
Keen, Sam: *Faces of the Enemy*, 17–18
"Keep the Home Fires Burning" (song), 247
"Keep the Hun Out" (poster), 10–12, 225
Khaki Girls series, 153, 282n24
Kipling, Rudyard, 68–69, 101, 219, 286n35; *A Diversity of Creatures*, 237; "For All We Have and Are," 218, 236; "The Rowers," 236–37; "Swept and Garnished," 237–40
Kris, Ernst, 272n33

Ladies' Home Journal, 35–36, 39, 40, 162, 164–65, 253
Lea, John: *Brave Boys and Girls in Wartime*, 284n41
Leighton, Etta V., 185
LeShan, Lawrence: *The Psychology of War*, 18–19
"Letters of a Japanese Schoolboy" (Irwin), 97, 280n31
Lewis, Wyndham, 3
Liberty Bonds, 185, *187*, *188*, 222; and the Liberty Loan Committee, 172–74, 175, 176, 177, 181; and "A Liberty Loan Primer," 172–75
Liberty Loans. *See* Liberty Bonds
Life and Labour of the People in London (Booth), 57–58
literary modernism, 3, 4–6. *See also* fiction
The Little American (film), 240, 243–47
"Little Americans Do your Bit" (poster), 192, *193*, 194
Lord of the Flies (Goldman), 171
Lusitania, 67, 68, 226–31, 244

magazines: and the domestic science movement, 40–43; and fiction, 66–67, 68, 69–76, 97–101, 113–16, 121–24, 281n7; and *Lusitania* reports, 67; and nonfiction articles, 35–36, 39–40, 46, 77, 91–92, 101–4, 164–65, 174–75; and poetry, 175–76
male duty, 78–80, 82, 91–97, 230–31, 247–53, 256. *See also* gender roles
The Man Who Stayed at Home (play). See *The White Feather* (Worrall and Terry)
The Margin of Happiness (Franks), 30–33, 38–39
Marshall, Logan: *Horrors and Atrocities of the Great War*, 228
"Mary and Marie" (Browne), 68, 69–70, 83, 225
Mary Louis and the Liberty Girls (Van Dyne), 282n24
"The Mating" (Gatlin), 101
McClure's (magazine), 68, 70, 71, 76–77, 97, 101, 174–76, 255, 256
Merritt, Albert N.: *War Time Control of Distribution of Foods*, 28–29
Metropolitan (magazine), 68, 91–92, 101, 113, 121, 281n7
Miller, Mark Crispin, 266
Mills, C. Wright: *The Power Elite*, 21–22
modernism, literary. *See* literary modernism
moral compulsion, 10, 12, 13, 14, 52. *See also* propaganda

Mr. Britling Sees It Through (Wells), 60–61
Mrs. Dalloway (Woolf), 4, 162
Mullendore, William Clinton: *History of the United States Food Administration*, 27–28, 29, 39
"My Daddy Bought Me a Government Bond of the Third Liberty Loan: Did Yours?" (poster), 185, *187*

National Security League, 183–85
Neagle, Anna, 110
"New York Stuff" (Gatlin), 71, 72–76
1984 (Orwell), 171–72, 269–70
Nineteen Nineteen (Dos Passos), 264–65
A Noble Woman (Protheroe), 234–35, 285n27
Not So Quiet . . . Stepdaughters of War (Smith), 4–5, 61–64, 147, 162
Notter, Florence: *Soldier Bob*, 196–97
novels, 3–4, 171–72, 235; and female stereotypes, 77–79, 82, 83–87, 117–21; and gender roles in Aunt Jane's Nieces series, 153–54; Ruth Fielding series, 124–34; "Somewhere" series, 135–53. *See also* fiction
Nurse Edith Cavell (film), 106, 110, 235
nurses, 166; in fiction, 113–16, 118–20, 153–54; images of, 106–13, 155. *See also* Cavell, Edith

"Oh please do! Daddy, Buy Me a Victory Bond" (poster), 185, *186*
"One Hundred Percent" (Ferber), 87–88, 90–91, 92
One of Ours (Cather), 106
"One of Ten Million" (Irwin), 67, 97–99
"The Order of the White Feather." *See* white feather campaign
Orr, Alfred Everitt, *25*, 26
Orwell, George: *1984*, 171–72, 269–70
"Our Daddy is fighting at the Front for *You*" (poster), 185, *188*
Our Hospital ABC, 201–3
"Over There" (song), 247
Owen, Wilfred, 59, 185; "Disabled," 95–96; "Dulce et Decorum Est," 278n86

Packard, Vance: *The Hidden Persuaders*, 14, 16–17, 265
Paget, Henry Luke: *Records of the Raids*, 216–17
Panopticon, 12–13
Parker, Cushman, 192, *193*
Paton, D. Noël, 55, 58
patriotism: and children, 171, 177, 183–85; and sheet music, 250; and transnationalism, 4; and the white feather campaign, 79–80, 82–83; and women, 61
Paus, Herbert, *190*, 191
Peel, Dorothy C.: *Eat-Less-Meat Book*, 57–58, 61
People's Home Journal, 43
Phoebe Marshall Somewhere in Canada (Trent), 135, 149, 151–53. *See also* "Somewhere" series
Pickford, Mary, 243
pledge cards, 28, 29, 34, 36, 61, 194. *See also* propaganda
Plumley, Ladd, 41
Ponsonby, Arthur: *Falsehood in War-Time*, 20–21, 51, 67–68, 169, 220, 267
Pope, Jessie, 278n86
posters, *7*, 24–26, 43, *44*, 52, *180*; and the American Red Cross, 110–11; and atrocity stories, *221*, 222–24, 225; British, *56*, *57*; and children, 169–71, 183, 185–91, 192–94; design of, 8; and food conservation, *47*, *48*, *50*, 52, 277n79; and Hun imagery, 10–12; about the *Lusitania*, 68, 229, *230*; and women, 46–47,

48, 49, 80, *81*, *89*, 224. *See also* propaganda
potty humor, 206, *207*
Pound, Ezra, 3
Poverty (Rountree), 57–58
The Power Elite (Mills), 21–22
Pratkanis, Anthony: *The Age of Propaganda*, 14
Price, Evadne ("Helen Zenna Smith"): *Not So Quiet . . . Stepdaughters of War*, 4–5, 61–64, 147, 162
propaganda: and advertising, 16–17, 51, 53, 58–59, 70–71, 76–77, 100, 154–62, *163*, 253–59, 265; and atrocity stories, 2–3, 6, 49, 51, 67–68, 220, 224–26, 271n3; British, *56*, *57*, 209, 211–13, 216–17, 227–28, 251–52; and children's books, 4, 9, 177–81, 196–97, 201–6, 211–13, 283n36, 284n41; and community standards, 120–21; definitions of, 10, 19–20; and the domestic science movement, 30–34; and Edith Cavell, 235–36; effects of, 216–17, 260–61, 267–70; and family relationships, 7–8, 26, 176–77, 218–19; fears of, 265–66; and films, 106, 110, 234, 235, 240–47; French, 4, 203–5, 206, *207*; German, 209, *210*; and moral compulsion, 10, 12, 13, 14, 52; origins of, 13, 266–67; and pledge cards, 28, 29, 34, 36, 61, 194; and poetry, 175–76, 218, 219, 236–37; and pop culture, 1–2, 8–9, 260; postcards, 106, *107*, *108*, *109*, *163*, 206–11; postwar attitudes toward, 263–65; and psychology, 13–19; recipe books, 33, 36, 37–38, 40–41, *50*, 51, 52–53, 57–59, 277n68; and sociology, 19–24, 26; songs, 8, 43–44, 80, 82, 112, 197–99, 247–53, *254*, 276n47; success of, during World War I, 6, 22, 29, 262–63; and textbooks, 37–38, 42, 191; and the white feather campaign, 79–80, 82–83. *See also* fiction; imagery; posters
Propaganda (Bernays), 265–66, 267
Protheroe, Ernest: *A Noble Woman*, 234–35, 285n27
The Psychology of War (LeShan), 18–19
Purity Crusade, 121

Quinn, Patrick: *The Conning of America*, 219–20, 231, 278n2

Raleigh, Henry Patrick, 10, 52, *221*, *222*
rape, 225–26. *See also* atrocity stories
The Rape of Belgium (Gibson), 77, 83
rationing, 27–28, 57, 277n77. *See also* food conservation
Records of the Raids (Paget), 216–17
Red Cross, 104, 126–28, 166, 191, 219; and the Junior Red Cross, 194–95, 219; and uniforms, 105
Rinehart, Mary Roberts: "Twenty-Two," 113–16, 281n7
Rogers, W. A., 229, *230*
Roosevelt, Theodore, 91–92, 113, 219, 281n7
"The Rose of No Man's Land" (song), 112
Rountree, Seebohm: *Poverty*, 57–58
"The Rowers" (Kipling), 236–37
Royal Society (Great Britain), 55, 57
Ruth Fielding and Her Crowning Victory, 125
Ruth Fielding at the War Front, 129–32
Ruth Fielding Homeward Bound, 125, 132–34
Ruth Fielding in the Red Cross, 126–29
Ruth Fielding series, 125–34. *See also* fiction

"The Salvation Army Lassie" (poster), 43, *44*
Samson, Joseph Ernest, 185, *186*

Sargent, Dudley A., 45–46
Sassoon, Siegfried, 95; "The Glory of Women," 96, 251
"Save your Child from Autocracy and Poverty" (poster), *190*, 191
Scott, Anna B., 46, 52
Severin, Louis, 234
sheet music. *See* songs
"She Helps Her Boy to Victory" (poster), *56*, 57
short stories, 67, 113–16, 121–24; and atrocity stories, 97–100; and female stereotypes, 68, 69–76, 87–88, 90–91, 92–96, 237–40. *See also* fiction
Smith, Helen Zenna (Evadne Price): *Not So Quiet . . . Stepdaughters of War*, 4–5, 61–64, 116, 147, 162
Smout, Edward, 80, 82, 252
Les Soldats de la Grande Guerre, 4, 203–4
Soldier Bob (Notter), 196–97
Soldier Painting Book, 236n36
The Soldier Painting Book (coloring book), 205–6
"Soldier's Home" (Hemingway), 226
"Somewhere" series, 3, 132, 135–53, 282n21. *See also* fiction
A Son at the Front (Wharton), 240
songs, 8, 112, *254*, 276n47; and food service, 43–44; and gender roles, 80, 82, 197–99, 247–53. *See also* propaganda
"Sow the Seeds of Victory" (poster), *7*, 8
Spaulding, Huntley N., 38
Spear, Fred, 68, 229
Stahr, Paul, 46
"A Star in the Window" (Gatlin), 92–95, 96–97
stereotypes, 213–15; "dangerous" married women, 71–76; gender, 66–67, 87, 100; German, 86, 130–31, 237–38, 240, 241, 278n2; racial, 204, 214–15, 217, 280n31. *See also* gender roles
Sterner, Albert, 110–11
Stevens, G. A., 176
"Sugar Means Ships" (poster), 46–47, 49
Sumner, Caroline Louise, 42–43
"Swept and Garnished" (Kipling), 237–40

Ten Little Sausages (Wood), 4, 211–13, *214*, *215*
Terry, J. E. Harold: *The White Feather*, 77–79, 82, 83–87
"That Family Called the U.S.A." (song), 252–53, *254*
"That's a Mother's Liberty Loan" (song), 250
"There's Nobody Home but Me" (song), 197–99
Thompson, W. H., 55, 58
Thrift Stamps, 181–83
Thuliez, Louise, 234
Tick-Mouse. *See* Captain Tick-Mouse series
Tönnies, Ferdinand: *Community and Society*, 22–24, 27, 68, 104, 260
toys. *See* war play
Trent, Martha, 3, 132, 135–53, 282n21
The Turn of the Screw (James), 171
"Twenty-Two" (Rinehart), 113–16, 281n7

Underwood, Clarence, 8, 99
uniforms: Red Cross, 105; United States Food Administration, *34*, 105
United States Food Administration, 222, 224, 253, 259, 278n85; and children, 172, 191–92, 195; and food conservation, 27–29, 31, 36–37, 38–40, 42–43, 46–47, 49, 51–54, 61, 65, 275n5; and uniforms, *34*, 105

Valerie Duval Somewhere in France (Trent), 139, 143–47. *See also* "Somewhere" series
Van Dyne, Edith (L. Frank Baum), 153–54, 282n24
Voluntary Aid Detachment (VAD) workers, 4–5, 61–64, 116–20

The War and Humanity (Beck), 228, 229, 232
War Cook Book for American Women, 36
war play, 9, 169, 196–97, 199–200, 209, 216. *See also* children
War Savings Stamps, 175, 177, 179, 181–82, 183, *190*
War Time Control of Distribution of Foods (Merritt), 28–29
War Time Recipes (Hill), 40, 53, 58–59
"A Way You'll Never Be" (Hemingway), 225–26
Wells, H. G.: *Mr. Britling Sees It Through*, 60–61
"We Need You" (poster), *111*
Wharton, Edith, 3, 240
"When You Fire Remember This" (poster), 229, *230*
The White Feather (Worrall and Terry), 71, 77–79, 82, 83–87
white feather campaign, 79–80, 82–83. *See also* patriotism
Wilcox, Ella Wheeler, 175–76
women: bitterness toward, 95–96; and the domestic science movement, 30–34, 37, 42, 53–54; and fashion, 102–3, 254–55; and food conservation, 27–29, 31, 35–37, 38–43, 45, 46–47, 49, 51–54, 58–59, 61, 65; images of, in propaganda, 80–95, 96–99, 106, 110, 219, 220, 224, 226, 235, 247, 279n20; and marriage, 113, 116, 119–20, 123–24, 134, 141–42, 147, 151; in novels, 77–79, 82, 83–87, 117–21, 124–54; in short stories, 68, 69–76, 87–88, 90–91, 92–96, 113–16, 121–24, 237–40; and war service, 4–5, 44–46, 61–64, 101–4, 105, 116–20, 154–62, 164–68. *See also* family relationships
"Women of Britain Say—GO!" (poster), 80
Women's Writing on the First World War (Goldman), 5
Women Writers and the Great War (Goldman), 5
Wood, Stacy H., 183
Wood, Stanley L.: *Ten Little Sausages*, 4, 211–13, *214*, *215*
Woolf, Virginia, 80; *Mrs. Dalloway*, 4, 80, 162
Worrall, Lechmere: *The White Feather*, 71, 77–79, 82, 83–87

Young, Winifred, 61. See also *Not So Quiet . . . Stepdaughters of War* (Smith)
"Your King and Country Want You (A Woman's Recruiting Song)" (song), 251

Studies in War, Society, and the Military

Military Migration and State Formation: The British Military Community in Seventeenth-Century Sweden
Mary Elizabeth Ailes

The State at War in South Asia
Pradeep P. Barua

An American Soldier in World War I
George Browne
Edited by David L. Snead

Beneficial Bombing: The Progressive Foundations of American Air Power, 1917–1945
Mark Clodfelter

Fu-go: The Curious History of the Japanese Balloon Bombs
Ross Coen

Imagining the Unimaginable: World War, Modern Art, and the Politics of Public Culture in Russia, 1914–1917
Aaron J. Cohen

The Rise of the National Guard: The Evolution of the American Militia, 1865–1920
Jerry Cooper

The Thirty Years' War and German Memory in the Nineteenth Century
Kevin Cramer

Political Indoctrination in the U.S. Army from World War II to the Vietnam War
Christopher S. DeRosa

In the Service of the Emperor: Essays on the Imperial Japanese Army
Edward J. Drea

The Age of the Ship of the Line: The British and French Navies, 1650–1815
Jonathan R. Dull

American Naval History, 1607–1865: Overcoming the Colonial Legacy
Jonathan R. Dull

You Can't Fight Tanks with Bayonets: Psychological Warfare against the Japanese Army in the Southwest Pacific
Allison B. Gilmore

A Strange and Formidable Weapon: British Responses to World War I Poison Gas
Marion Girard

Civilians in the Path of War
Edited by Mark Grimsley and Clifford J. Rogers

Picture This: World War I Posters and Visual Culture
Edited and with an introduction by Pearl James

Death Zones and Darling Spies: Seven Years of Vietnam War Reporting
Beverly Deepe Keever

For Home and Country: World War I Propaganda on the Home Front
Celia Malone Kingsbury

I Die with My Country: Perspectives on the Paraguayan War, 1864–1870
Edited by Hendrik Kraay and Thomas L. Whigham

North American Indians in the Great War
Susan Applegate Krouse
Photographs and original documentation by Joseph K. Dixon

Citizens More than Soldiers: The Kentucky Militia and Society in the Early Republic
Harry S. Laver

Soldiers as Citizens: Former German Officers in the Federal Republic of Germany, 1945–1955
Jay Lockenour

Deterrence through Strength: British Naval Power and Foreign Policy under Pax Britannica
Rebecca Berens Matzke

Army and Empire: British Soldiers on the American Frontier, 1758–1775
Michael N. McConnell

Of Duty Well and Faithfully Done: A History of the Regular Army in the Civil War
Clayton R. Newell and Charles R. Shrader
With a foreword by Edward M. Coffman

The Militarization of Culture in the Dominican Republic, from the Captains General to General Trujillo
Valentina Peguero

Arabs at War: Military Effectiveness, 1948–1991
Kenneth M. Pollack

The Politics of Air Power: From Confrontation to Cooperation in Army Aviation Civil-Military Relations
Rondall R. Rice

Andean Tragedy: Fighting the War of the Pacific, 1879–1884
William F. Sater

The Grand Illusion: The Prussianization of the Chilean Army
William F. Sater and Holger H. Herwig

Sex Crimes under the Wehrmacht
David Raub Snyder

In the School of War
Roger J. Spiller
Foreword by John W. Shy

The Paraguayan War, Volume 1: Causes and Early Conduct
Thomas L. Whigham

The Challenge of Change: Military Institutions and New Realities, 1918–1941
Edited by Harold R. Winton and David R. Mets

To order or obtain more information on these or other University of Nebraska Press titles, visit www.nebraskapress.unl.edu.

CPSIA information can be obtained
at www.ICGtesting.com
Printed in the USA
LVHW091901130819
627504LV00005B/42/P

9 780803 224742